D0113517

# CONTRACTS IN THE REAL WORLD

Contracts, the foundation of economic activity, are vital, fascinating, and misunderstood. Through a series of engaging stories – involving such captivating individuals as Maya Angelou, Clive Cussler, Lady Gaga, Paris Hilton, Martin Sheen, and Donald Trump – this books corrects the misunderstandings. Capturing the essentials of this subject and reviewing the classic cases, the book explores recurring issues people face in contracting. It shows how age-old precedents and wisdom still apply today and how contract law's inherent dynamism cautions against exuberant reforms. The book will appeal to the general reader and specialists in the field alike, and to both teachers and students of contracts.

Lawrence A. Cunningham is the Henry St. George Tucker III Research Professor at the George Washington University Law School. He has been a professor of law and business for more than twenty years at Boston College, George Washington University, and Yeshiva University. Cunningham is the author of many books, notably *The Essays of Warren Buffett: Lessons for Corporate America*, and editor for many years of the leading treatise on contract law, *Corbin on Contracts.* His writing has appeared as op-eds in *The New York Times*, *The Financial Times*, and *The National Law Journal*.

# Contracts in the Real World

## STORIES OF POPULAR CONTRACTS AND WHY THEY MATTER

### Lawrence A. Cunningham

*George Washington University Law School*

CAMBRIDGE
UNIVERSITY PRESS

# CAMBRIDGE
## UNIVERSITY PRESS

32 Avenue of the Americas, New York NY 10013-2473, USA

Cambridge University Press is part of the University of Cambridge.

It furthers the University's mission by disseminating knowledge in the pursuit of education, learning, and research at the highest international levels of excellence.

www.cambridge.org
Information on this title: www.cambridge.org/9781107607460

First published 2012
Reprinted 2012, 2013

*A catalog record for this publication is available from the British Library.*

*Library of Congress Cataloging in Publication data*
Cunningham, Lawrence A., 1962–
    Contracts in the real world : stories of popular contracts and why they
matter / Lawrence A. Cunningham.
        p.  cm.
    Includes bibliographical references and index.
    ISBN 978-1-107-02007-8 (hardback) – ISBN 978-1-107-60746-0 (pbk.)
    1. Contracts – United States – Cases.  I. Title.
✓ KF801.C615    2012
    346.7302–dc23  2011052115

ISBN  978-1-107-02007-8  Hardback
ISBN  978-1-107-60746-0  Paperback

*For Stephanie,*
*My Dream Come True*

# CONTENTS

# ANNOTATED CONTENTS

## 1. GETTING IN: CONTRACT FORMATION

Tools to distinguish enforceable promises from others – seals, writings, deals, and reliance – and to evaluate intention to bargain: offer, acceptance, and mutual assent.

### A. Gifts, Bargains, Reliance: MLK and BU

Why bargains but not promises to make gifts are enforceable as contracts and how to tell the difference, using the case of Martin Luther King's donation of his papers to Boston University.

### B. Ads or Offers: Pepsi and Harrier Jets

The difference between an unenforceable ad and an enforceable offer, using the case of a consumer's effort to hold Pepsi to a deal for a military fighter jet based on a humorous television commercial.

### C. Frolic or Acceptance: Boasts on "Dateline NBC"

The difference between mere talk and valid offers that can be accepted to form a contract, using the case of a law student taking up prominent criminal defense lawyer J. Cheney Mason's boast on "Dateline NBC" about the strength of his defense in a capital murder trial.

## D. Mutual Assent: Spyware and Secret Clauses

Why mutual assent is required to form contracts and how it is tested, using controversial cases of software users subject to restrictions buried electronically or appearing inside the product's packaging.

## E. Policies or Pacts: The Cleveland.com Blogger

The rising struggle about whether corporate policies, especially about privacy on the Internet, are enforceable as contracts, using the example of a blogger at Cleveland.com and analogizing today's challenge to contract law's resolution during the 1990s of disputes about whether employee handbooks are enforceable as contracts.

*Synthesis*: Why neither formal rules and pure objectivity nor pure context and subjectivity are sufficient to determine the existence of an enforceable contract.

## 2. FACING LIMITS: UNENFORCEABLE BARGAINS

Boundaries of enforceable contracts, which exclude those merely disguised as bargains and those bordering on illegality or violating prevailing sense of public policy.

## A. Unconscionability: Gail Waters's Annuity Swap

Why courts rarely examine the fairness of exchange but will probe contracts on massively lopsided terms plagued with bargaining irregularities, using the example of an impressionable young woman's agreement to sell for $50,000 cash an annuity contract with a cash surrender value of $189,000.

## B. Blackmail: Michael Jordan's Paternity

Why courts resist enforcing bargains amounting to blackmail and how to distinguish those from valid contracts, highlighting the context of patrimony, and illustrated using a case involving Michael Jordan.

## C. Palimony: The Rapper 50 Cent

Why courts struggle against enforcing contracts for personal services among unmarried cohabitants except when other elements of a bargain appear conspicuously, using the example of claims of a paramour against the rapper 50 Cent.

## D. Gambling: Octogenarian Powerball Sisters

Why courts defer to people's freedom of contract yet still identify a class of cases as illegal bargains that courts would not enforce, using the case of two elderly sisters who made an agreement about lottery tickets.

## E. Making Babies: Baby M, Baby Calvert

Continuing struggles in law, society, and technology concerning human reproduction, addressing contracts involving multiple participants in child bearing, contrasting competing approaches states take, from banning, to regulating, to endorsing this field of human endeavor.

*Synthesis*: Why neither pure freedom of contract nor excessive judicial second-guessing of the legitimacy of contracts is desirable.

## 3. GETTING OUT: EXCUSES AND TERMINATION

Legitimate grounds to excuse an otherwise enforceable contract, such as mutual mistake, impossibility, infancy, mental illness, fraud, and express termination clauses – albeit not including hysteria resulting from public outrage or private embarrassment.

## A. Mistake and Warranty: Madoff's Ponzi Scheme

Why problems existing but unknown when a deal is made, owing to mutual mistake or warranty, can justify excusing contractual obligation, using the case of a divorcing couple's settlement agreement based on the existence of a Madoff account that turned out to be fictional.

## B. Impossibility and Force Majeure: Donald Trump

Why problems arising from supervening events like fire, flood, and other catastrophes that make performance impossible or impracticable can justify excusing contractual obligation, using the case of Donald Trump's effort to delay loan repayment duties in light of the 2008 financial crisis.

## C. Infancy: Craig Traylor of "Malcolm in the Middle"

Why minors and mentally ill persons have the right to elect to affirm or disaffirm otherwise valid contracts they make, using the case of child actor Craig Lamar Traylor who elected to disaffirm a contract with his personal manager, Sharyn Berg.

## D. Outrage: AIG's Employee Bonuses

Why public outrage is not a ground to rescind a bargain, and how the terms of a contract govern whether it must be performed or not, using the example of the bonuses AIG paid employees during the 2008 financial crisis.

## E. Embarrassment: The New York Mets and Citi Field

How contracts can be used to promote business relationships with parties who can become an embarrassment and why this does not excuse the obligation, using the example of the contretemps over the deal Citicorp made to name The New York Mets' home field, at the crest of the 2008 financial crisis.

*Synthesis*: Why ancient doctrines like *caveat emptor* (let the buyer beware) or *pacta sunt servanda* (promises are kept) are vital but cannot be absolute, and how contracts and contract law rather than politics and ideology rightly define the terms of bargains people make.

## 4. PAYING UP: REMEDIES

Remedies for breach of contract, primarily compensation for disappointed expectations, along with limits on remedies.

## A. Interests and Limits: Paris Hilton and "Pledge This!"

Contract law's remedies for breach of contract designed to protect interests in expectancy, reliance, and justice, subject to limitations requiring losses to be shown with reasonable certainty and foreseeable as a result of breach, using the example of Paris Hilton's agreement to promote the raunchy film "Pledge This!"

## B. Compensation: Paris Hilton and Hairtech

Differences between how contract claims award remedies to compensate and tort claims that can include damages to punish, using the case of claims by Hairtech International against Paris Hilton for failing to promote hair care products as promised.

## C. Markets and Mitigation: Redskins Season Tickets

Standard market references contract law uses to measure damages from breach and associated limitations on recovery for losses that can be avoided with reasonable diligence, using the case of claims by the Washington Redskins against season ticket buyers who breached their agreements to buy tickets.

## D. Stated Remedies: Sprint's Early Termination Fees

The possibility of contracts stating the remedy for breach and how courts police these for excess, using the case of early termination fees in cell phone service contracts.

## E. Specific Performance: Tyson Chickens and IBP Pork

Limited times that courts require contract parties to perform their promises specifically, as opposed to paying money damages, when money would not be adequate to protect an interest because of unique features of the bargain, using the case of a merger agreement between Tyson Foods and IBP.

*Synthesis:* Why awarding money damages in most cases works while holding out the possibility of specific performance in extraordinary cases, as well as the possibility of restitution when all else fails.

## 5. REWINDING: RESTITUTION AND UNJUST ENRICHMENT

A body of law intertwined with contracts, called restitution, available to promote justice when contract law's standard tools break down, recognizing obligations where contract law might not and awarding remedies to prevent unjust enrichment.

### A. Gratuity or Exchange: Caring for Aunt Frances

Difference between those conferring benefits gratuitously and those doing so in the expectation of compensation or reimbursement, using the example of family caretakers.

### B. Mere Volunteers: Battling Alaskan Beetles

Limits of restitution, not extending to cover mere volunteers, using the example of a prospective buyer of Alaskan timberland voluntarily preparing a site study amid Alaska's beetle epidemic that threatened the state's forests.

### C. Trailing Promises: Lena Saves Lee's Life

Why promises made after someone else has conferred a benefit are rarely valid, using the case of one neighbor saving another neighbor's life.

### D. Novel Ideas: The Making of "The Sopranos"

When no contract is formed but one person shares ideas with another who exploits them for gain, a claim in restitution can arise so long as the ideas were novel but not otherwise, using the example of a municipal judge's claim to a share of the profits from the hit HBO television series "The Sopranos."

## E.  Off-Contract Remedies: Rod Stewart at the Rio

When a contract is too indefinite to resolve a dispute over entitlement to money, off-contract remedy of restitution to prevent unjust enrichment can apply, using the example of a $2 million advance paid to Rod Stewart for a concert he could not perform because of complications arising after his throat surgery.

    *Synthesis:* Why formal rules of contract should be resisted to enable the flexible protection of interests that the doctrine of restitution enables.

## 6.  WRITING IT DOWN: INTERPRETATION, PAROL, FRAUDS

The significance, problems, and requirements of putting a deal in writing.

## A.  Plain Meaning I: Eminem's Digital Records

How courts interpret written contracts, evaluating whether contractual expressions manifest a plain meaning or require additional evidence, using the case of rapper Eminem's claim against his record producer about whether recordings marketed as iTunes and ringtones are "sales" or "licenses."

## B.  Plain Meaning II: Dan Rather's Last Broadcast

Example of plain meaning interpretation that complements the preceding story, showing how telltale linguistic cues convey a plain meaning, using the example of CBS's termination of Dan Rather following controversial news broadcast about President Bush's Vietnam-era military service two months before the 2004 presidential election.

## C.  Parol Evidence: The Golden Globes

Why complete and final written agreements prevent consideration of evidence about previous or contemporaneous deal making, using the example of a production contract for the Golden Globes.

### D.  Scrivener's Error: Who Owns the L.A. Dodgers?

Effects of fraud and mistake on determining obligations, using the example of scrivener's error in preparation of postnuptial agreement between Jamie and Frank McCourt about ownership of the Los Angeles Dodgers baseball team.

### E.  Statute of Frauds: Cliff Dumas's Phantom Radio Deal

Limited but important circumstances where contracts must include a writing to be valid, along with exceptions and how the requirement is met, using the example of country music radio personality Cliff Dumas's employment with a local radio station.

*Synthesis:* Why "putting it in writing" is not always the surest path to contractual certainty, but how it remains an appealing way to iron out the details, contract law taking the pragmatic middle ground between those who invest full faith in written expression and those incapable of believing that sometimes words have plain meanings.

## 7.  PERFORMING: DUTIES, MODIFICATION, GOOD FAITH

What having a contract entails and how duties may be adjusted during performance.

### A.  Implied Terms: Butch Lewis and Maya Angelou

The role good faith can play to fill in gaps in indefinite, incomplete, or tentative agreements, using the case of the entertainment impresario Butch Lewis's deal to promote the poet Maya Angelou's work as greeting cards with Hallmark, in a deal that generated hundreds of millions of dollars for the card company and many millions of dollars in royalties.

### B.  Express Terms: Clive Cussler's Movie "Sahara"

The relation between express contract terms and standards of good faith, using the case of best-selling adventure novelist Clive Cussler's deal with billionaire Philip Anschutz's Crusader Entertainment to make a movie of Cussler's book, "Sahara."

### C. Unanticipated Circumstances: Deutsche Building

Why unanticipated circumstances can justify departing from literal terms of a contract, but how promises extorted by duress are unenforceable, using the example of Bovis Lend Lease's fixed-price contract to demolish the Deutsche Bank building in Lower Manhattan, rendered dangerous by 9/11.

### D. Accord and Satisfaction: Lady Gaga

Why parties may settle bona fide disputes by contracts called "accord and satisfaction," using the example of disputes between music producer Rob Fusari and pop performer Lady Gaga.

### E. Adjustment: Conan and "The Tonight Show"

Renegotiation of contracts, role of good faith, covenants not to compete, and remedies using the 2010 dispute between Conan O'Brian and NBC over "The Tonight Show."

*Synthesis*: Why the prevailing scope of the duty of good faith and respect for the express terms of a bargain properly balance the need for flexibility in contractual relationships with aversion to holding contracting parties to standards of conduct to which they did not assent.

## 8. HEDGING: CONDITIONS

Why and how parties limit the scope of their promises with conditions, express or implied, and how contract law's tools reinforce bargains and protect their fruits rather than encourage parties to walk away and scatter losses.

### A. Interpretation and Effect: Kevin Costner's Bison

How to determine whether a contractual expression makes a promise, whose breach entitles the injured party to remedies, or states a condition, whose non-occurrence excuses duties, using the case of Kevin Costner's commission of fine rural American sculpture inspired by his film "Dances With Wolves."

## B. Order of Performance: Charlie Sheen and Warner

How to minimize problems arising from finger-pointing about who breached first with constructive conditions to regulate the order of performance, using the example of the saga of actor Charlie Sheen's role on the Warner Brothers television show "Two and a Half Men."

## C. Partial or Total Breach: Sheen and Warner II

Why contract law encourages parties to use self-help and other steps to promote performance and protect the bargain, highlighting different calibers of breach, especially partial and total breach, continuing the example from the saga of Sheen and Warner.

## D. Waiver: Sheen and Warner III

How parties can make minor adjustments, but not major modifications, to their ongoing deals by waiver, opening disputes about whether some commitments are promises or conditions, rounding out the saga of Sheen and Warner.

## E. Substantial Performance: Sandra Bullock's Lake House

Why a party in default can recover anyway, at least if they substantially performed, compensating the other side in money, using the example of Sandra Bullock's contract to build a mansion in Austin, Texas.

*Synthesis*: Why parties should be encouraged to use self-help, backed by the strength of judicial enforcement.

## 9. CONSIDERING OTHERS: THIRD PARTIES AND SOCIETY

The limited rights and related duties third parties have concerning contracts to which they are strangers.

## A. Beneficiaries: Supply Chain Abuse at Wal-Mart

Scope of rights of third parties to enforce contracts to which they are strangers, highlighting the case of foreign employees against Wal-Mart for violations of local labor laws by its suppliers.

## B. Assignment: JP Morgan's Cablevisión Loan

Scope and limits of party's rights to transfer contract interests, using the example of JP Morgan's attempted sale of a loan contract to a competitor of the borrower.

## C. Interference: New England Patriots and StubHub

Limitations on the rights of third parties to interfere with the contracts of others, using the example of the New England Patriots challenging the online ticket service StubHub for arranging sales of Patriots' season tickets.

## D. Torts: Katie Janeway's Tragic Accident

Why courts police bargains that purport to exculpate people from civic obligation, like negligence, using the example of contracts purporting to relieve sports and recreational facilities from liability for grossly negligent behavior.

*Synthesis:* Why law rightly limits the rights of strangers to contracts to enforce them and protects the interests of parties in contractual relationships from impairment by assignment or by tortious interference from others and law's interest in standards of behavior that may trump freedom of contract.

# ACKNOWLEDGMENTS

I am indebted to many people whose help on this book was valuable. For helpful comments on many chapters, thanks to my colleagues at The George Washington University Law School, H. Jefferson Powell and Michael Selmi, and to the following readers: Ian Ayres (Yale University), Miriam A. Cherry (Saint Louis University Law School), Ronald K. L. Collins (University of Washington), Susan Heyman (Roger Williams University), David A. Hoffman (Temple University), Tom C. W. Lin (University of Florida), Jake Linford (Florida State University), James Steven Rogers (Boston College), Andrew Sutter (Rikkyo University), Jennifer S. Taub (Vermont Law School), Douglas J. Whaley (The Ohio State University), and several anonymous reviewers commissioned by Cambridge University Press and other prospective publishers.

For enthusiastic and astute editorial support, I am grateful to John Berger of Cambridge University Press, and for general editing of portions of the manuscript, as well as helpful comments and encouragement, I owe thanks to Ira Breskin, Fred Cuba, Marion Cuba, Lucy Martucci, and Susan Schulman.

For spectacular copyediting of the entire manuscript, exuberant thanks to my former Contracts student, Stephanie Resnik, George Washington Law School class of 2012. For additional editorial assistance on selected chapters, thanks to another former Contracts student at George Washington, Zachary Stern, class of 2010, and for research assistance, thanks to two others: Chris Davis, George Washington Law class of 2010, and Christa Laser, class of 2011.

For assistance concerning documents and other materials for the stories, I appreciate the help of lawyers and paralegals involved in the cases, including: Andrew R. Damgaard (Janklow Law Firm, Lawrence, South Dakota, in *Detmers v. Costner*); David George (Connelly Baker Wotring, Houston, Texas, in *Kolodziej v. Mason*); and Richard Emery and Ellen Wood (Emery Celli Brinckerhoff & Abady LLP, New York, in *Simkin v. Blank*).

Above all, for reading, commenting, and editing, plus listening, and for everything, forever and always, thanks and love to Stephanie Cuba.

# INTRODUCTION

The wedding celebration of Leo and Elizabeth Facto took place on a humid August night in a New York City suburb. The ceremony was complete and their reception in full swing. They had rented a beautiful banquet hall, where champagne flowed, a band played, and a photographer preserved the memories. As the 150 guests kicked up their heels, one hour into the gala, an electric power failure gripped the region. The air conditioning shut down, the music died, and picture taking stopped.

Their night ruined, the Factos sued the banquet hall for a refund of the $10,000 they paid months earlier when they signed their rental agreement. The Factos, like many people, thought a full refund was in order. After all, the Factos deserve sympathy, as they will never have their big celebration. The banquet hall countered that it was blameless for the regional power outage. It argued that the Factos had signed a contract to pay the $10,000 and they should be bound to that.

The judge decided the case based on well-established principles of contract law that govern with an even hand.[1] The court noted that the banquet hall could not control the power grid, yet the outage made it impossible for the hall to perform its side of the deal. That meant the hall was excused from its duty to do so. But contract law also provides that when one side is excused from performing because of an uncontrollable event, the other side is excused too. So the Factos were likewise freed from their duty. However, to be fair, the court also ruled that the couple had to pay for the services they received. The hall was entitled to payment for decorations, candles, tables, and the food and

1

beverages it served before the power outage; the Factos got a refund of the balance.

Contract law has wrestled with dilemmas like this for a long time and has forged well-worn paths through them. Solutions to contemporary problems, such as those the Factos encountered, can be found in cases that are scores or even hundreds of years old. Many people, among experts and the general public alike, wrongly think that such classic contract law cases makes the subject dusty and dull. They say the old cases are fossils of interest mostly because they reveal law's pathological streak and that contemporary legal education that teaches these specimens is outdated and out of touch.[2] This book's stories show that the classic cases are alive, well and bear directly on modern disputes that arise everyday, among ordinary folks such as the Factos as well as among the famous – from Coretta Scott King to Paris Hilton and Donald Trump; from poet Maya Angelou to novelist Clive Cussler; musicians Eminem, Lady Gaga, 50 Cent, and Rod Stewart; movie stars Sandra Bullock and Kevin Costner; and television personalities Conan O'Brien and Dan Rather.

Inherently interesting for their personalities and distinctive business or social settings – such stories stoke earnest discussions among neighbors and coworkers, in real time and online – these tales reveal contract law's remarkable capacity to use ancient principles to resolve today's puzzles. As the old saying goes, the more things change, the more they stay the same: Contract law principles timelessly thrive in the face of novel problems. Our credit card agreements differ from eighteenth-century promissory notes, but raise similar issues, like whether the rate is usurious and if late fees are part of the bargain. Attitudes shift about family life, transformations follow technological innovation, and standard form contracts proliferate. While people of goodwill debate the implications, most answers and general principles of contract law are readily adaptable to meet the needs in this ever-changing world.

Despite long-settled principles, moreover, a huge gap separates people's beliefs about contracts from the reality of contracts, a gap too often exploited by parties spinning the media, politicians grandstanding, and Internet and water cooler know-it-alls polluting what could be meaningful conversation. Many people think that promises must be kept, come hell or high water.[3] They say promises are sacred and suppose that judges force people to perform them – as if Portia might have ordered Antonio's pound of flesh paid to Shylock in Shakespeare's "The Merchant of Venice." Many believe judges punish those who breach promises. Some think that a valid contract must be signed, sealed, and delivered – as in the title of Stevie Wonder's popular song. Hourly workers think companies can only fire them for "just cause."[4]

This book's tour of American contracts stories in the news will reveal how all these beliefs are mistaken. The gap between common belief and contract reality not only gives the devious or the ignorant tools to mislead others; it entices visionaries to recommend changes to contract law, often to conform to their political tastes. Moralists see in promise making a higher order of behavior that is sacrosanct and prescribe that promises must be kept.[5] Economists think promise making can be measured solely in utilitarian terms. So they dictate choosing among alternative actions, such as performing a promise or breaching it, by comparing costs and benefits.[6] Some on the political left suspect that contract law privileges the rich over the poor and the powerful over the weak. They urge a more egalitarian revision. Their foes on the political right declare that contract law is too paternalistic and yearn to oust normative law from the market altogether.

These positions can have considerable allure, for different reasons. Approaching the world with a measuring device like a utility function, and hunting for the efficient solution, offers the satisfaction of a definite course of action. Taking a contextual approach to problems and appreciating the plight of others brings the satisfaction of empathy. Despite allure, by showing how the settled doctrines of contract law have long served our widely accepted social and business goals, this book's stories illuminate the flaws in these revisions. The book displays this body of ideas as holding a sensible center against extreme political positions and misguided populist intuitions.

To appreciate today's clarity in contract law and its place in history, it is useful to recognize legendary figures dating back more than a century. In the 1870s, C. C. Langdell, as Dean of Harvard Law School, designed a simple way to organize the vast field of law, still used to this day. He thought that underlying law's complexity were a handful of basic ideas. Examining leading cases organized around these ideas would reveal law's elements and rhythms.[7] Common law actions, meaning those courts resolve one by one, were of greatest interest to Langdell and are the focus of this book. In the United States, following English traditions, common law is developed by state courts as disputes arise. Originally referring to law "common" to all citizens, today this system yields some variation among states, but general principles tend to prevail.[8] Although the common law evolves as society and the economy change, judges draw on precedents when evaluating new cases, under the principle of stare decisis.[9]

Langdell organized the welter of cases on numerous topics according to basic questions: how, what, and why. The question of *how* isolates the procedures private parties follow when resolving disputes using civil litigation – like the Facto's wedding fiasco. This is the practice of the lawsuit, arranged into the subfield of study called civil procedure. The question of *what* addresses the stakes in a lawsuit, pivoting around entitlement to property. This involves drawing the lines of ownership, such as between what belongs to the Factos and what belongs to the banquet hall. Most pertinent, the question of *why* investigates justifications courts give when requiring property to change hands.

The answer to "why" is because of a judgment that one party instead of another is entitled to a sum of money or other property. Dean Langdell identified two sources of these obligations. One arises from behavior required of all people living in a civil society, called the law of torts, epitomized by the idea of negligence. The other comes from self-imposed undertakings, usually by a promise or an agreement, called the law of contracts. These two fields, torts and contracts, define the scope of civil obligation that courts may enforce. Civil obligation contrasts with criminal law. The substance of criminal law consists of invasions by a person of the rights of another or of the public (like treason) so serious as to require public force (the police and district attorney), not just private remedy, to redress. Such public interests also appear in constitutional law, which sets basic rights of individuals, as against government, plus the powers of the states in relation to each other, and to the federal government.

Contract law asks the vital question: Of all the promises made in the world, which should be recognized as enforceable in court? Equally important, it asks, among enforceable obligations, what remedy should be awarded upon breach? There are many promises contract law views as unenforceable. For example, contract law does not recognize social promises such as dinner dates as warranting enforcement,[10] nor does it enforce most promises to make gifts. Instead, contract law concentrates on bargained-for transactions – such as promises to borrow and lend money or rent a car or banquet hall. There are also bargains that are enforceable even though a promise is not made. A customer who drops off suits at a dry cleaner owes the price for the service when performed, whether any promise was made or not.[11] A doctor who treats an unconscious person prone in the street is entitled to recover the reasonable value of services rendered, even though the patient obviously promised nothing.[12]

The substance of contract law expresses a political philosophy. In a capitalist society, contracts and contract law are essential. Where people are free to own and exchange property, contracts and contract law establish ownership and facilitate commerce. "Freedom of contract" describes an approach of deference to private autonomy and individualism. It means courts have a limited, albeit crucial, role: to decide whether contractual liability exists and order appropriate remedies for breach. Freedom of contract can be a wonderful way to unleash creative energies and expand productive capacity and well-being. Yet contractual freedom is neither unchecked nor unbridled. Government regulation provides social control over individuals by curtailing licentious pursuits of self-interest. Governmental regulation aims to protect people from the unscrupulous who would take advantage of contract law's freedom. "Freedom *from* contract" provides a way to limit such exploitation. This gives courts a broader role. They decide not only questions of liability and remedy, but police against objectionable bargains.

Conflicts can arise between private autonomy and state regulation but, in contract law, there is remarkable harmony between the two: You can bargain for anything you want – almost. But that does not stop people from advocating that contract law should move toward the extremes. Devotees of pure capitalism, on the political right, campaign for uncompromising devotion to freedom of contract and resist state regulation that limits individual autonomy or contractual possibilities in any way. Opponents of rampant capitalism, on the political left, vigorously object to such rugged individualism, pushing for substantial social control and stressing freedom *from* contract. They exhort judges to review bargains for fairness or impress standards of behavior on people even if they did not agree to accept them.

Contract law in the United States reflects neither extreme. U.S. citizens may be conservative or liberal, Republican or Democrat, even libertarian or socialist. But the country, as a whole, is none of those things and neither is its contract law. The country's practices are capitalist and democratic, capacious notions stressing both entrepreneurship and responsibility.[13] The nation's contract law gives enormous but not unlimited space for freedom of contract. Of course, contract law is dynamic, adapting as society and the economy change. And the philosophies of particular judges in individual cases affect their analysis and sometimes the resolution of a dispute. But contract law's evolution and its application by particular judges has vacillated within stable, practical boundaries.[14] These boundaries are well defined by two other titans in the law of contracts: Samuel Williston and Arthur Corbin.

In 1920, Williston, a Harvard colleague of Langdell's, published a monumental treatise on the entire law of contracts and kept it updated until his death in 1963. In 1950, Arthur Corbin, a professor at Yale, promulgated an equally magisterial and comprehensive treatise based on earlier writings throughout his career. These works – still kept up to date by successor editors – have influenced generations of lawyers and judges addressing contract disputes.[15] Williston's philosophy dovetailed with that of the eminent jurist, Oliver Wendell Holmes, Jr., and Corbin's resonated with that of the esteemed judge, Benjamin N. Cardozo.

Williston epitomized a formalist approach to law and reflected what some call the "classical" school of contract. It looks to whether parties in a transaction were giving and getting something, emphasizing a concept called "consideration" as the signal of an enforceable contract. This school of thought held unenforceable not only promises to make gifts or attend dinner, but promises merely inducing another party to take some action. In this view, the remedy for breach of a bargain is to pay the injured party money to put them in the same economic position they would have enjoyed had the other performed. This classical conception of contract law dominated well into the twentieth century and remains a force today.

Corbin took a realist approach to law and offered a more pragmatic conception of contract. Although agreeing with Williston on many points, Corbin recognized, as courts increasingly did in the twentieth century, a wider range of circumstances that create contractual obligations. Williston's bargain model of consideration remained, but loosened so that even some promises to make gifts could be enforced, so long as there was an identifiable return, like naming a college endowment.[16] It recognized reliance on a promise as a basis of contractual liability, in a novel doctrine commonly called "promissory estoppel."[17] Compensation for disappointed expectations remains the primary measure of remedy. But recognizing promissory estoppel gave equal dignity to measuring remedies by out-of-pocket costs incurred relying on a promise.[18]

These twentieth-century developments that Corbin captured and helped shape reflected broader social developments as well, moving law's orientation from a formalist to a realist conception. For example, classical contract's relative strictness, limiting the scope of contractual obligation, was accompanied by an equivalent strictness of enforcement: If a contract was hard to get into, it was also hard to get out of. People could be bound to contracts that were made based on mutually mistaken assumptions, or even where performance became impossible. But as the ambit of contractual obligation expanded, so did grounds for excusing it, like mutual mistake about the terms of a trade, or impossibility of performance, such as a power outage in a rented banquet hall. Similarly, classical contract law venerated written records, limiting the scope of obligation to what was plainly meant within a document's four corners. Corbin and his realist descendants were more willing to consider evidence supplementing these written expressions.

An example of this shift appears in a classic case from the 1920s.[19] In the fall of 1923, the Laths proposed selling their Schenectady (New York) farm to the Mitchills.[20] The parties discussed how the Laths would remove an unsightly ice house they owned on the property of a neighbor. Their written contract took an elaborate form, containing a wealth of recitals about price, insurance, water supply, a land survey, a deed, and broker's commissions. It said nothing about removing the ice house. After the deal closed, the Mitchills renovated the place for use as a summer home and sued the Laths for failing to remove the ice house. The Laths stressed that the two couples had written up an elaborate contract that said nothing about any ice house. The Mitchills tried to persuade the court to look beyond the writing to the discussions they said the couples had about the ice house.

The court sided with the Laths. Judge William Andrews, an acolyte of Williston, explained that the written agreement, with its wealth of recitals, looked complete. Had the parties made a deal about removing an ice house, he would naturally have expected to see it in the writing. Therefore, the Mitchills were not even allowed to present at a trial any testimony about their negotiations with the Laths. In dissent, Judge Irving Lehman, more in tune with Corbin, was skeptical. When deciding whether the contract was complete, he took the negotiations into account and, with them in mind, said he would *not* naturally expect a side deal about the ice house to be included in the writing.

Judge Andrews reflected the era's dominant view: classical, formal, "four-corners." Lehman was ahead of his time, reflecting the ascendant view: contemporary, realistic, contextual. But even these oppositions are neither extreme nor ironclad, as Cardozo, a realist, joined the majority opinion in the case, siding with Andrews, not Lehman. The positions of these judges in this typical case show that most of the disagreements within contract law are differences with a practical rather than an ideological edge. The case was not about the rich or poor, the powerful or the oppressed, or a fight between freedom and control. Like most issues contract law addresses, it was about a pragmatic question: What weight to give a written contract compared to oral negotiations? Healthy debate continues about this and many other questions that divided titans like Williston and Corbin, although the range of credible debate is substantially bounded by positions those two staked out.

Unbounded is the range of subjects contracts involve, which is as large as life. Contract law addresses all exchange transactions and the universe of promises. Given such a sprawling enterprise, expect to find occasional tensions or contradictions between cases or within doctrines, or variation among states. Despite such findings, however, which tend to be clearest at microscopic levels of inspection, contract law shows a surprising degree of coherence across settings and geography.

Many have tried to provide a grand theory of contract law, but it is unsurprising that contract law's vastness defies tidy explanation using any single account. True, much of contract law is based on promises, but not all promises are recognized as legally binding;[21] much of contract law probes whether people have consented to some exchange, but it is likewise true that not every consented deal is valid, and liability can attach even though consent is not obvious.[22] It is particularly difficult to explain everything about contract law in terms of protecting people when they rely on others[23] or determining which arrangements are the most economically efficient,[24] although both reliance and efficiency are often relevant. If pressed, the best way to account for the vast run of contract law doctrine is pragmatism – a search for what is useful to facilitate exchange transactions people should be free to pursue.[25]

Famous books have been published that consciously demonstrate not contract law's coherence, but its tensions, contradictions, and the dissolution of Langdell's revered categories, including the venerable distinction between torts and contracts.[26] Other approaches include the "law in action" movement, which insists that in contracting, business reality is more important than the law.[27] Proponents joined critics of Langdell's "case method" to debunk the practice of learning contracts from common law opinions, saying that was akin to learning zoology by focusing on unicorns and dodos.[28] Although influential, these tidings did not transform the field, which is still readily learned by the reading of opinions in individual cases and stitching them together into a tapestry of knowledge. The stories in this book take a similar approach, each one explaining its setting and then stating and resolving the conflict. They explore recurring issues people face in contracting and, in line with the concept of stare decisis, show how previous cases and their rationales apply to evaluate arguments.

Remarkably, this book recounts only forty-five main stories, along with as many supplemental tales, yet its insights are relevant to billions of people and contracts. The great majority of deals are made and completed without giving contracts or contract law the slightest thought. Only a tiny fraction trigger disputes of the kind these stories tell. Much as we breathe without thinking about the indispensability of oxygen, however, those invisible qualities of contract law enable doing deals without conscious thought on the subject. Keeping it that way means that people should appreciate how principles germinated generations ago remain vital to resolve ongoing challenges, know enough to discuss stories of contracts in the news intelligently and check those advocating extreme changes. This book, by telling entertaining stories capturing the essentials of this subject, aims to promote those goals.

# 1 GETTING IN

## Contract Formation

*The great variety of contract theories since the Romans attests to the fact that the power of making promises has occupied the center of political thought over the centuries.*

– Hannah Arendt

## A. GIFTS, BARGAINS, RELIANCE: MARTIN LUTHER KING, JR. AND BOSTON UNIVERSITY

Dr. Martin Luther King, Jr. is among the most consequential figures in America's civil rights movement. As an activist and leader, he corresponded with luminaries of his time and wrote passionately. His voluminous papers have historical significance, so valuable that many have bid hefty prices to buy them. Most spectacularly, in June 2006, King family members planned to auction the bulk of his papers to the highest bidder at Sotheby's in New York City. Civic leaders in Atlanta, where King was born and raised, worried about the papers landing in private hands, never to be available for public reviewing or scholarly research.[1] To avert that fate, distinguished civic-minded citizens, led by Atlanta Mayor Shirley Franklin, engineered a $32 million loan to a new foundation to buy the papers. The foundation deposited the papers for permanent public access with Atlanta's Morehouse College, where King studied as an undergraduate.

The Morehouse College episode was not the first drama surrounding where King's papers would reside, nor was it the most controversial. That distinction goes to an earlier batch of his papers that King deposited in the 1960s with Boston University, where he earned the PhD that made him "Dr. King." A July 16, 1964 letter that King wrote and signed, and on which he followed up by delivering many papers, read, in part:

> I name the Boston University Library the Repository of my correspondence, manuscripts and other papers.... It is my intention that after the end of each calendar year, [additional] files of materials ... should be sent to Boston University. All papers and other objects which thus pass into the custody of Boston University remain my legal property until otherwise indicated....
>
> I intend each year to indicate a portion of the materials deposited with Boston University to become the absolute property of Boston University as an outright gift from me, until all shall have been thus given to the University. In the event of my death, all such materials deposited with the University shall become from that date the absolute property of Boston University.

Dr. King was assassinated on April 4, 1968. He left no will. Decades later, after years of BU's custodianship, Dr. King's widow, Coretta Scott King, challenged the archive arrangement in Massachusetts court.[2] Mrs. King argued that the letter and Dr. King's delivery of the materials showed he had merely loaned them to BU. She said he made no promise to do more, and that any promise he did make was merely to make a gift, as opposed to a legally valid commitment. BU contended just the opposite, saying the promise was clear and binding.

The King case raised profound issues in a struggle dating as far back as the Middle Ages: how to distinguish enforceable statements from those that are not. A long-standing social and moral norm treats promises as sacred.[3] An important strand of philosophy considers promise keeping a social or civic duty. If these principles were followed, law would be obliged to enforce all promises as contracts, which, of course, it cannot. It would simply be impracticable for any court system to handle, and undesirable for judges to resolve, every fight over a breached promise. Courts are therefore more circumspect about what makes for a legally binding contract.

Mrs. King stressed the lack of formality in Dr. King's statements. His letter, though signed, was merely a gesture of kindness. For example, he did not take the trouble of having any witnesses attest to it, getting it notarized, or affixing a waxed seal on it to evidence an intention that it be legally binding.[4]

BU urged more substantive tests than this emphasis on formalities. True, such formal tests can be probative of intent, and the law for centuries, in America and Europe, looked to such formalities. But modern law appreciates that such formal tests become diluted or supplanted over time. The seal can become a mere habit, meaning nothing, and people gradually adopt other norms of bargaining, from shaking hands to writing letters. Fixating on such formalities could enable legitimate claims to be defeated.

BU stressed two more useful tests to determine the enforceability of a promise. The first is based on an intuitive sense of a bargain: whether parties agreed to an exchange that one side disappointed. Called "consideration," this has been our law's most important test to determine the enforceability of a contract since the eighteenth century.[5] Unlike a seal or notary, consideration offers both a formal and a substantive test. The presence of an exchange – a quid pro quo – establishes an intention and cautions against impulsively made promises.

The second ground BU urged was reliance, an alternative reason to enforce a promise, which gained increasing recognition throughout the twentieth century. Reliance refers to a change of position made on the basis of a promise someone else made. This doctrine, often called "promissory estoppel," means that unsealed, unwritten, and unbargained-for promises can be enforced when the person making them should expect another to rely on them and did so. Today, this is an available alternative to consideration to justify enforcing a promise, so long as the reliance is reasonable.[6]

The fight in the King case, then, was whether BU gave consideration for Dr. King's commitment of his papers to it or, alternatively, Dr. King made a promise on which BU foreseeably and reasonably relied. Mrs. King argued that Dr. King's statement was not binding because it lacked consideration. In his letter, Dr. King indicated that, in the future, a portion of the deposited materials were "to become" BU's property "as an outright gift" until all papers had been given. To Mrs. King, that language amounted to a mere gratuitous promise to make a gift – not a binding deal. Mrs. King emphasized the letter's qualifying language, when Dr. King wrote that all papers BU takes into custody "remain my legal property" until further steps occurred.

In opposition, BU argued that Dr. King's promise was supported by consideration and by the University's reliance. The statement that deposited property would become BU's by gift must be read alongside the statement that, upon Dr. King's death, all the property would "become from that date the absolute property of" BU. Dr. King delivered property upon signing the letter and another installment the following year. BU took possession of the materials and cared for them. The delivery signaled BU's reciprocal obligation and amounted to consideration, a trade: the papers in exchange for appropriate curating. Alternatively, that same language and context justified the interpretation that Dr. King made a promise that he should have foreseen BU would rely on. By archiving the material in its special collection for many years, the University did reasonably rely on that promise.

## A Charitable Pledge

Although the King-BU dispute presented a close call, a well-known case decided by the same Massachusetts court the previous decade provided guidance.[7] Like the King case, it involved a clash between a charitable organization and one of its deceased donor's widows. The donor, Saul Schwam, suffered a long illness and was often visited by his rabbi, Abraham Halbfinger from Congregation Kadimah Toras-Moshe, in the Boston neighborhood of Brighton. On many of these visits, Schwam promised the rabbi, with witnesses present, to give the synagogue $25,000. The synagogue planned to use the money to transform a storage room into a library in Schwam's name. Before the money was paid, however, Schwam died without a will providing for its payment. The synagogue claimed its $25,000 against Schwam's estate. The court refused to allow it.

The promise was unenforceable because it failed to meet contract law's requirements: either consideration or reliance (nor was it signed, sealed, or notarized). Where the synagogue saw a bargain – cash for naming the library – the court saw only a gratuitous, unenforceable pledge. The synagogue never promised to name the library for Schwam – or even to build it. The rabbi merely said that was the plan. There was simply no indication that the library naming induced Schwam to make his pledge, nor was there any evidence that the synagogue relied on Schwam's promises. All it did was make an entry in its budget of $25,000 for the storage room renovation. This action signaled a hope and a wish, but not reliance or consideration.

The King case differed in several ways. True, Dr. King's letter could be read merely as a promise to make a gift. Taken alone, that would only stimulate hope and wish. But Dr. King also delivered materials to BU, which BU then maintained. That delivery could suggest that Dr. King intended by his letter to seek BU's custodial care of the papers and to transfer them to BU. In contrast, Mr. Schwam never delivered anything. Even though he repeatedly promised Rabbi Halbfinger to make a gift to the synagogue, he never completed the gift.

BU hosted a commemorative convocation celebrating receipt of Dr. King's first installment of papers. There, Dr. King gave a speech that explained why he made the donation. His appearance and comments supported treating the promise as one that BU would be entitled to enforce based on its reliance. BU indexed the King papers, archived them for researchers, and made them available for study. The University also trained staff to care for the papers and to help researchers. These actions were undertaken reasonably in reliance on the letter and were the letter's foreseeable result. In contrast, again, the Kadimah Toras-Moshe synagogue had not taken any similar actions in reliance. Given the absence of any return promise or firmer commitments, it would not have been foreseeable or reasonable to do so.

BU thus won its case against Mrs. King, in an opinion written by Judge Ruth Abrams, the first woman to serve on the 300-year-old Supreme Judicial Court of Massachusetts. Dr. King's promise was supported either by consideration BU supplied or by BU's reasonable reliance. BU still houses its collection of Dr. King's papers in its library – and the papers are extremely valuable, as Atlanta's $32 million purchase of Dr. King's other papers attests. Even though some believe charitable pledges like these should always be enforced, whether or not supported by reliance or consideration, most courts apply these venerable tests, in all contract disputes, to sort out which promises merit enforcement.[8]

### Estopping Aretha Franklin

Whereas BU won the case concerning Dr. Martin Luther King's papers under both theories urged – a bargained-for contract and promissory estoppel – it is more common for cases to accept one or the other. Typically, promissory estoppel is invoked when a bargained-for exchange cannot be shown. A simple example involved Aretha Franklin at the peak of her amazing singing career.[9] She negotiated for several months in 1984 with a Broadway musical producer, Ashton Springer, to perform the lead in a play about the renowned gospel singer, Mahalia Jackson. Franklin and Springer agreed on nearly every detail: a twelve-week performance run with compensation set at $40,000 per week, expenses up to $5,000 weekly, and a 20 percent stake in profits. This was all spelled out in a written document stating it would be binding once Franklin signed.

Franklin never signed, but Springer spent considerable time and at least $200,000 planning the production based on Franklin's assurances that she was in. The court agreed with Franklin that the two had not formed a bargained-for contract. But the court also agreed with Springer that Franklin was liable under promissory estoppel. Franklin unequivocally promised Springer that she was doing this production and that it was her highest professional priority. Franklin most certainly foresaw that Springer would act on those assurances, including juggling the production planning to coincide with Franklin's own schedule. This reliance was reasonable. The court therefore ordered Franklin to pay Springer $200,000 in damages. "Sing Mahalia Sing" ran on Broadway during most of 1985, starring Jennifer Holliday.

## B. ADS OR OFFERS: PEPSI AND HARRIER JETS

Twenty-one-year-old John Leonard thought he had a deal to buy a Harrier jet, an advanced military aircraft, for less than $1 million.[10] The Harrier jet played a decisive role in Operation Desert Storm in 1991, helping the U.S. Marine Corps repel Iraqi dictator Saddam Hussein's invasion of Kuwait, and was also used extensively by the British Air Force. Visitors to London in 2010 could see a retired Harrier jet hanging in the Tate Britain Museum. This plane, known in aviation circles as a V/STOL for vertical/short take-off and landing, is designed to attack and destroy surface targets in broad daylight or pitch darkness. The jet carries tons of military ordnance, including ballistic missiles, yet floats like a butterfly in air.

One day while watching television, Leonard saw a Pepsi Cola ad about goods called Pepsi Stuff – shirts, jackets, sunglasses, and the like boasting Pepsi's logo. The idea was simple: Packages of Pepsi include tokens with point values consumers could redeem for goods. An additional cash payment could buy additional points to supplement the tokens. In the ad, not only did those kinds of goods appear with their price tags in "Pepsi Points," but also a military fighter plane, the Harrier jet. It flew in at the ad's end, with the screen flashing its price tag in Pepsi Points. The ad was evocative.

It is a sunny suburban morning, birds chirping, a paperboy on his route. A military drum beat introduces the title, *Monday 7:58 am.* A well-groomed teenager prepares for school, wearing a shirt with Pepsi's logo, as the words *T-Shirt 75 Pepsi Points* roll on screen. Another angle shows the teenager in a hipleather jacket, while *Leather Jacket 1450 Pepsi Points* appears, and the military drums beat in the background. As the kid leaves his house, he dons a pair of sunglasses, the words *Shades 175 Pepsi Points* scrolling across the screen. A voiceover says, "Introducing the new Pepsi Stuff Catalog," and the camera zooms on a *Pepsi Stuff Catalog.*

The camera changes to three boys sitting in front of a high school building. One studies the Catalog; the others drink Pepsi. The three look skyward, as the background military boom amplifies, inducing a sense of pending drama. Winds of gale force scatter paper in a physics classroom.

The jet swoops into view, landing next to the school, near a bike rack. Students take cover, and the wind's power strips an unlucky teacher of his clothing. The young pilot, looking cool without a helmet, opens the jet's door, holding a Pepsi. As the pilot disembarks, he quips, "Sure beats the bus." The military drumroll pounds again, as this tag line appears: *Harrier Fighter Jet 7,000,000 Pepsi Points.*

The promotion's Pepsi Stuff Catalog displayed goods and points they cost, including T-shirts, jackets, and glasses – but not the Harrier jet. The Catalog's directions, order form, and rules required at least fifteen original Pepsi Points to redeem any good, but permitted a consumer to buy additional points for $.10 each. At first, John Leonard thought he would drink gallons of Pepsi to get the points needed for the Harrier jet. But he soon realized that was unreasonable. So he raised the required cash to meet the price, $700,000.

Leonard sent Pepsi its order form, with fifteen original points and a check for the remaining amount. Pepsi responded that Leonard must be kidding. After all, the spot was merely a commercial advertisement, not an overture to form a sales contract. In addition, the jet in the ad was obviously a joke. Pepsi returned Leonard's check, explaining: "The Harrier jet in the Pepsi commercial is fanciful and is simply included to create a humorous and entertaining ad. We apologize for any mis-understanding or confusion that you may have experienced and are enclosing some free product coupons for your use."

Leonard's lawyers replied that they were not kidding. To them, the ad offered the Harrier jet for 7 million Pepsi Points or its equivalent in points plus dollars. Leonard, they argued, accepted that offer, forming a contract. Again, Pepsi demurred, only this time an executive at its ad agency, Raymond E. McGovern, Jr. of BBDO New York, wrote: "I find it hard to believe that you are of the opinion that the Pepsi Stuff com-mercial really offers a new Harrier jet. The use of the Jet was clearly a joke that was meant to make the commercial more humorous and entertaining. In my opinion, no reasonable person would agree with your analysis of the commercial."

Despite Pepsi's response, the company later changed the spot to make clear it was merely presenting commercial advertising and just joking. Meanwhile, Leonard and Pepsi litigated. Pepsi observed that a common way people form contracts, and what law looks for, is a combination of an offer to make a bargain and an acceptance of it, complete with consideration. It stressed that ads are not usually treated as offers because reasonable people usually interpret them as announcements, not proposed deals. Typically, ads are broadcast to a large number of people and amount to notices of products on sale or requests to consider something and perhaps to negotiate.

## "First Come, First Served"

An ad can become an offer by making that intention clear, targeting it to a particular individual or group of people, using plain language of commitment, or an invitation to act without further communication. A classic example is a department store ad telling potential customers that "three brand new fur coats are on sale for $1 this Saturday at 9 A.M. sharp, first come, first served."[11]

When such an ad prompted Morris Lefkowitz to go to the store, tendering his dollar for a coat, the store refused, saying the ad was only open to women. Yet that is not what the ad said and its delineation of the terms signaled not merely a broadcast to the public at large, but a specific deal on the table. The ad amounted to an offer because its language limited the quantity offered (to three coats) and limited the number of people who could act on it ("first come, first served"). The store thus made an offer that Morris accepted, forming a binding contract.

The Pepsi ad was not within this exception, the company convincingly argued. It communicated to the world at large, without any limitation about who or how many in the world could accept. It was indefinite about the plane, and other goods for that matter, instead referring to the Catalog. The ad said nothing about steps people must take to accept any offer. These features are characteristic of marketing advertisements, not offers to form binding contracts. Any concern that merchandisers might advertise deceptively is addressed by federal and state consumer protection laws.

## Orders at the U.S. Mint

An ad is even less likely to be construed as an offer when an order form is part of it, as in the Pepsi case. For example, the U.S. Mint circulates brochures and order forms advertising Statue of Liberty commemorative coins. Collectors who submit orders do not form a binding contract by doing so. When the Mint, faced with unexpected high demand, could not fulfill its orders, it did not breach any contract.[12] A contract would be formed only once the Mint accepted an order and processed payment. A customer's order form is an offer that the advertiser can accept – or not. In the Pepsi context, Leonard's letter and form were an offer, not an acceptance, and Pepsi rejected it.

## Jesting

Even communications in the form of an offer or an acceptance may not be treated that way when circumstances indicate that they are made insincerely, as in jest. Television actors solemnly uttering scripted words of promise and commitment obviously are not bound to resulting bargains.[13] Act out a ruse in private with a colleague who is in on the joke; no contract results.[14] Of course, fail to let your colleague know it is a joke, and you may be bound.[15] But in the Pepsi case, no reasonable person could avoid apprehending a joke, even if the ad could somehow be seen to assume the form of an offer.

Making Leonard's case somewhat plausible was how Pepsi targeted its Pepsi Points campaign to a lowbrow demographic that would actually desire the products. So it should have expected to encounter the likes of Leonard, perceiving an offer. Pepsi's about-face – changing the ad – could thus be portrayed as an admission of that perception's validity. But the particular views of Leonard and his cohort are idiosyncratic compared to what ordinary common sense suggests. The argument may make his case plausible but not necessarily persuasive. Further, Leonard could not pinpoint his claim as prompting Pepsi's ad change. Companies regularly change marketing materials for many purposes.

For all these reasons, no contract was made, held distinguished Judge Kimba Wood of the federal trial court in New York. The ad is merely a commercial and nothing in it warrants special treatment. Exaggeration is the ad's artistic move, just as ads promoting the transformative properties of ordinary things like cars, beer, and pizza are commonly known to be puffery.[16]

Pepsi called its commercial "zany humor," which Judge Wood thought apt. The ad suggests that Pepsi can transform routine experiences like going to school into a thrill, evoking military drama. The jet's helmetless pilot is hardly the Marine Corps type. His comment about how flying the plane beats the bus, the judge wrote, tongue in cheek,

"evinces an improbably insouciant attitude toward the relative difficulty and danger of piloting a fighter plane in a residential area."[17]

## C. FROLIC OR ACCEPTANCE: BOASTS ON "DATELINE NBC"

J. Cheney Mason is a high-profile and outspoken criminal defense
lawyer in Florida.[18] In 2006, Mason represented Nelson Ivan Serrano,
a wealthy businessman who, prosecutors said, orchestrated a plot to
kill his former business partner, George Gonsalves, and three others in
a Florida manufacturing plant in 1997. During the widely publicized
capital murder trial, Mason gave a challenge in a television interview
aired on "Dateline NBC."

In the capital murder case, state prosecutors said Serrano, traveling
under several aliases, flew from Atlanta to Orlando, rented a car, then
drove 66 miles to the plant and killed the four people, execution style.
Then, the state said, he promptly drove 50 miles to the Tampa airport,
flew back to Atlanta and, in 28 minutes, drove from the Atlanta airport
five miles to La Quinta Inn on Old National Highway. A surveillance
tape showed him in La Quinta, both at midday and in late evening.
Serrano used that tape as an alibi. Mason argued there was no way
anyone could get off a plane at Atlanta's crowded Hartsville-Jackson
airport and be at La Quinta hotel 28 minutes later.

On "Dateline NBC," the host, Ann Curry, posed the vital question – whether there was enough time for Serrano to make that trip in
28 minutes – and gave an answer: "[T]he defense says no." On air, an
excited Mason declared: "And from there to be on the videotape in 28
minutes? Not possible. Not possible. I challenge anybody to show me,
and guess what? Did they bring in any evidence to say that somebody
made that route, did so? State's burden of proof. If they can do it, I'll
challenge 'em. I'll pay them a million dollars if they can do it."

Dustin S. Kolodziej, a law student at South Texas College of Law
living in Houston, had been following the Serrano trial on television
between classes. He saw the Dateline show featuring Mason. Two
phrases caught his attention: "I challenge anybody to show me" and
"I'll pay them a million dollars if they can do it." On December 10,

2007, Kolodziej made the full trip in the required time, videotaping his steps, from Atlanta to Orlando to Tampa and back to Atlanta and, within 28 minutes, getting off the plane, walking through the terminal, getting into a car, and arriving at La Quinta on Old National Highway. When Kolodziej demanded payment, however, Mason refused.

Kolodziej claimed this breached a unilateral contract, a bargain occurring when the offer proposes to pay or do something in exchange for the performance of a designated act (as distinguished from merely promising to perform it). Mason called Kolodziej's claim ridiculous. He contended that he made his statement in jest, to prove a point, as any reasonable person would know. He also said he directed the statement to the prosecutors, daring them, not the general public. Mason was wrong that Kolodziej's claim was "ridiculous," but neither was it an obvious winner.

Companies or people may offer payments in exchange for someone doing something, like disproving a trade claim or finding a lost pet. Sometimes called "prove me wrong" cases, the commercial illustration appears in an immortal 1892 English case, amid an influenza epidemic.[19]

### The Curious Carbolic Smoke Ball

Inventive geniuses concocted cures, hawking them under product labels like Clarke's World Famous Blood Mixture, Sequah's Prairie Flower, Epp's Glycerine Jube-Jubes, the Carbolic Smoke Ball, among many others. The Smoke Ball was especially curious.[20] It was an apple-sized ball containing powdered carbolic acid, with an opening covered by gauze. When squeezed, the powder puffed out a smoke cloud that the user then inhaled.

Probably seen today as an obvious screwball gimmick, the product's promoters were serious about the ball's properties. In their ad campaign, they showed endorsements from the rarified likes of British royalty – well-known earls, duchesses, countesses, and physicians to a prince, a knight, and the queen. One full-page ad in the *Pall Mall Gazette* for the Smoke Ball said:

> £100 reward will be paid by the Carbolic Smoke Ball Co. to any person who contracts the increasing epidemic influenza ... after

having used the ball three times daily for two weeks according to the printed directions supplied with each ball. £1,000 is deposited with the Alliance Bank, Regent Street, shewing our sincerity in the matter.

Louisa Carlill read the ad, bought the ball, and used it. She then, of course, got the flu. She claimed that a contract existed and the company had to perform by paying the reward. True, ads are usually not offers, but this was no ordinary ad. It promised payment if a user got the flu. The ad was an offer of a reward for an action – using the ball – not merely inviting a consumer into a store for discussion. Unlike ordinary advertisements, those offering rewards invite anyone who does the act to form a contract. Mrs. Carlill therefore earned the £100, the court said.

There is a practical justification for this result. Consider when people advertise rewards for the return of lost pets. It is unnecessary, and undesirable, for anyone who sees such an ad and is willing to search first to sit down with the owner and hammer out an agreement. And there is a difference between cases such as pet rewards and smoke balls compared to cases like Pepsi Points. Like reward ads for lost pets, the smoke ball ad was not jocular. It manifested the company's interest in a bargain – depositing reward money in the bank as "shewing its sincerity." Consideration exists: The bargain is an exchange of that money for the action the company induced the woman to take, using the product.

The Dateline example is a variation on the smoke ball theme. Mason, the lawyer, made a statement, akin to the ad, seeking an action and promising payment based on it; Kolodziej, the student, did the act and demanded payment. Yet the case differs from the smoke ball case in an important way: Mason did not deposit any payment with a bank to show his sincerity. But that does not automatically negate his sincerity. Many similar on-air dares have been found to be valid offers:

- A tax protestor appearing on television declared: "If anybody calls this show and cites any section of the code that says an individual is required to file a tax return, I'll pay them $100,000."[21]
- A gambling company executive testifying at a public hearing about the integrity of his product, a punchboard, said: "I'll put $100,000 to anyone to find a crooked board. If they find it, I'll pay it."[22]

- The head of the Jesse James museum asserted that the outlaw did not die in 1882 as legend has it but lived under an alias many years afterward, at the site of the museum; he offered $10,000 "to anyone who could prove me wrong."[23]

## The Hole in One

Analogous cases are common in charity events, especially golf tournaments. Local businesses contribute prizes to players achieving feats, such as a hole-in-one. In this context, signs promising cash or a new car for making a hole-in-one are offers that players accept by acing. Signs manifest an offer to bargain; acing is accepting. The result is a binding contract. That is so even if the sponsor mistakenly left signs up after tournament day. In bargain terms, the sponsor gets the benefit from promotion, like brand awareness, and the golfer does something not required – even if the stroke benefits him by a lower score.[24]

So attorney Mason was wrong that it is ridiculous to see his statement as an offer. After all, he was on "Dateline NBC" while defending a capital murder defendant. That was no laughing matter. And there is good precedent for characterizing his rewards statement as an offer, a "prove me wrong" challenge.

Many observers thought the case an easy one on the facts. They saw it as a simple deal: The lawyer made a bet, lost, and should pay. But it is a much closer call, of course, even if Kokodziej's claim was not "ridiculous." Weaker was Mason's other claim, that any offer he made was limited to the prosecution. It would be odd to make such an offer to an adversary in a legal dispute. Mason's defense also failed in the courtroom: Jurors found Serrano guilty, and a death sentence was handed down in 2007.

As for Dustin Kolodziej, the law student, he is like many first-year students: He learned some relevant law and acted on it. The facts made for a close case. Kolodziej's lawyer, David George, put it well: "This is the kind of thing only a law student would do. It reads like a question on a law school test. This case will likely be studied in law school."[25] As of this writing, after two years of skirmishing over where the case should be heard, it is still pending in a Florida court.

## D. MUTUAL ASSENT: SPYWARE AND SECRET CLAUSES

Spyware is computer code that enables electronic surveillance. When installed on a computer, it can allow third parties surreptitiously to track all of the user's Internet activity. Some unscrupulous companies disseminate it by bundling it with other products. Sometimes those products are accompanied by contracts limiting user rights to sue the purveyor. Fights erupt about whether those are binding.

In a famous case at the dawn of the Internet era, Netscape offered to let users download free software from Web pages, conventionally subject to a license restricting use. Most users are unable to download without seeing the license. When installation begins, an icon opens in a window showing the user the agreement's text, along with instructions: "Do you accept all terms of the license agreement? If so, click the *Yes* button. If you select *No*, setup will close." People most often click *Yes* and are bound by its terms.

Netscape's program was software that enabled Internet browsing and was distributed using that click protocol to assure user awareness of its licensing terms. Netscape offered a companion product, called SmartDownload, that plugged into its browser feature to enhance it. Yet Netscape offered this product in an unconventional way. Users could download the software without seeing a license or any mention of one. Instead, the license appeared in a low part of Netscape's Web page, hidden beneath the download button.

After thousands of users downloaded the product, some discovered it contained spyware. Many found this objectionable and in violation of federal privacy laws.[26] When they sued Netscape to challenge this practice, Netscape said users were bound by a licensing contract directing them to private arbitration and forbidding filing the lawsuit. The users denied that the purported contract was binding.[27] The users emphasized a subjective test, which explored whether they had actual knowledge of an offer and its terms and whether they actually intended to accept those terms. They said Netscape made no offer of terms that any user accepted. What Netscape claimed was an offer was located in the Internet, hidden from view, and not attached to the product. It was impossible for users, unaware of the linked license, to accept any such offer. When users clicked the download button, they did not intend to agree to anything – indeed, they did not even *know* about anything they could possibly agree to.

Netscape countered with an objective test, asking whether reasonable people would know of an offer and its terms and whether a party's actions manifested an intention to accept those terms. Netscape emphasized it is unnecessary for people accepting offers to have actual knowledge of the offer or subjectively intend to accept it. For centuries, Netscape asserted, people have been held to contract terms, regardless of whether they read and understood them.

## Two Ships *Peerless*

The users' argument would have been welcomed throughout the nineteenth century, when there was much talk that an agreement required two subjective intentions, called the "meeting of the minds." The subjective test is illustrated by a famous case of the period.[28] The case concerned a deal to exchange cotton at a stated price for investment. The parties agreed that the cotton would be delivered to Liverpool from Bombay on a ship named *Peerless*. Alas, neither party knew there was more than one ship named *Peerless* plying that route, which sailed at different times.

As a result, each thought the deal was based on a different *Peerless*. The error was pivotal. In that era, the identity of a ship determined its arrival time, which in turn determined the value of goods on board (today the problem of similarly named vessels is resolved by assigning unique radio call letters).[29] Although outward manifestations suggested mutual assent, subjective knowledge and intent differed. For that reason, the parties had formed no contract, held the court.

Returning to the late twentieth century, Netscape argued that an exclusive focus on subjective intent could be perilous. People could sign contracts, exhibiting outward manifestation of intent, yet maintain a hidden intent to be unbound. If the deal turned out well, they could insist they outwardly and inwardly intended a deal and uphold it; if it turned out poorly, they could cite the inward intent and escape.

Netscape rightly observed how early-twentieth-century observers doubted our ability to discern such subjective intentions, and emphasis gradually shifted to outward manifestations. Under its proffered objective standard, Netscape argued that Internet users downloading software have some knowledge that licenses may restrict use. They knew that the appearance of the scroll bar on Netscape's Web page indicated further material on that page; knew how to operate the scroll bar; and knew that most software is governed by license agreements. Objectively speaking, Netscape argued, reasonable people had enough knowledge to alert them to the existence of the license agreement, or at least some agreement, governing use.

Yet exclusive emphasis on outward manifestations can be perilous too, holding people to bargains they did not intend, as the *Peerless* case suggested. As a result, contemporary judges use a synthesis, with outward manifestations the primary determinant, while allowing people's testimony about subjective views to be heard.[30] In the Netscape dispute, it thus mattered what users subjectively intended when clicking on SmartDownload, not solely that they downloaded, installed, and used it.

Contract law has always recognized an escape hatch from apparent manifestation of assent, by not binding people to inconspicuous terms of which they are unaware, in a document whose contractual nature is not obvious. True, people are bound to writings they sign, whether they read them or not. But people are not bound when terms are not presented to them or do not appear to propose a binding contract. Receipt of a physical document containing terms may be enough to give people notice of terms, but they must receive the document.

The action of clicking, downloading, installing, and using software does not manifest assent unless the terms are clearly accessible. It is insufficient that the license appeared on the next scrollable user screen. That is not the same as saying people are held to the terms of documents they sign, whether they read them or not. This "writing" was not presented to users or signed by them. The apparent agreement was to terms whose contractual nature was inconspicuous.

Accordingly, the users did not assent, held Judge Sonia Sotomayor for a federal appellate court in New York, several years before her promotion by President Barak Obama to the U.S. Supreme Court. The users were free to maintain their lawsuit asserting that Netscape violated federal privacy law – which the parties eventually settled on undisclosed terms.

Compare the olden *Peerless* case with the modern Netscape case –
and they show how archaic problems reappear in new forms. Yet no
two cases are identical, and the most recent precedent for the Netscape
case pointed in conflicting directions. The precedent involved a company, ProCD, which compiled information from telephone directo-
ries onto computer discs sold under the brand name SelectPhone. The
company knew different buyer groups use the information differently:
business buyers to expand customer pools; social buyers to connect
with old friends. So it priced the product higher for businesses than
for individuals. The versions offered to consumers included contract
terms, inside the box and on the disc, limiting use to noncommercial
purposes.

Matthew Zeidenberg, a computer science graduate student in
Madison, Wisconsin, bought a consumer-use version of SelectPhone at
a store, paying cash and walking home with the box. The box adverted
to a set of terms inside but did not articulate the exact restrictions. The
terms were inside the box, however, and inserting the enclosed disc in a
computer, the software displayed the term prohibiting commercial use
upon every start of the program. Despite the restrictions, Zeidenberg
posted the information on his Web site and sought advertisers there to
generate revenue.

ProCD sued for breach of contract, citing the clause in the box
and on the disc restricting commercial use of the product. Zeidenberg
contended the restriction was not part of their contract, which he said
was formed when he paid for the product and the store handed it to
him. At the time of purchase, he stressed, he did not know of the terms,
so they could not be part of any contract. There would be no mutual
assent, as contract law has long required.

Frank Easterbrook, the federal judge in Chicago appointed by
President Ronald Reagan, thought otherwise. He accepted ProCD's
argument that the contract was formed later, once Zeidenberg used the
product after taking it home and having a chance to examine its terms.[31]
True, contracts are usually formed by haggling over terms before cash
changes hands. But many are formed by exchanging money before
communicating detailed terms, including those for insurance, airline
tickets, and prescription medicine.

Contract law recognizes that agreements can be made in many ways, so long as they sufficiently show a deal. Those making offers can set the terms however they like. That power is reflected in an august slogan calling that person "master of the offer." That person sets the ground rules, including specifying how an offer can be accepted. A software seller thus sets the terms and buyers accept or reject.

When ProCD proposed a deal priced with related restrictions, it made an offer. That offer was not simply to buy goods at the outset. Rather, the offer was to use the goods and, by use, assent to the terms. A contract can thus be formed at the store upon sale or at home after using. It was up to ProCD, as master of the offer, to dictate which it would be. The transaction at the register was not a contract, because Zeidenberg was not merely accepting an offer of the product for cash, but an offer of the product, along with the terms inside, for cash. Zeidenberg, by using the product without objecting, accepted.

Zeidenberg's acceptance is analogous to download offers on the Internet, where users are invited to click *Yes* to signal they accept the terms. Cases like ProCD seemed to favor Netscape's stance, but they actually support Netscape users' case. After all, in ProCD's case, the box of software noted it was subject to the terms listed inside. The license appeared on the screen and required assent before each use. The license was in the software manual and on the CD-ROM. These details made ProCD an easy case on which to conclude that a contract was formed. In contrast, the Netscape users never saw – and they could not reasonably have seen – the clause at all. There was no chance to click *No*.[32]


## E. POLICIES OR PACTS: THE CLEVELAND.COM BLOGGER

Like most traditional print newspapers, the *Cleveland Plain Dealer* migrated in the early 2000s to provide news online, at Cleveland. com. Following trends, the site let people post comments to its articles, signed or anonymous. The site posts governing company policies, including protecting personally identifiable information. Site users click a "terms-of-use" link to signal assent to the policies.

In early 2010, some eighty anonymous comments came from "lawmiss," many discussing cases pending before a state court judge, Shirley Strickland Saffold.[33] After determining that many comments were made using the judge's state-issued computer, the newspaper disclosed the judge's identity as the comments' author, without her permission. Judge Saffold claimed the newspaper's disclosure breached the company's commitment to protect the identities of users on its site. Similar cases multiplied during this period, making this wave of litigation among the hottest contemporary contract law topics.

The Cleveland.com story echoes the hottest practical topic in contract law from the 1990s, namely whether corporate employment policies could be enforced as contracts. Saffold could point to how judges handled that flood of unprecedented cases to resolve her own battle with Cleveland.com about whether corporate privacy policies stated on the Internet are contracts. Before the 1980s, the common law of contracts was clear: Corporate policies stated in employee handbooks were not offers to form contracts and, regardless, would not be binding for lack of consideration. Employers were free to fire employees at will, following a centuries-old tradition with deep roots in Anglo-American culture and law.[34] Rulings like that are highly favorable to companies such as the *Cleveland Plain Dealer* wishing to resist having their online privacy policies seen as contracts.

During the late 1980s and early 1990s, however, human resources departments spruced up these handbooks to express warmer commitments to employees of job security in compelling language. Employees, seduced by the handbooks' promises, increasingly relied on these statements when choosing jobs, and many viewed them as binding contracts. As a result, contract law gradually shifted its stance. The handbooks could manifest employer intention to offer a binding contract. By reporting for work each day, employees accepted the offer and supplied the requisite consideration.

## Mobil Coal's Employee Handbook

A 1991 case illustrates this shifting landscape in the workplace and how law adapted in ways relevant to today's online policy disputes.[35] Mobil Coal Company of Wyoming published an employee handbook one year before hiring Craig McDonald as a mine technician in August 1987. The handbook told employees to read its contents carefully, then declared that the handbook was not a contract and that the employment relationship was terminable by the company at will. But it also said the best way to promote healthy employee-company relations is through consultation, adding that during any job dispute, the company would always give employees a consultation and a five-step discipline schedule.

The company fired McDonald in June 1988, amid rumors that he had sexually harassed a colleague. Investigation into the allegations and the firing did not follow the handbook's procedures. McDonald sued for breach of contract, asserting either a binding bargain supported by consideration or, alternatively, an enforceable promise based on reliance. In a bewildering series of rulings, the judges on the Wyoming courts took various positions on whether McDonald had made out a traditional claim for breach of contract or a claim for the more modern promissory estoppel. In the end, a divided Wyoming Supreme Court said he had made a plausible claim for promissory estoppel but failed to make out a claim for old-fashioned breach of contract. Courts countrywide similarly struggled when deciding what, if any, claims an employee in cases similar to McDonald's might be able to win.[36]

When judges like those in Craig McDonald's case became willing to treat employee claims as valid, employers got the message. The glossy brochures boasting of job security that proliferated in the 1980s and 1990s returned to the form of practical guides of earlier eras. Companies took greater care in handbooks to say what they meant and to mean what they said, clarifying that employment could still be terminated at will.

Courts struggled during this process of change with traditional doctrines to evaluate whether to enforce promises as contracts. That meant new encounters with old contract law tools such as offer, acceptance, and consideration, as well as mutual assent. Contract law tools worked because the employee manuals common before the 1980s did not warrant enforcement as contracts, but many that came afterward did.

The Cleveland.com case shows that a similar shift is afoot concerning corporate policies about the privacy interests of consumers, especially online.[37] Corporate policies do not readily meet the usual tests required to establish contracts, such as bargained-for consideration or reasonable reliance.[38] As courts struggle with this novelty, however, they forge pathways to recognize privacy policies as contracts. A harbinger appears in a 2007 case unwittingly linking the old employee handbook cases to today's privacy cases – of help to online users such as Judge Shirley Strickland Saffold, and a caution to online companies such as Cleveland.com.[39]

## Breaching Promises of Secrecy

Millions were to be made by Alan Meyer, a Kansas real estate developer with expertise in residential projects. In February 2005, his longtime business acquaintance and loan officer, James Duff, suggested that Meyer meet David Christie to discuss an opportunity to build a residential complex called The Bluffs. Thanks to that introduction, the two formed a joint venture in March 2005 to finance and build The Bluffs, expecting riches to follow.

That summer, however, Duff heard from the president of Security Savings that Meyer may have made fraudulent statements in his loan applications, lacked collateral for some loans, and faced financial difficulties. Duff relayed that to Meyer, who denied the claims, stressing that he was prepared to meet any financial challenges coming his way. Duff also passed on such rumors to Christie. When Christie later applied for a loan at Security Bank, the bank declined, saying that Meyer was in default on his loans and the bank would not lend to anyone associated with him. Christie then severed the joint venture with Meyer and finished The Bluffs without him, earning the expected millions.

Meyer sued Security Savings for breach of contract. He pointed to the bank's express privacy policies, asserting an implied contractual duty to maintain confidentiality, which it breached by divulging information to Christie and Duff. Security Savings contended that no contract existed and that there was no consideration for any. The bank stressed that Meyer's claim was founded on its privacy policies and cited long-standing law that such policies are not binding contracts, invoking the famous line of employee handbook cases. They remained clear, even after cases like MacDonald: Contracts are not created by an employee handbook describing a supportive environment and boasts of a commitment to employee retention and fair pay, so long as they are accompanied by conspicuous disclaimers of such assurances.[40]

The bank cited contemporary cases echoing the long-standing law that Web site policies also do not constitute binding contracts. For instance, after September 11, 2001, the National Aeronautical and Space Administration (NASA) asked Northwest Airlines for passenger data to research airline security, and Northwest turned it over – without asking passengers' permission.[41] Information included names, addresses, credit card numbers, and itineraries. Once they discovered what has transpired, the infuriated passengers sued. A principal claim was breach of contract, asserting that the disclosure violated Northwest's privacy policy stated on its Web site. But the courts were impatient with this argument, stressing that Web site policies are not contracts or offers to form contracts. They are mere corporate policies, not offers or promises.

But the court in Alan Meyer's case against Security Savings was not convinced by this reasoning. After all, it overlooked the important line of employee handbook cases epitomized by Craig MacDonald's case that qualified the traditional stance. The precedent also missed the mark because Meyer's case against Security Savings was far stronger contractually than the airline passengers' case. Meyer had a long-term banking relationship with Security Savings; the bank requested confidential information and he provided it. In doing so, he relied on the bank to keep information confidential in accordance with its policies. The policy was part of the bank's offer to lend, which Meyer accepted by supplying the requested information. That meant the privacy policy formed part of the bargained-for exchange.

This analysis helps assess the claim that Judge Shirley Strickland Saffold made against the *Cleveland Plain Dealer*. The newspaper made its privacy policy clear on its Web site. Its purpose could not be other than to bid users to post comments on it. It presented terms of use, manifesting an intention to be bound by them. So stimulated, users contribute posts online – something they do not have to do – constituting acceptance and supplying consideration.

Sweeping assertions that Web site policies cannot be contracts are misleading. They can be enforceable contracts or promises when meeting traditional tests of manifested intention, assent, and either consideration or reliance. Aware of such precedents and arguments, and how they do not automatically resolve disputes over online privacy, Judge Saffold and Cleveland.com settled their dispute on undisclosed terms. The problem and related challenges thus remain alive and well.

Law continues its long-standing struggle to identify what promises should be enforced as contracts. Today's contract law takes a pragmatic approach. It makes bargains the primary signifier of an enforceable deal, with reliance a sturdy fallback. That stance contrasts with competing beliefs and prescriptions. At one extreme, many believe that having a document notarized is necessary and sufficient to make it legally binding. A pure formalism would endorse that approach. That would return contract law to the heyday of the seal, insisting on some formal ceremonies to form a contract. At the other end of the spectrum, some believe that a handshake, or sometimes even a nod of the head, is all that it takes to make a bargain binding, and that even promises to make gifts are binding. There are those who insist that searching in the context of every interaction is necessary before concluding that a valid contract is formed. People have differing opinions on whether advertisements are or should be seen as offers to contract.

Unlike what many people think, for years, contract law has concentrated on enforcing promises made in bargains or inducing reliance – but not promises to make gifts. Bargains are enforceable when manifesting an intention to be bound, according to how reasonable people would understand it. This rules out jokes and ordinary advertisements – yet includes boastful rewards reasonably seen as inducing action. Freedom of contract lets people form contracts on the terms they wish, and law holds people to those terms as long as they had a chance to learn them. Venerable contract law still offers rich and dynamic doctrine adaptable to novel problems, from proliferation of glossy employment handbooks to digital corporate policies. This freedom of contract is not absolute, however, and contract law polices objectionable terms, as the next chapter explores.

# 2  FACING LIMITS

## Unenforceable Bargains

*A legal order can indeed be characterized by the agreements which it does or does not enforce.*

– Max Weber

## A. UNCONSCIONABILITY: GAIL WATERS'S ANNUITY SWAP

When Gail Waters was twelve years old, she had a bad accident and fought a resulting legal battle for six years, finally settling for cash. With that money, she bought an annuity from Commercial Union Insurance Company. It would pay annual amounts totaling $694,000 over its twenty-five-year life and could be surrendered on any given day for cash of $189,000. At twenty-one, Gail became involved with an ex-convict, Thomas Beauchemin, who turned her to drugs and ran up $6,000 in charges on her credit card, hitting its limit. Thomas, aware of Gail's annuity, put the idea into her head of selling it to some friends of his, David DeVito, Robert DeVito, and Michael Steamer, for $50,000.

Thomas worked out details for Gail, who was then naïve, insecure, and vulnerable. The others used a licensed lawyer for the trade. They sealed the swap and signed the papers in a parking lot of a restaurant. As part of the deal, the DeVitos and Steamer forgave debts Thomas owed them of $7,000. Later, Gail regretted the deal and refused to turn over the annuity. She asked a Massachusetts court to declare it invalid.[1]

The DeVitos and Steamer invoked a fundamental principle of contract law: Courts typically do not inquire into the adequacy of consideration. Instead, they let people make exchanges on whatever terms they wish. The idea that courts do not inquire into the adequacy of consideration is as old as the idea of consideration itself, enforced as early as 1587.[2] People can trade hats for cars, documents for cash, or feathers for skyscrapers. Relative magnitudes are irrelevant, so even the "slightest consideration is sufficient to support the most onerous obligation."[3]

Several justifications explain. After all, in most commercial transactions, there is a rough equivalence of values given and received – such as a car for cash. The law recognizes the importance of leaving room for people to make trades for many different reasons, such as to gain advantages, real or perceived. Because people assign different values to identical things, it would undermine principles of a free market to have judges second-guess the equivalence of trades. So our courts never have.

But Gail could stress an equally esteemed exception: the doctrine of unconscionability. For centuries, Gail urged, the consideration device has alerted courts to features of an exchange that make it so obnoxious as to be unenforceable. Unconscionability bears kinship to the ancient prohibition against usury – charging outrageous interest on loans – a practice long ago made illegal by statute in most states. Yet courts rarely refuse to enforce bargains because the consideration is unconscionable.

Favoring the DeVitos and Steamer were two famous examples of judicial reticence. One involved speculators heading to Alaska during the Yukon gold rush at the turn of the nineteenth century, the other citizens fleeing from Greece after the Nazi invasion of World War II.

## Chasing Alaska Gold

The initial 1870 discovery of gold in what is now Alaska stoked intense interest in the territory, widening with the extensive gold deposits found throughout the area in the ensuing decades, from the town named for prospector Joseph Juneau to gold strikes in the Klondike. Prospectors rushed in, entering the port at Valdez, trudging up steep

paths, acquiring properties, and establishing gold mines that made fortunes for many, although others lost their shirts or lives. The game was
high-risk, and the legal infrastructure for buying and selling properties
was inchoate.

Among the prospectors on the Alaskan gold rush was John Tuppela,
who spent many years in the early 1900s acquiring mining properties
in the area worth $500,000 (about $10 million in today's currency).[4]
Tuppela was of uncertain mental stability, however, and at one point
was adjudged insane and committed for four years to an asylum back
home in Portland, Oregon. While he was institutionalized, Tuppela's
court-appointed guardian, managing his affairs, sold his Alaskan mines
without his knowledge.

After Tuppela's release, a local lawyer told him it was unlikely he
would win a legal battle to reverse his guardian's sale. Demoralized,
unemployed, and destitute, the gold miner in May 1918 ran into an old
friend, Henry Embola, whom he had known for thirty years. Embola
loaned Tuppela $270 (some $4,000 in today's dollars) to support him
and, in September 1918, arranged to let him stay in the Seattle home
of his brother-in-law, Herman Lindstrom. Tuppela wanted to return
to Alaska to rejoin the rush and recover his gold mines, yet could ill
afford it. He reached out to prospective investors to back the venture, but found no takers. Defeated, Tuppela finally turned to Embola.
Acknowledging his existing debt, Tuppela proposed that if Embola
would lend him another $50 (nearly $1,000 today), he would go to
Alaska to recover his mines and, if recovered, Tuppela would pay
Embola $10,000 ($140,000 now).

Embola immediately accepted that offer and handed Tuppela the
cash. The money enabled Tuppela to get to Alaska, where he waged an
intensive legal battle, winning back his mines in January 1921. Tuppela
wanted to pay his friend the $10,000, but before he could do so, he
lapsed back into mental illness, and his newly appointed guardian
repudiated the deal. Embola sued for the money.

The guardian, on Tuppela's behalf, said the contract lacked adequate consideration – and that it was unconscionable and usurious. The
contract was not usurious, however, because whereas statutes make
illegal a loan that charges excessive interest, this was not a loan. It was,
instead, an investment, akin to those popularly referred to during the

gold rush as a "grubstake." And although the Embola-Tuppela contract paid off big, the odds were dubious when they made it. Success
depended on Tuppela's ability to persuade an Alaska court to render
his guardian's property sales invalid – a proposition as uncertain as
any grubstake.

Tuppela and Embola's arrangement was not a simultaneous
exchange of different amounts of money, but rather an exchange of
cash one day for the promise of a different amount of cash later, if
an uncertain event occurred. True, if the exchange emitted an air of
unconscionability, the court would refuse enforcement. Courts may
sense unconscionability when the values exchanged are wildly disproportionate. But grubstake contracts like that between Tuppela and
Embola often involve asymmetrical payoffs. It was for Tuppela, sane
and sound when he made the promise, and later when he wanted to
uphold it, to make that judgment – and he made it, thinking it both fair
and advantageous.

The same could be said for Gail. She preferred immediate cash in
a lump sum to a financial instrument paying periodic amounts or the
trouble of formally surrendering it to Commercial Union Insurance
Company. Yet there is a world of difference between a grubstake for
which values are unknown and an annuity whose current cash value is
known with certainty. Unlike the Embola-Tuppela deal, the arrangement between Thomas and Gail was akin to the simultaneous exchange
of unequal amounts of cash. But the validity of Gail's contract was
supported by an even more extreme case arising from the Greek tragedy of World War II.[5]

### Escaping Nazi Greece

Nazis invaded Greece on April 6, 1941. Despite valiant resistance,
Greek forces surrendered on April 23 of that year. The surrender brought vicious reprisals, destruction, and price inflation. Even
before the invasion, Greece had suffered from a deficiency in agri-
culture, farming only one-fifth of arable land and importing most
food requirements. The Nazi occupiers confiscated food and cut off
imports, plunging average daily calorie intake of Greek citizens to 900

per individual. Hundreds of thousands died from malnutrition. People were desperate to escape.[6]

One hopeful escapee was Eugenia Demotsis, who borrowed money in April 1942 from George Batsakis to flee the ravage. A letter bearing Eugenia's signature, and addressed to George, said she received US$2,000 from him, which she would repay, along with 8 percent interest, after the war was over and she had arrived safely in the United States. Eugenia later claimed this letter was forged and that George in fact loaned her 500,000 Greek drachmae, not U.S. cash, which amounted at the time to a mere $25.

Once in the United States, Eugenia refused to pay and George sued, seeking $2,000 plus 8 percent interest, which amounted to a sum more than eighty times the $25 she claimed she received. A jury split the difference, awarding George $750 plus interest. George appealed, and a Texas court, using the traditional test of bargained-for consideration, upheld the contract as it appeared in the writing – the full $2,000 (plus interest).

Even accepting what Eugenia said as true about the document being forged, 500,000 drachmae had some value to her at the time the exchange of funds was made. It did not matter whether the value to her was the $25 exchange rate that day, the $750 the jury seemed to estimate, or the $2,000 recited in the letter. The court therefore held the exchange to be valid without regard to whether the document was forged or which amount was in fact loaned.

As in the Tuppela case, the bargain's context matters: Eugenia was desperate to get out of Greece, and the 500,000 drachmae, even if only worth 25 dollars, could have had substantial value to her at the time, buying her escape. Eschewing the woman's claim of forgery and invoking a standard phrase, the court said: "Mere inadequacy of consideration will not avoid a contract."[7]

The DeVitos and Steamer could recite that same principle in their dispute with Gail: It is for each of the parties, not a court, to decide whether it is fair and advantageous to trade a financial instrument worth $189,000 for $50,000 cash. In exchange for trading in the annuity, Gail got the advantage of not having to follow required procedures to surrender the annuity contract and shed any credit risk that

Commercial Union Insurance Company would pose over the annuity's twenty-five-year term. Courts long have said that even the transfer of a document, known to be without any value, supplies consideration for a trade of anything in return, despite its value.[8]

To prevail, Gail Waters needed to persuade the court that the disproportionate amounts signaled that no real bargain was intended. She could rely on a long line of extreme cases where consideration on one side is a nominal amount like $1. This type of imbalance alerts judges that the arrangement may be a joke, ruse, scam, or worse, signaling a lack of intention to enter into an enforceable contract.

### The Christmas Dollar Joke

A marvelous example of nominal consideration is a chestnut from Michigan in the early 1900s.[9] At Christmas 1895, the Fischer family gathered. Amid the festivities, the father, William, said to his daughter, Bertha, a younger woman of uncertain mental stability, "I want to give you, as a Christmas present, our home." He handed her the deed, which included a covenant against encumbrances except two mortgage loans he promised to pay when due. At that time, mortgage loans totaled $8,000 (more than $200,000 in today's dollars) and William's net worth was $50,000 ($1.3 million today). Bertha took the deed and read it. At that moment, one of her brothers handed her a dollar, and she gave that to her father, who took it.

Many years later the father died, leaving few assets and the two unpaid mortgages. The banks foreclosed on the home to recover their loans. Bertha objected, saying the home was hers and that she was entitled to a remedy from her father's estate for breach of his promise to repay the loans. But while the court agreed that the delivery of the deed completed the father's gift of the home to the child, there was no consideration for his promise to pay off the mortgage loans. The court viewed the dollar Bertha handed her father as a joke. The consideration for the father's promise was love and affection in the family setting, not the dollar.

The problem with Bertha's Christmas dollar was not its amount, but its setting. The context of the event left no doubt the father was giving Bertha a gift – he said as much when handing over the deed. The dollar, or other nominal consideration, can signal a lack of contractual intention, especially when it is obvious that values in a purported exchange are wildly imbalanced. Although the consideration doctrine is not a safeguard against improvidently made contracts, it helps identify cases where there was no bargain in fact. The objectively variant sums hint that no bargain occurred. The ratio suggests abuse or deception in the deal's procedures rather than substance and invites probing the background leading to contract formation, including who proposed an exchange, who presented the terms, how they were documented, and the relationship and sophistication of the parties.

In Gail Waters's case, the court agreed with her and held the contract unconscionable. Gail's trade of $50,000 cash for an instrument worth $189,000 cash was not dispositive – that imbalance alone may not warrant upsetting a contract. But that objective mismatch did signal a potential lack of bargain. Probing its background, the court stressed that Thomas proposed the deal, suggested its terms, gained $7,000 from it, and worked on both sides as a go-between.

Gail relied on Thomas, with whom she was romantically involved, while the DeVitos and Steamer used legal counsel. Gail gained little or no advantage in the exchange and the DeVitos and Steamer took little or no risk. It was negotiated in a parking lot. Thomas unduly influenced Gail. She did not assent in any meaningful way. There was no bargain. Meeting an ancient test for unconscionability, it was a deal no fair person would suggest and no rational person would accept.[10]

## B. BLACKMAIL: MICHAEL JORDAN'S PATERNITY

Michael Jordan, the legendary basketball star for the Chicago Bulls, met Karla Knafel, a lounge singer, in the spring of 1989.[11] After several months of long-distance phone conversations, Jordan and Knafel got together in December 1989. Jordan was married, but Jordan and Knafel engaged in unprotected sex at that time and once again in November 1990. Throughout that year, Knafel dated other men and had unprotected sex with at least one. She became pregnant and, inferring the date of conception back to November, claimed Jordan was the father.

During the spring of 1991, the Bulls were heading for another NBA championship and Jordan was earning millions from the team and from product endorsements. It was in Jordan's interest to keep the extramarital affair and his possible paternity from the public. Knafel later claimed that Jordan suggested she get an abortion, which she refused to do. Jordan ultimately offered to pay her $5 million, upon his retirement from basketball, if she would keep the matter confidential and not file a paternity suit. Knafel accepted. After she gave birth in July 1991, Jordan paid the bills and gave Knafel $250,000. In exchange, she kept quiet and never filed a paternity suit. A month later, Jordan determined through blood testing that he was not the baby's father.

When Jordan retired from playing professional basketball, Knafel asked him to pay up. Jordan refused and instead sued to have the alleged contract declared illegal and unenforceable. Jordan argued that, as a matter of public policy, all contracts involving paying money in exchange for silence are extortionate. Knafel contended that to hold the contract extortionate would unwisely render all settlement agreements containing confidentiality clauses invalid as against public policy. The court rejected both extreme positions. Confidentiality agreements may have some special features, but are presumed valid and are common in settlement agreements. On the other hand, some are suspect, such as those commanding silence about harmful products, threats to public safety, criminal enterprises, or those constituting blackmail – often targeted to the rich and famous.

### The Blackmail of David Letterman

An example of such suspect deals confronted David Letterman, host of the popular CBS television show, "Late Night."[12] A once-respected CBS news executive, Robert Halderman, knew that Letterman was having extramarital affairs with staff members. Using an assortment of evidence – pictures, letters, and one woman's diary – Halderman wrote a screenplay depicting Letterman facing public humiliation from the disclosure. Halderman gave that evidence and the screenplay to Letterman's limousine driver on September 9, 2009. One week later, Halderman told Letterman's lawyer, Jim Jackoway, he would go public with it unless Letterman paid him $2 million. Letterman promptly called the police, who assisted him in preparing a bogus check for $2 million. After Halderman deposited that check, police arrested him for attempted grand larceny. He spent six months in jail, followed by four years of probation.[13]

In contrast to Jordan and Knafel's case, no valid contract could possibly have been formed between Halderman and Letterman in the circumstances because there was no other relationship between them.[14] The deal was based solely on a spontaneous threat from a stranger to extract cash for silence. Such cases involve money for silence, and nothing else. To recognize these as valid contracts would encourage people to engage in behavior that criminal law seeks to deter.[15]

## Child Support

Knafel contended that her contract with Jordan was more like the valid bargain found in an old-fashioned case involving Hilda Boehm and one Louis Fiege, who had a romantic relationship in the 1950s.[16] Hilda got pregnant, named Louis as the father, and claimed he agreed to pay child support if she refrained from filing a paternity suit. Louis denied all of this, pointing to later blood tests proving he was not the father, contradicting Hilda's confident assertions of paternity.

Ancient common law declared that fathers of children born out of wedlock had no legal duty to care for them. Courts often found a father's promise to provide financial support unenforceable for lack of consideration. After many states enacted paternal support statutes, however, such promises could be supported by consideration if the mother gave up valid rights to pursue statutory paternity proceedings. A statute applicable in the case of Hilda and Louis authorized mothers to sue putative fathers for support, persuading the court that there is no public policy objection to bargains such as theirs.

Even though such precedents were helpful to Knafel, she was not home-free in her dispute with Jordan because any such bargain must still meet standard contract law tests for enforceability. With money-for-silence deals suspect, the place to look for consideration is foreswearing legal action. Cases dating to early English law recognized as consideration a promise not to sue, so long as the claimant held an honest and reasonable belief in the validity of the claim being sworn off.[17] Courts refused to recognize giving up "entirely baseless" claims as consideration but validated claims so long as they were "colorable" or "tenable" or "possible." To paraphrase one court's poetic summary of the cases: Consideration includes giving up a claim that makes a mountain out of a mole hill, but there must be some mole hill to begin with.[18]

Knafel and Jordan thus disputed whether they had settled a molehill's worth of quarreling. Knafel stressed that in paternity cases, consideration is provided by a mother giving up valid statutory rights, putting her claim squarely in the line of cases running back to that of Hilda and Louis. Taken at face value, that could have spelled the end of the Jordan-Knafel case in her favor, but the famous Jordan made a novel argument that lured Knafel into a damning concession.

Jordan contended that their contract was unenforceable because it was induced by Knafel's fraud. Fraud in the inducement of a contract occurs when someone knowingly misleads another into a bargain they would not likely make otherwise. Knafel resisted the assertion of fraud by stressing that she believed in good faith that Jordan was the baby's father. She claimed that the authenticity of paternity was not so important to Jordan that, without her statements, he would have acted differently. Jordan countered that the paternity issue was an inducement to his promise: Had he known he was not the baby's father, he likely would not have agreed to pay to avoid a suit or obtain confidentiality. True, Jordan feared damaging his public image, which induced him to agree, but that was not the sole motivating factor.

The court agreed with Jordan. To accept Knafel's claim that Jordan's agreement was not induced by the paternity issue would suggest that the two had haggled over and settled nothing by their agreement. But that would make the case equivalent to that of the blackmail of David Letterman – silence for money. Concerning the paternity issue, Michael Jordan's fame and fortune, and the fling he and Karla Knafel had, did suggest reasons to be more skeptical of Knafel's story than that of the claim Hilda Boehm made against her obscure partner, Louis Fiege.[19]

## C. PALIMONY: THE RAPPER 50 CENT

The rap artist 50 Cent, whose real name is Curtis Jackson, secured his first recording contract in October 2003.[20] It came with a $300,000 advance.[21]To boost his professional image as a rapper, he bought a Hummer and a Connecticut mansion once owned by boxer Mike Tyson. The mansion boasted a state-of-the-art recording studio, and the rapper hired a full-time caretaker and professional cleaning crew to maintain it. In 2004, Jackson bought another house in Valley Stream, the small village in New York's Nassau County where his grandmother and other relatives lived; in December 2006, he added to his real estate holdings a $2 million house at 2 Sandra Lane, Dix Hills, on Long Island, New York. By then, he had sold tens of millions of recordings, toured the world, and amassed hundreds of millions of dollars in net worth, as chronicled in his 2005 autobiographical film, "Get Rich, or Die Tryin."

This success came after hard knocks. Jackson had dealt crack cocaine as a teenager. In 1995, at age twenty, he was released from jail and became involved with Shaniqua Tompkins in his hometown of Jamaica in Queens, New York. The two had a son, Marquise, out of wedlock in 1996. Jackson and Tompkins had no money and no real home, living with his grandmother or hers. In May 2000, Jackson nearly died when he was shot nine times during a gangland ambush. He was in the hospital for weeks, followed by months of rehab spent at his mother's house, near the Pocono Mountains in Pennsylvania. Before the shooting, Jackson had been negotiating with Columbia Records; following it, the record company stopped returning his calls.

Jackson, however, persevered. In November 2001, he launched a recording company, Rotten Apple Records. The rising rap star Eminem brought Jackson's 2002 self-produced record to the industry's attention.[22] As a result, Interscope Records offered Jackson the 2003 deal that propelled him to fame and fortune. With money flowing in and Jackson leading the high life, Tompkins asserted her right to a share. But Jackson's relationship with Tompkins was tumultuous. They did not always live together and fought often, sometimes physically.

When Jackson bought the Dix Hills house in 2006, both agreed it was the best place to raise Marquise, then almost ten years old, and Tompkins pled with Jackson to put it in her name. Although Jackson promised to do so, he never did. After the relationship soured, Jackson tried to evict Tompkins from the Dix Hills house. During that battle, the house burned to the ground under circumstances that authorities considered suspicious. The house had been insured against fire, but the policy lapsed for nonpayment of the premium a few weeks before. In response to Jackson's eviction lawsuit, Tompkins asserted a claim of her own: that the two had a contract entitling her to $50 million.

Tompkins claimed that in September 1996, one month before Marquise was born, she and Jackson made a deal. She claimed that Jackson promised her, in exchange for putting up with him and helping him through tough times, that when he "makes it big," he would take care of her for the "rest of her life," sharing everything he ever owns equally. They were "down for life," Tompkins recalls Jackson saying. In exchange, Tompkins said, she agreed to support him until he "got it together." Tompkins alleged that formed a binding contract. She elaborated this claim:

> I agreed to continue to live with him, maintain his home, perform homemaking and domestic services for him as well as support him mentally, emotionally and financially to the best of my abilities. I also agreed to accompany him to social and other events.... Jackson agreed that he would vigorously pursue a professional recording career with the understanding that our combined efforts could result in the accumulation of substantial wealth and assets that we would divide and share equally.

Tompkins said they were in love at that time. She explained:

> He was a corner crack dealer parolee. He did not have anything.... So I was going to be with him whether he was 50 Cent, with a hundred million dollars, or Curtis Jackson, working for sanitation, making $50,000 a year. I would have been with him, because I loved him. It was not about him saying that he would give me everything he had. It is when you love a person, you don't – it is not about the monetary. If you're a prostitute, then it is a monetary thing. We were two people in love with each other.

Jackson denied making any lifetime promise and argued that, even if he had, it was unenforceable. Instead, Jackson argued, these were merely expressions of support by two unmarried lovers. Their commitments sprung from mutual regard and affection – not money – and even if done for money, they resembled arrangements law historically frowned on.

Jackson could cite many precedents, from decades earlier, that refused to enforce as contracts agreements between paramours (unmarried cohabitants). Tompkins countered that the deal went beyond ordinary domestic management and could cite other, more modern cases recognizing the enforceability of contracts between unmarried cohabitants. The Jackson-Tompkins dispute was thus wedged between these lines of authority.

Before the 1960s, courts were disinclined to enforce contracts like this, for the two reasons Jackson urged. Well into the twentieth century, a social stigma attached to unmarried cohabitation and law reflected that distaste by refusing to recognize bargains made in those settings as valid contracts. The law's main discomfort around these types of bargains stemmed from concerns about whether the deal was a type of disguised prostitution. Early cases called this type of consideration – money for sex – meretricious, referring to a harlot's traits. Because prostitution was and remains illegal by statute throughout the United States, courts refuse to enforce these contracts; this repugnance extended to include deals made among unmarried cohabitants.

## Lee Marvin's Lover

Social norms have, of course, evolved. Pejoratives such as meretricious and the association of such living arrangements with prostitution are outdated. Even so, resulting legal change is halting and varies among states. The most hospitable stance appears in a famous, trailblazing, and controversial California case from 1966.[23] Actor Lee Marvin had lived for seven years with a paramour, Michelle Triola, while the two shared duties and wealth. After they split, Lee refused to pay more, and Michelle sued. Even though Michelle could not identify any express contract or promise between the two, the California Supreme Court recognized an implied obligation of mutual support – treating the arrangement akin to how law traditionally treats married couples when divorcing.

Although not all states follow that approach, most, like New York, where Jackson and Tompkins disputed, have reversed the historical hostility toward unmarried cohabitation so that such contracts are not automatically invalid. Most states now regard express contracts in these settings as they do others, enforcing those supported by consideration and manifest mutual assent to be bound. But relics of the past persist. Courts struggle in paramour cases to determine whether the evidence shows a bargain. They must discern whether promises were made with or without expectation of payment and whether primarily out of love and affection or with an intention to make a deal.

Jackson argued that the arrangement Tompkins asserted was all about love and personal affection and not any sort of exchange transaction intended as an enforceable bargain. The promises Tompkins made addressed daily attention, support, companionship, and household chores; in exchange, Jackson promised to take care of her for life. Those are the things couples do for each other in day-to-day living without intending, expecting, or manifesting a bargain.

Tompkins contended the deal was not only about love, but also amounted to a bargain, noting that Jackson's promise did not depend on whether the two were living together or involved romantically. Although originating in love, the promises were a bargained-for exchange, she argued.

The court ultimately sided with Jackson, drawing on this writing from the leading New York case:[24]

> As a matter of human experience personal services will frequently be rendered by two people ... because they value each other's company, or because they find it a convenient or rewarding thing to do. For courts to attempt through hindsight to sort out the intentions of the parties and affix [legal] significance to conduct carried out within an essentially private and generally non-contractual relationship runs too great a risk of error.... There is, therefore, substantially greater risk of emotion-laden afterthought, not to mention fraud, in attempting to ascertain by implication what services, if any, were rendered gratuitously and what compensation, if any, the parties intended to be paid.

Applying those insights to the dispute between Tompkins and Jackson, the court concluded:

> Providing loving care and assistance to her boyfriend and the father of their son before and after he was shot and seriously injured, does not transform her relationship to one founded upon contract. To conclude otherwise would transform the parties' personal, yet informal relationship to that of a marriage.

Although the Lee Marvin case in California approved exactly that result, it is not followed in New York or most other states, which treat the cases like other contract cases, not like typical divorce cases. And that meant there was yet another reason that Tompkins' claim failed: Jackson's asserted promise, speaking only of "care for life," lacked definiteness, an essential element of a contract. The vagueness signals that the parties were expressing wishes, hopes, and feelings, not forming expectations of remuneration for services rendered. As the judge put it, this was an "unfortunate tale of a love relationship gone sour."[25]

## D. GAMBLING: OCTOGENARIAN POWERBALL SISTERS

Judges have long been averse to enforcing bargains founded in illegal activity, ranging from prostitution to murder. But some behavior once widely condemned as criminal, such as adultery, gambling, or possessing marijuana, becomes decriminalized or legalized. While society's attitudes slowly change, judges sometimes struggle with whether to enforce bargains based on those activities.[26]

Gambling has been an especially interesting setting in recent years. After all, millions of Americans play the lottery, often teaming up with siblings or colleagues to buy tickets with agreement to share the winnings.[27] Most lottery tickets are worthless, but when they pay off, fights often break out and at least one of the parties asserts the deal was illegal and unenforceable. That is the sad story of the octogenarian sisters, Terry Sokaitis and Rose Bakaysa.

Terry and Rose grew up in the 1920s in a family of ten children in New Britain, Connecticut, a small middle-class town near Hartford famous for its Polish community and locally referred to as "Hard Hittin' New Britain." The sisters were close. Both married; Terry raised six kids; Rose's husband died in 1981. After Foxwoods Casino opened in 1986, the sisters gambled there several times weekly, Terry playing Black Jack, Rose the slots. They informally shared all of their winnings.

In January 1995, Terry hit a poker jackpot paying $165,000. She shared that nearly equally with Rose, giving her $75,000. In April of that year, Terry proposed signing a winnings-sharing contract, perhaps to ensure that Rose would be likewise obligated to split her winnings in the future. An accountant typed and printed the terms, proclaiming the sisters were "partners in any winning" in slots, cards, or lotteries, with gains "to be shared equally." The sisters signed and notarized the writing. Terry and Rose continued their trips to Foxwoods, bought lottery tickets, and shared winnings.

In 2004, however, Rose faced health challenges requiring surgery and weeks in rehab. Terry visited daily. During her visits, Terry borrowed some money from Rose. After leaving the facility, Rose still needed assistance and so stayed for three weeks with Terry. In exchange, Rose forgave Terry an earlier $650 loan she had made. After Rose went home, she phoned Terry to say she and their brother Joe were coming over to recover the $250 Rose had lent her in the rehab facility. Terry said she had borrowed only $100 and told Rose not to come because she had no money anyway.

A disputed dialogue ensued. Rose reported a heated yelling match whereas Terry recalled a calm chat. Rose said Terry hollered "I don't want to be your partner anymore," and Rose said "okay." Their brother Joe reported conflicting versions of events, possibly because of how his own fortunes may have turned on later interpretations of what really happened. Rose, upset by the call, contacted Joe and said, "Terry doesn't want to be my partner anymore," and Joe responded, "I'll be partners with you."

The sisters never spoke again. Terry bought some scratch lottery tickets afterward but less often, preferring to put any extra money she had in the church collection basket. She also sent Rose a check for $250. Rose began buying tickets with Joe, biweekly, always selecting the same number to bet.

On June 15, 2005, Joe bought Powerball tickets that won $500,000, promptly calling Rose to share the news. They split the winnings as agreed, each receiving five days later checks for $175,000 (the other $150,000 going to the government, as income tax). They did not tell Terry, however, who learned about it from her daughter, Eileen, Rose's godchild, to whom Rose had given $10,000 as a gift from the winnings. Within weeks of hearing the news, on August 19, 2005, Terry sued Rose for breach of contract. They fought a pitched and ultimately tearful battle in a tortured case lasting five years until its final resolution on May 11, 2010.

The first skirmish in the sisters' legal battle was over the validity of their 1995 winnings-sharing contract. Rose argued it was invalid because it violated a state statute rendering void any contract whose consideration was money won in a bet. Terry denied that the consideration was money won in a bet. The deal involved an exchange of promises – to buy together and share winnings. Given that no winnings existed when the contract was formed, that fruit was not the consideration – the exchange of promises was. So, Terry argued, the contract was valid.

Terry coupled that hair-splitting defense with a more practical one: Even if the consideration was money won in a bet in apparent violation of the statute, the statute cannot make contracts like these illegal, because many other state statutes legalize gambling in various forms. Read literally, the statute would void all kinds of bargains made every day and lawfully statewide, like betting on horse races, at jai alai frontons, and in tribal casinos.

Every legal wager is a gambling contract, including the very lottery ticket being fought over – a contract in which buyers pay the purchase price in exchange for the lottery commission's promise to pay the holder of the winning ticket. The parties to it engage in a gamble, and the consideration is a "money bet." Taken at face value, the statute would bar anyone from buying state lottery tickets. Looking at all the other statutes legalizing various forms of gambling, the Supreme Court of Connecticut determined that the statute voids only contracts for gambling unauthorized by those statutes. As a result, the court held that even if Terry and Rose's bargain were a gambling contract, it was outside the statute's proscription.[28]

But after losing the gambling defense, Rose vouched a firmer defense in the trial of her case with Terry. She said the two, although originally bound to the lawful contract written up in 1995, had mutually rescinded it during the disputed 2004 telephone conversation. The trial judge, Cynthia Sweinton, accepted that argument, characterizing Terry's declaration, "I don't want to be your partner anymore," as an offer to rescind the deal, which Rose accepted by saying, "okay."[29] The two were legally free of each other.

Judge Sweinton thus found for Rose, concluding her opinion with: "There is something in this tragedy that touches most people. While the court may be able to resolve the legal dispute, it is powerless to repair the discord and strife that now overshadows the once harmonious sisterly relationship." Judge Sweinton also reprinted a tear-jerking letter Terry wrote to Rose during the case:[30]

Rose,

I hope you get this letter because I have plenty to say – the most important thing is I am so sick over what is happening with you and I going to court. None of this would have happened if you were not so greedy. All I know is we should both be ashamed of ourselves. We are sisters. Going to court is not right. All I know is I am entitled to my share of the money and you know it.

I remember when I was pregnant. We went to Raphel's and you bought me my dress. It was navy blue and it had pink flowers on it. You and I used to go to the casino all the time and to Old Saybrook and look at all the houses and get hot dogs out there at the restaurants.

Well Ro Ro, I don't know what is going to happen. I want you to know I will always love you. But if you wanted to hurt me you did. My kids are so good to me and they do send me any money I need. They can't do enough for me so I guess I am rich with a lot of love and that is something you can't buy.

I hope you feel good and have good health. I have a disease that is incurable. It is called neuropathy. I can't walk at all. It is really painful. But Ma always said other people have worse problems so I just ask God to let me be able to handle it all.

Take care of yourself. Mom would be sick over all of this. It would never happen if you at least shared some of the money with me. Do you think I would have done that to you? Never.

See you in court.
Terry

## E. MAKING BABIES: BABY M, BABY CALVERT

William and Elizabeth Stern, a married couple living in New Jersey, wanted a baby. The Sterns met when both were PhD students at

University of Michigan and married in 1974. Because of financial factors and Elizabeth's work toward a medical degree, the couple deferred starting a family until 1981. By then, however, Elizabeth had learned that she may have multiple sclerosis, a condition that can complicate pregnancies. But having kids was particularly important to William, who was the only survivor of a family lost to World War II's Holocaust. The Sterns considered alternative options after seeing an ad for so-called "surrogacy parenting" run by a New York fertility center.

Mary Beth Whitehead had seen a similar ad. She was motivated by the chance to help other couples and, as she was married and had children herself, by the opportunity to earn additional money for her family. The fertility center arranged a meeting between the Whiteheads and the Sterns, and on February 6, 1985, the two couples signed a contract. The Sterns would pay Mrs. Whitehead $10,000 to be artificially inseminated with Mr. Stern's sperm in exchange for conceiving, carrying, delivering, and surrendering a baby to the couple for adoption. The agreement said that the Whiteheads would do whatever it took to terminate their parental rights to the baby. Separately, Mr. Stern agreed to pay $7,500 to the fertility center for its services.

After several months of attempted inseminations, Mrs. Whitehead eventually became pregnant by Mr. Stern's sperm. The result, on March 27, 1986, was the birth of a beautiful and healthy baby girl, fondly referred to in court proceedings and media as Baby M. Keeping the surrogacy arrangement confidential at the hospital, the Whiteheads looked the part of proud parents. They even had the birth certificate show the newborn's name as Sara Elizabeth Whitehead, listing Richard Whitehead as the dad.

From the moment of birth, Mrs. Whitehead bonded with the baby and felt it was impossible to part with her. When the Sterns told Mrs. Whitehead, at the hospital, their plans to name the baby, the woman burst into tears, explaining her reluctance to give up the infant. The baby, after all, looked much like the Whitehead's other daughter. Even so, several days later, on March 30, the Sterns visited the Whitehead's home, and Mrs. Whitehead relinquished Baby M into their custody. The Sterns were delighted. They had outfitted a room for her and prepared for a life of joy. They shared the news with their entire circle of family and friends. They named her Melissa. They understood the strain Mrs. Whitehead was undergoing, but they scarcely imagined the coming drama.

Mrs. Whitehead fell despondent. She did not sleep and could not eat. She felt an imperative to reclaim her child and, eventually, went to the Sterns' home to explain. The Sterns were surprised, and grew frightened. Mrs. Whitehead implored how she could not live without the baby, begging to have her for at least a week as a coping mechanism. The Sterns, worried that Mrs. Whitehead might commit suicide, acceded to her request, believing she would keep her word and return the baby shortly.

But Mrs. Whitehead reneged. She insisted the baby was hers. For months, the Sterns sought futilely to recover the infant. After their pleas failed, they sued and got a court order directing authorities to go to the Whitehead residence, recover the baby, and deliver it to them. When the authorities, along with the Sterns and police officers, arrived at the Whitehead home to do that, some confusion arose as to whether they had located the correct baby, whether her name was Melissa or Sara Elizabeth.

Amid the commotion, Mr. Whitehead went outside and Mrs. Whitehead handed the baby to him through a window. The couple absconded to Florida with her. At first, they stayed at the home of Mrs. Whitehead's parents and then, on the run for four months, at twenty other homes and hotels. From Florida, Mrs. Whitehead occasionally called Mr. Stern by phone to discuss the dilemma. Mr. Stern recorded these conversations. They reveal an intensifying and ultimately enraged dispute about the merits of the bargain and its broader human dimensions of morality and power. Mrs. Whitehead made incendiary threats, including of suicide or infanticide, if the Sterns persisted in their quest. Meanwhile, the Sterns won a Florida court order directing local police to recover the baby from the Whiteheads for the Sterns.

The two couples then fought an intense custody battle in New Jersey courts, disputing the validity of their contract. The trial spanned two months, with thirty-two days of live action, and drew heavy press attention. On February 3, 1988, the New Jersey Supreme Court held that the contract was invalid as an illegal bargain under state public policy.[31] Instead, the court followed an ancient test in child custody cases that looks solely at what the court perceives to be in the best interests of the child. That resulted in awarding custody to Mr. Stern, along with visitation rights to Mrs. Whitehead.

In striking the contract down, the court referenced the state's statutes regulating child adoption. They prohibit most payments for adoptions and give birth mothers a chance to change their minds. These safeguards were intended to negate "the evils inherent in baby-bartering," which the court called "loathsome" for many reasons. The contract ran afoul of these principles, because the Sterns paid both the Whiteheads and the fertility clinic and the contract made an irrevocable, pre-birth commitment to surrender the child and parental rights. The court stressed: "There are, in a civilized society, some things that money cannot buy"; there are "values that society deems more important than granting to wealth whatever it can buy, be it labor, love or life."

The Baby M case was the first of its kind in the United States. The story was promptly made into a film, and the court's opinion is a landmark. It was the dawn of the late twentieth century's rapid advances in human reproductive technology. Methods now include many more variations than the relatively simple artificial insemination featured in the Baby M case, such as in vitro fertilization, embryo and gamete freezing and storage, gamete intrafallopian transfer, and embryo transplantation. Such developments provoke ongoing struggles about medical ethics and legal validity of associated contracts.

The legal debate put the state of contract law governing these arrangements in flux. In the years since the Baby M case, some states have passed statutes regulating such arrangements. Validity now depends on complying with stated requirements. Statutory requirements address matters such as compensation and when commitments become binding (before or after birth). Many states have not passed statutes, however, leaving it for judges to navigate cases one by one in the grand common-law tradition. New Jersey adheres to the firm stance of the Baby M case, making the contracts illegal there; judges in other states, including in California, take the opposite stance, treating these contracts as they do all others.

In the leading California case, a married couple, Mark and Crispina Calvert, wanted a baby.[32] But Crispina had a hysterectomy in 1984, making child-bearing impossible, even though her ovaries could produce eggs. On January 15, 1990, the couple signed a contract with Anna Johnson. A zygote – an embryo created by Mark's sperm and Crispina's egg using in vitro fertilization – would be implanted in Anna. The rest of the arrangement mirrored that of the Baby M case: Anna would carry the child and deliver it over to the Calverts after labor; Anna would relinquish parental rights; and the Calverts would pay Anna $10,000.

After a healthy birth, Anna wanted to keep the baby. California statutes, like those in New Jersey, addressed the subject only obliquely. Unlike New Jersey, however, the California court saw nothing in its state's statutes to prevent enforcing the contract. The court saw the contract as one where a childless couple made use of modern technology to help them procreate in a way that nature could not. To the court, Anna had willingly signed up for the role of surrogacy, nothing more. The deal was to yield a child for the Calverts to rear, not for the Calverts to donate a zygote to Anna.

The court saw "no reason" why "Anna's later change of heart should vitiate the determination that Crispina is the child's natural mother." A California parentage statute recognizes that maternity can be founded in genetics or birthing, without making one more important than the other. The court considered the choice of the parties to the contract to be worthy of more respect than any judicial choice made by second-guessing. The best interests of the child are paramount, but parties to reproductive technology contracts are abler than courts to determine what those are, the court reasoned.

Whatever conclusions they reach, validating or invalidating these arrangements, judges usually concede that better solutions are likely to come from legislation. As magisterial as the common law of contracts is, many of society's vexing puzzles should be resolved by the legislative branch of government. Yet legislatures struggle too. The statutes that have been enacted tend to support a lawful framework to form valid contracts governing these arrangements, but laws have not been passed in every jurisdiction.

So it may be left to contract law and judicial statements of public policy to handle these cases, in California, New Jersey, and elsewhere. Judges can still rely on the ancient common-law test about the best interests of the child. That test seemed to work out well for Melissa

Stern, Baby M. In May 2007, for its twenty-fifth anniversary, *USA Today* named Ms. Stern one of the top twenty-five "lives of indelible impact," during that period.[33]

People often think that fairness is a court's chief concern, but that is not always true in contract cases. Others think all contracts are enforced as made, but that is not quite right either. As a matter of policy to promote freedom of contract, courts usually enforce contracts as written, without specific review of the terms. If terms show a contract was formed, courts enforce them. Some deals, however, are struck on surprisingly lopsided terms, like a simultaneous exchange of different amounts of money or as the product of extortionate threats. Courts struggle with whether to enforce bargains that appear in unconventional settings, such as parenting, or romance, where bargains are unlikely; or involve activities that are illegal or unsavory, like gambling or prostitution. Deals suggesting lack of true bargain or verging on illegality provoke judicial attention – and are often ruled unenforceable.

Visionaries on the left and right alike object to this balanced approach. Devotees of a greater formalism rebuke any judicial second-guessing of the bargains people make. It should be irrelevant whether a trade is made of different amounts of money or for nominal consideration like $1. People should be free to strike bargains on any subjects they wish with equal dignity – whether deals about paternity, palimony, gambling, parenting, or human reproduction. Promoters of a greater contextualism would give judges broader license to police not only bargains signaled to be suspect by the form or amount of consideration, but a wider range of terms deemed objectionable. That could include authorizing a more probing evaluation, on the grounds of public policy, of contracts that may be not only the product of extortion, but about babies, among paramours, or between sisters playing slots.

These stances are problematic in opposite ways. Greater formalism has the virtue of promoting freedom of contract and increasing the security of exchanges. But expand that freedom infinitely, and any space for social control is lost. It is difficult to deny that there is at least some utility in some avenues of social control – almost certainly for anti-extortion laws, but probably for the regulation of other activities strongly affecting the public interest. In contrast, excessive zeal for social control constricts a desirable space for freedom of contract. By inviting judicial second-guessing of all bargains, such zealotry would destroy certainty about the security of exchanges.

Reasonable people may differ about where to draw the line between freedom of contract and social control, and it certainly changes over time as social norms evolve and can vary between states. Contract law's exact division may not always be clear and can be contested on any given issue. But it seems pragmatic and prudent to enable a wide scope for freedom of contract accompanied by a modicum of oversight to thwart extremes and police gray areas. That, in any event, is the best description of prevailing contract law and seems an apt description of contract law as it has stood for generations. Moreover, these are not the only tools available to mediate between the extremes. Just because people make a valid contract does not mean it must be performed come hell or high water, as the next chapter shows.

# 3  GETTING OUT

## Excuses and Termination

*The best laid schemes of mice and men often go awry.*

– Robert Burns

## A. MISTAKE AND WARRANTY: MADOFF'S PONZI SCHEME

On December 11, 2008, Bernard Madoff, revered as a savvy investor, confessed to his sons that he had perpetrated one of the largest
financial scams in history, involving an estimated $65 billion. His sons
turned him in – and one of them committed suicide on the first anniversary of his father's arrest.[1]

Beginning in the 1980s, thousands of sophisticated investors, from
hedge fund managers to university investment officers, entrusted millions to him and his firm, Bernard L. Madoff Investment Securities.
He turned others away, increasing his allure, and delivered unmatched
returns to those in on the action.

Madoff's confession revealed, however, that his firm had crafted a
Ponzi scheme, using later-invested funds to repay earlier investments
in escalating magnitude reaching billions of dollars. For two decades,
Madoff had provided fraudulent monthly statements to investors
meticulously portraying fictional securities holdings and trades. On
June 29, 2009, Madoff was sentenced to 150 years in prison.

Among investors stung by Madoff's scam were Steven Simkin, a
prominent New York real estate attorney with the firm of Paul, Weiss,
Rifkind, Wharton & Garrison, and Laura Blank, a distinguished lawyer

working for the City University of New York and heiress to the fortune
of the neckwear manufacturing company, J. S. Blank.

After thirty years of marriage and raising two children, Steven and
Laura separated in 2004, not long after Laura's mother had died. To
finalize their divorce, on June 27, 2006, Steven, who lived in Scarsdale,
and Laura, who lived in Manhattan, signed an agreement dividing their
property, virtually all of which was considered jointly owned because it
was obtained during their lengthy marriage.

In their negotiations, the couple listed their marital assets, including
four cars, the Scarsdale and Manhattan homes, and millions in bank,
securities, and retirement funds, including their investments with
Madoff. The homes and cars aside, it appeared that the couple's total
assets amounted to $13.2 million. The agreement provided that Steven
would keep most assets in exchange for paying Laura $6.6 million in
cash. Thirty months later, when Madoff's Ponzi scheme was exposed,
they discovered that the value of the investments was overstated by
$5.4 million because of it.

After Madoff was arrested, Steven wanted to rescind the settlement
agreement with Laura and redo that part of their deal.[2] He sought
payback from Laura of $2.7 million, half the amount of their over-
valuation of the Madoff account. Laura refused. Steven said the $5.4
million was a fiction, although they did not know it in 2006. So, Steven
argued, Laura got a windfall. For her part, Laura argued that they were
not mistaken at all in 2006, because the account did exist then. From
Laura's perspective, the losses arose only in late 2008, after Madoff
confessed. By 2008, of course, Steven was the account's sole owner.
The arguments of both sides had some intuitive appeal. They also both
found some support in the law, because the precedents can be hard to
reconcile. The case was therefore a close one, but Steven ultimately
had the better of the argument.

People entering bargains are generally held to them, but an exception applies if both parties were mistaken when they made their deal
about a basic assumption that materially affects the exchange. In such
situations, under the doctrine of "mutual mistake," either side can void
it, so long as the risk of the basic assumption was not taken by one
party alone.[3]

## The Forged Dime

A good example involved a coin deal.[4] Beachcomber Coins paid $500 to another coin dealer, Boskett, for a rare dime supposedly minted in 1916 in Denver, signified by a "D" etched on the coin's reverse ("tails") side. Boskett had acquired the dime, along with two modest coins, for $450. He told a Beachcomber representative he would not sell it for less than $500. The representative studied the coin for some time before buying it.

Afterward, another buyer offered Beachcomber $700 for it, subject to getting a genuineness certificate from the American Numismatic Society. The Society declared that the "D" on the coin's reverse side was counterfeit. Beachcomber wanted to rescind its deal with Boskett, citing mutual mistake. Boskett refused, claiming that customary coin-dealing practice called for dealers buying coins to do their own investigation and take all risks: caveat emptor, Latin for "let the buyer beware." The New Jersey Supreme Court held that the case fit the mutual mistake excuse to a tee and, accordingly, rescinded the sale.

Both sides assumed the coin was a genuine Denver-minted dime. This assumption was central to the pricing, and both were mistaken about it. True, contracts can allocate risks of mistake to one side or the other. That happens when parties throw up their hands about whether some assumption is true or false. When people say things like "we're not sure," "we're uncertain," or "it is a matter of judgment," they are consciously allocating a known risk.

In the coin case, however, both sides committed to a specific deal about mintage, neither indicating uncertainty about its authenticity and both assuming the coin was the real thing. Two factors reveal that both parties thought the coin was real: one, Boskett bought the coin for just less than $450, and two, Beachcomber's rep examined it and then forked over the hefty price.

Sometimes standard practice reveals what risks people take. The coin seller's assertions about the custom among coin dealers – buyers investigating and taking all risks – could reveal that. The second buyer, after all, took the trouble to submit the coin to the American Numismatic Society for certification. But such practices were not so regularly observed among coin dealers that the seller was entitled to expect the buyer to follow them.

The Madoff account is much like the dime. The parties in each case thought something was real – an account with securities in it, a dime minted in Denver. Both were mutually mistaken because of someone else's fraud and traded something different from what they thought they were swapping. Enforcing either contract would let happenstance of fraud, rather than intention, determine what bargains are made and how gains are distributed.

Neither case involves questions about what the dime or the account are really worth, how value fluctuates in markets, or how different people may assign different values. A mere change in the market value of exchanged property does not justify excuse for mutual mistake. Beachcomber could not rescind its coin deal by saying the rare coin market had plummeted, and Steven could not rescind his agreement with Laura based solely on a decline in the stock market.

Laura said there was no mistake when she and Steven signed their contract in 2006. They thought there was an account, and there was, she said. Steven withdrew funds from it in 2006 and added funds before 2008. An account can exist, although money deposited into it is not the same money that is paid when funds are withdrawn. Even after December 2008, the account "existed" in many senses. The account was the basis for Madoff customers to claim under a securities investor protection fund and it determined which customers had to return redemptions to the fund.

For Laura, the basic assumption of her bargain with Steven was that the account could be redeemed and she saw no mistake about that. In 2006, they both got the benefit of that bargain. As for conscious risk taking, Laura noted how everyone knew Madoff was opaque, had some special secret method, and delivered outsized returns. As a "sophisticated transactional lawyer," she said, Steven could not say he fully understood the Madoff investment, and an agreement to take that account showed conscious acceptance of all its risk.

Steven countered that the case was a "textbook example of a mutual mistake." If a real account existed, there would be no mutual mistake, Steven allowed, and value declines would be his risk to take. But no real account ever existed. It was irrelevant whether the fictional account had some value for some time. Even though withdrawals could be made, the money would have been stolen from others. In Ponzi schemes, new money from later marks is used to repay old money from earlier ones.

Steven added that nothing he or Laura could have done would have changed anything – Madoff had duped the world's savviest investors. In addition, the requirement of conscious risk taking was missing. The two did not throw up their hands about whether the Madoff account was real, and Steven never assumed the risks of the investments.

## The Fertile Cow

By textbook example, Steven had in mind the landmark case that put mutual mistake firmly on the books. It involved the sale of a blooded, polled Angus cow named "Rose 2d of Aberlone."[5] Both parties – the seller, Hiram Walker, who ran the liquor business that distributes Canadian Club Whiskey, and T. C. Sherwood, a prominent banker who became Michigan's first banking commissioner – assumed the cow was barren and useless as breeding stock. The contract price was $80.

Right before the cow was to be delivered, however, she produced a calf. Now valued as a breeder, Rose 2d of Aberlone was worth $750. The court held that the seller could rescind, as the mistaken belief that the calf was barren was the basic assumption of the deal, indicated by the pricing of the cow, showing that the two had a specific set of bovine attributes in mind that turned out to be incorrect. Mutual mistake applied because mistaken beliefs about a bargain would result in the incorrect distribution of benefits.

The same was true in the story of Steven and Laura. Their bargain was to split economic value both parties thought to be $5.6 million. They were both innocently mistaken about that. In reality, there was nothing to split. There were no investments, securities, or returns or losses, and without those attributes the idea of an account is a nullity. Fraudulent institutional account statements are not a risk parties reasonably perceive or should prudently guard against in forming contracts. To hold parties to those terms after discovering the error is to hold them to a bargain they did not intend to make.

Laura's arguments resemble the coin seller's. Both urged caveat emptor, or "let the buyer beware," and argued that the risk of fraud was on the buyer. Caveat emptor remains critical in contract law and American culture. But saying that all assets come with inherent risks that every buyer must live with is a draconian, seventeenth-century relic – absolute caveat emptor – that would eviscerate any doctrine of mutual mistake. Law outgrew such absolutism long ago. Now, contract law embraces a pragmatic approach to determining what risks people take in contracts. Parties must live with those they meant to take, but not with those they did not.

## The Fake Stradivarius

A renowned case about violins illustrates another route to the same result.[6] Efrem Zimbalist, the internationally acclaimed violinist and father of two accomplished actors, collected violins made by old masters. One afternoon during the Great Depression, Zimbalist visited the home of eighty-six-year-old George Smith, also a collector of rare violins, although not a dealer. Zimbalist asked if he could see Smith's collection and the old man obliged.

The violinist picked up a violin and, calling it a Stradivarius, asked what Smith would take for it. Smith said he was not offering to sell any violins, but since he was aging, he would let that one go for a lower price than dealers would – $5,000 (about $65,000 today, a steal when similar violins today fetch many multiples of that at auction sales). The player picked up another, called it a Guarnerius, and asked the same question about price. Smith said he would sell them both for $8,000. Zimbalist agreed, offering $2,000 down and the rest in monthly $1,000 installments. Smith accepted.

Zimbalist signed a note acknowledging receipt from Smith of "one violin by Joseph Guarnerius and one violin by Stradivarius dated 1717" and promising to pay the balance as agreed. Smith signed a bill of sale certifying that he sold Zimbalist "one Joseph Guarnerius violin and one Stradivarius violin dated 1717" on the agreed terms. The violins, in fact, were imitations, each only worth $300.

Even though both men believed violins were made by Antonio Stradivari and Joseph Guarneri and the writings described them as such, Smith never made any promises or representations about the violins' authenticity. So Smith, citing caveat emptor, demanded payment of the balance; Zimbalist claimed mutual mistake and attempted to rescind the contract.

At the time, caveat emptor ran strong in the courts, leaving little elbow room for the excuse of mutual mistake. Upheld under caveat emptor were sales of knockoff paintings both parties thought to be by famous artists, deals for facsimile stones thought to be precious, and sales of a cheap timber called peachum thought to be the exotic brazilletto. Caveat emptor prevailed even when a seller's advertising, catalogs, and bills of lading described the more valuable item the parties thought they were trading. Although some cases noted that the sellers had informed the buyers of the risk they were assuming, or that the buyers had a chance to examine the goods, these points were not needed for courts to enforce caveat emptor.

The cases did, however, leave room to enforce warranties when sellers clearly made them. These warranties permitted buyers to rescind the sale of a forged painting the seller described as made by the Venetian painter Canaletto, as well as a sale the seller described as involving a pure copper compound that was actually a mixture. Over time, courts recognized that sellers make warranties and take risks, and that not all deals put all risks on buyers. The absolutism of caveat emptor began to yield.

The evolution even left room for rescission when the described and actual goods were of equal quality, such as a deal for the sale of flour described as Haxall that was actually Gallego (and no Haxall flour existed). This new flexibility morphed into the modern doctrine of mutual mistake. The two excuses – breach of warranty and mutual mistake – often apply to the same bargains, as the flour deal illustrates. The contract could be rescinded using either breach of warranty or mutual mistake.

Warranty and mutual mistake are therefore independent grounds to rescind a contract, even though they can both appear in a single case. That happened with Efrem Zimbalist's violins. Because the documents showed an intention to trade violins of particular makers, the bill of sale amounts to a warranty that the seller breached. Together, the bill of sale and the promissory note show that both parties were honestly mistaken about the identity of the subject matter. Therefore, no valid contract arose. It was irrelevant that Smith made no representations and committed no fraud.[7]

Like the violin case or the cattle deal, Steven and Laura's divorce settlement agreement was a case of mutual mistake, as a matter of contract law. Although ancient cases put caveat emptor in a rarified place, modern doctrines mediate it. Bargains that amount to happenstance, rather than actual intentions of both parties, can be rescinded. When parties make a deal based on a shared central assumption that proves to be wrong they are entitled to rescind it. The doctrine of mutual mistake protects the benefit of bargains people intended to make while freeing them from those they did not.[8]

Perhaps the best argument Laura offered was from outside of contract law. She argued that, whatever contract law might provide for the general run of contracts – such as those between coin dealers, cattle traders, and violin collectors – special rules govern divorces. In the divorce setting, the finality of agreements is so important, given the emotional stakes, that the standard for rescission should be stricter and even divorce agreements such as the one she and Steven signed should be upheld. As of this book's publication date, New York's Court of Appeals had not ruled on the merits of this argument.[9]

## B. IMPOSSIBILITY AND FORCE MAJEURE: DONALD TRUMP

Donald Trump, the billionaire real estate developer, thought the so-called Great Recession of 2008–2009 so calamitous as to count as an "act of God." He was in the midst of building what would be Chicago's tallest skyscraper, a combination luxury hotel and condominiums. To finance the project, Trump borrowed $640 million from lenders led by Deutsche Bank in February 2005. By the end of 2008, Trump had only sold condos netting him $204 million, along with others under contract that would yield another $353 million. That left him facing a shortfall of nearly $100 million when he was obligated to repay his lenders $40 million per month. Trump cited the Great Recession as an excuse to delay making monthly payments. The banks refused to accept the excuse from timely payment, so Trump – a prolific litigant – went to court.[10]

Unfortunately for Trump, there was no mutual mistake between him and the banks that would excuse his prompt monthly repayment duties. No one was mistaken about conditions that existed when Trump and the banks made their bargain. But circumstances changed and law has long recognized excuse from contract for some kinds of surprising supervening events loosely called forces majeure, from the French meaning "superior forces," or acts of God. If you rent a banquet hall for your wedding, and it burns down with no one at fault, you and the hall are both excused from the agreement;[11] when Hurricane Katrina destroyed New Orleans in September 2005, contracts to buy or sell homes and businesses there were excused.

Recognized forces majeure include fire, flood, lightening, famine, and deep freezes that destroy the subject matter of a contract. Death excuses promises made to render personal service to others. People are not held to deals when it becomes objectively impossible to perform them, at least so long as they did not have reason to foresee the risk and did not address it in their contract.[12] Trump would stress that man-made calamities can also excuse bargains when, although something is possible to perform, it would be idle to perform it given a deal's purpose. A rental agreement for a hotel room to watch a parade can be excused if the parade is canceled, although the room could be occupied, under the aptly named doctrine "frustration of purpose" – unless, of course, the contract states otherwise.[13]

In extreme cases, a party can be excused when the economics of a deal make performance impracticable. But that excuse is usually limited to prevention by governmental authorities restricting some activity and does not let people out of bargains that prove more costly, even as a result of events like war.[14] The excuse does not cover a bargain to transport goods, like oil from Texas to India, although a wartime blockade prevents the cheapest route and the alternative costs twice as much.[15]

Deutsche Bank and Trump's other lenders stressed the narrowness of these excuses, reflected in a long-standing principle of contract law called *pacta sunt servanda*, a Latin phrase meaning "promises are kept."[16] Akin to venerable caveat emptor, the traditional idea is that people make bargains and must stick to them, all risk being taken when they make their deal, whatever those risks are. Back in England of

1647, this stance was rigid. "Yet, he ought to pay his rent," is a famous legal conclusion from that year's grand case of *Paradine v. Jane.*[17] A tenant had to keep a promise to pay rent, even though the premises were uninhabitable as they were located in a war-ravaged region occupied by marauding bandits and battling armies of the German Prince Rupert. Courts for the next two centuries firmly invoked pacta sunt servanda, as they did caveat emptor.[18] There was no way out, however burdensome performance might be.

But just as modern law gradually relaxed strict caveat emptor to recognize mutual mistake, it softened pacta sunt servanda to recognize excuses based on impossibility, frustration, and impracticability. And it is easy to see why: Contracts allocate risks, but not necessarily *all* risks. They do not allocate risks that people did not think about or could not reasonably foresee. When those types of risks occur, there is reason to excuse the obligation, not insist on it. Otherwise, law would hold people to bargains they did not intend to make. Still, the impulse to keep promises and enforce valid bargains remains strong, and excuses based on impossibility, frustration, and impracticability are narrowly defined and typically require calamitous events.

As Donald Trump knows, these limits on excuse from changed circumstances prompt people to allocate risks expressly in contracts. A common method is a provision naming what events count as excuses, called a "force majeure clause." In these clauses, parties can list any sorts of events they wish, including both man-made and natural causes. Here is an example: "If either party to this contract shall be delayed or prevented from the performance of any obligation through no fault of their own by reason of labor disputes, inability to procure materials, failure of utility service, restrictive governmental laws or regulations, riots, insurrection, war, adverse weather, Acts of God, or other similar causes beyond the control of such party, the performance of such obligation shall be excused for the period of the delay."

## The Uninsurable Roller Rink

That clause appeared in a lease Kel-Kim Corporation made for a vacant supermarket it planned to use as a public roller-skating rink.[19] The ten-year lease required it to keep liability insurance in minimum amounts to cover accidents and injuries. Insurance was no problem for the first half of the lease term. But then the insurance market toughened amid a proliferation of liability claims, making it cost-prohibitive for Kel-Kim to obtain the minimum insurance. In court, Kel-Kim said its duty to keep insurance should be excused, either by contract law's general impossibility doctrine or by virtue of the parties' specific force majeure clause.

But the court held that Kel-Kim's duty was not excused under either escape hatch. Excuse from impossibility is limited to cases where the subject matter of a contract is destroyed or the means of performance so impaired that performance is objectively impossible. To be considered "impossible," the situation has to be unanticipated so that it could not have reasonably been foreseen and addressed in the contract. In Kel-Kim's case, the property had not been destroyed and astronomical insurance costs can still be paid and are easy to foresee and address in a contract. The contract expressly addressed insurance and required Kel-Kim to maintain it. If the parties wanted Kel-Kim to be excused from obtaining insurance if some events should occur, they needed to explicitly say so in the contract. They did not.

Nor was Kel-Kim's problem included in the contract's force majeure clause. The clause addresses problems that could arise in daily operations, concerning things like labor, materials, and utilities. It does not address insurance or Kel-Kim's ability to get it. True, the clause ends with a catch-all referring to "other similar causes beyond the control of such party." But that general wording relates to the specific listing – "similar causes" – so only events of that sort may qualify as excuses.

Donald Trump's position was analogous to Kel-Kim's. Accordingly, his claim would fail under contract law's general impossibility excuse. It was not impossible for him to repay the banks on time. Even if he did not have the money, the impossible act must be objectively impossible – something no one could do, like revive a dead person or deliver a building that has burned to the ground. Trump's claim would therefore also fare no better than Kel-Kim's under the force majeure clause in its lease. To make his claim persuasive, his loan agreement's force majeure clause would have to include something like: "riots, insurrection, war, adverse weather, Acts of God, *national financial crisis of magnitude unprecedented in modern time,* or other similar causes." But banks do not agree to that kind of risk allocation.

On the contrary, force majeure clauses in business agreements, including commercial loan agreements, usually say that the excused duties exclude duties to pay money. These clauses begin by saying something like: "If Borrowers shall be delayed or prevented from the performance of any obligation, *other than the payment of money,* through no fault of their own ..."

Despite weaknesses in Trump's arguments, he got accommodations from Deutsche Bank in the repayment schedule amid the Great Recession, stretching the case out through settlement in July 2010, after the financial storm passed. As Trump fought that battle, millions of other American borrowers struggled to repay their real estate loans as well. People wondered, if Donald Trump could be excused from repaying his loans on time, why could not they? Some of these were Trump customers, including those buying condos in his Chicago development project. When asked whether they should be excused, Trump said no. He explained: His contract included a force majeure clause that their contracts lacked.[20]

But the clause in Trump's contract did not give him the excuse to delay payment. The difference between Trump and mortgage borrowers was not the contracts or contract law, but scale. Banks compete vigorously to get Trump's billions in business; they care proportionately less about individual loans in the hundreds of thousands of dollars. Thus, banks have an incentive to settle their dispute with him and permit a change in his payment schedule. The law, however, is clear: As the court in the seventeenth-century case of *Paradine v. Jane* might have said, even in a financial crisis, Donald Trump must pay his debts.

## C. INFANCY: CRAIG TRAYLOR OF "MALCOLM IN THE MIDDLE"

Craig Lamar Traylor, the American actor known for his role as best friend of the title character in the hit television show "Malcolm in the Middle," entered into a contract when he was ten years old with Sharyn Berg, as his manager. He later wanted out and invoked a long-standing principle letting minors disaffirm otherwise valid contracts they have made.[21] The contract, called an Artist's Manager's Agreement, covered two pages and was signed by Craig's mother, Meshiel, but not by Craig. Executed in California in January 1999, the agreement called for Berg to serve as Craig's exclusive personal manager in exchange for a commission of 15 percent of Craig's acting earnings for the next three years and income from merchandising and promotional activities.

In June 2001, Craig landed a regular acting role on "Malcolm in the Middle." The money rolled in – and so did large tax bills and other expenses. As a result, in September 2001, Craig's mother wrote Berg to cancel the agreement. Meshiel explained that she and her son could not afford to pay the commissions. Berg declared that action to be a breach of contract by both Craig and his mother. During the ensuing litigation and arbitration, Meshiel hired, fired, or lost a series of four different law firms, many of whose bills went unpaid. In 2005, an arbitrator determined that the parties had a valid contract and that Craig and Meshiel owed Berg $150,000 in past commissions plus $400,000 in projected commissions based on earnings from planed syndication of the show. The parties agreed to modify that award – which implied that the teenaged Craig stood to earn about $3.7 million from his role on the show – to pay a lower but still substantial amount in a series of installments.

Inexplicably, however, during years of legal wrangling, the several law firms representing Craig, as well arbitrators and at least one judge, overlooked a fundamental question in the case: whether Craig, as a minor, wanted to ratify or disaffirm his contract with Berg (and, later, the modified arbitration award). It was not until Craig was represented by Robert Pafundi, in the summer of 2005, that Craig became aware of this election. He promptly exercised it. At first, the other lawyers in the case and even a California trial judge denied Craig's request. Finally, an irate appellate court invoked contract law's "infancy doctrine" to let Craig disaffirm his contracts. His mother, however, remained bound.

The infancy doctrine is a way for a minor, someone less than eighteen years of age, to escape contractual obligations. The ancient doctrine sets limits on the freedom people have to contract with minors. It reflects how freedom of contract is an exercise of maturity, judgment, and experience – traits not every child can be presumed to possess. A similar paternalistic impulse governs contracts made by mentally ill people, who may likewise elect to disaffirm otherwise valid contracts.[22]

The infancy doctrine also reflects a general principle that parents bear considerable, albeit not absolute, responsibility for their minor children. The public policy impulse to protect children is paramount, so that it applies even when it imposes hardship on the other party to a minor's contract. Sell your car on credit to a minor who defaults, and the law will not necessarily help you recover either your money or your car.[23] The stance helps protect minors against adults who may intentionally seek to exploit them, although minors have the right to disaffirm even the fairest contracts made with the most scrupulous adults.

Accordingly, judges have for centuries been prepared to intervene on behalf of minors, and the mentally ill, who wish to disaffirm contracts.[24] So long as the minor made no misrepresentation about age and committed no other civil or criminal violation, courts readily accept minor elections to disaffirm most contracts. Minors, as well as the mentally ill, may also elect to affirm their contracts and bind their counterparties. The election belongs to them, not to the other side.

Berg argued various exceptions to the infancy doctrine. She first claimed Traylor was bound despite the infancy doctrine because his mother, a competent adult, had assented to the contract for him. There are a few cases where that argument works, but they are limited to subjects where parental decision making is particularly important, such as health care determinations or medical treatment. A rationale for the health-related exception is that medical providers would not contract with minors knowing that disaffirmance is possible. The only way to induce medical providers to make such contracts is to let parents bind themselves as well as their children to the contracts. But that exception is narrow and did not apply to Craig and Berg's personal managerial services contract.

Berg urged another exception to the infancy doctrine, where parents can bind their children to contracts addressing qualifications to participate in scholastic events, including sporting contests. This exception commonly applies to contracts containing provisions releasing schools from responsibility for injuries a child may suffer when participating in athletic events. For example, the parents of a high school cheerleader bound her to a contract releasing a school district from responsibility for injuries suffered while participating.[25] But this line of cases likewise had no bearing on Craig's contract, about the payment of commissions on acting earnings, having nothing to do with scholastic athletic injuries.

Finally, Berg urged an exception to the infancy doctrine that bars minors from disaffirming contracts involving supplying goods and services that are necessary for the child's sustenance.[26] This is a venerable exception, but it did not quite fit the story either, because Craig's contract was not about things he needed to live, but the management of his acting career.

Berg's arguments lost for yet another reason. The written contract addressed what would happen if Craig elected to disaffirm it: It said that in that case, his mother, Meshiel, would remain bound to pay the commissions. Berg, as well as Meshiel, thus contemplated that Craig had the right to disaffirm and said what would happen if he did. As many courts have written, including the judge in Craig's case, "those who provide a minor with goods and services do so at their own risk." And Berg addressed that risk by making Meshiel liable even if Craig was not.[27]

Berg could have done one more thing when she made her initial deal with Craig. A California statute authorizes people making contracts with child entertainers to have them preapproved by a state judge. Once approved, the infancy doctrine goes away and people like Craig are bound to their deals just as if they were adults.[28] Berg, as a professional agent, should have known about this statute and availed herself of the procedure when making her contract with Traylor.

## D. OUTRAGE: AIG'S EMPLOYEE BONUSES

In September 2008, the U.S. government seized control of American International Group, or AIG, the massive global insurance company that ran a complex financial products business. To avert an AIG bankruptcy that could have threatened the financial system, the government committed $85 billion of capital and seized an 80 percent ownership stake in the company.

In March 2009, headlines nationwide reported that the company was about to make $165 million in cash bonus payments to 400 employees in AIG's financial products business, ranging from $1,000 to $6 million apiece. The U.S. unemployment rate was approaching 10 percent, and many Americans were outraged that they were footing the bill for AIG's seizure, let alone extravagant bonuses. Public backlash was swift and political uproar intense.

Amid the wrangling, the company persistently asserted that its employee bonus contracts were ironclad agreements obligating it to make full payment. On the other side, members of Congress threatened to confiscate the payments by imposing punishing excise taxes on recipients. Senator Charles Grassley, the Iowa Republican, even told AIG executives they should commit ritual suicide over the imbroglio. AIG employees reported receiving death threats. President Barak Obama directed his Treasury Department to "pursue every single legal avenue" to abrogate or limit the company's payment obligations. Andrew Cuomo, New York's attorney general at the time, demanded more information from AIG about how the deals were made and their purpose.[29]

The contracts were made in early 2008, many months before AIG's financial troubles led it to decide to close its financial products business. At that point, it appeared that the business was prospering and the market for financial products so competitive that it risked losing important talent to competitors. To retain them, AIG used the bonus scheme, promising bonus payments in 2009 and 2010 so long as the worker was still on board. Employees thus both bargained for and relied on that promise.

Before anyone analyzed the employment contracts, the heated political environment sidetracked debate into polarized camps, one making nebulous assertions, the other hysterical threats.[30] The loudest voices were outraged by what they saw as the obscene size of the bonuses, made to a company now funded by taxpayers. They endorsed a heavy governmental hand, suggesting that the government should prevent paying the bonuses, even if that meant breaching the contracts. If the government prevented the bonuses, employees who wanted payment would have to sue, shouldering costs and critical publicity. Likewise impassioned opponents of the bonuses argued that without the government's funding, AIG employee claims to bonuses could be worthless with AIG in bankruptcy and its limited resources paid to other claimants.

Some misinterpreted the bonuses as payments under contracts triggered by achieving performance goals, like profitability. It was difficult for many to understand how employees of an operation losing significant money and on the brink of insolvency, but for government funding, could be entitled to anything. Intuitive as that sounds, these bonuses were promised simply to retain people – a promise to pay so long as employees kept their end of the employment bargain and remained at the company. Equally ill-informed, some reports suggested that the plans were adopted when the company expected to close the business, a view that suggested the retention tools were important to keep people from fleeing the company when its prospects looked dim.

A vocal minority detected a mob mentality in the populist uproar opposing the bonuses. They began from the premise that government should not have bailed out AIG and should not meddle in its affairs after it had. For them, this meant rejecting government involvement in evaluating the bonus contracts. This vociferous group saw the AIG employees as unfortunate political punching bags and objected to what they saw as attaching strings to the government bailout. Attaching strings would lead companies who might need or benefit from financial support to decline. None of these feuding positions was based on the actual terms of the contracts, however, or relevant to any applicable contract law.

The company repeatedly touted the sanctity of contracts, insisting that the contracts required it to pay the bonuses and that there was no legitimate way around it. As the debate heated up, however, that stance was insufficient to convince the public. So AIG launched a more serious defense, leaking a fascinating memo in March 2009.[31] It warned that not paying the bonuses would amount to breach of contract, with devastating consequences.

The memo said a breach would expose AIG to punishing penalties under state worker protection laws. It cautioned that reneging on the payments could amount to "constructive discharge" of employees, meaning they could walk off the job while still demanding pay.

The memo stressed that nonpayment could trigger so-called cross-defaults under other contracts – meaning one contract is deemed breached if breach of any other contract occurs. It cautioned that if certain employees left, international banking authorities could appoint replacements.

The memo also made a business case for bonus payment. It stressed the peculiar expertise these employees possessed that was indispensible to the operation, and who could not be replaced in short order. It detailed the progress these employees had made reducing the company's risk in the six months since its financial meltdown began. It explained how AIG had reduced the size of this complex financial products business, including shrinking its workforce from 450 to 370 employees. The memo concluded by promising to use best efforts to reduce compensation during 2009.

Despite its harrowing warnings, the AIG memo was far from thorough. All the legal warnings hinged on highly technical concerns that could go either way but were presented as one-sided fait accompli. For example, worker protection law it cited was from one state, did not necessarily apply to every AIG employee contract, and has a "good faith" exception that was relevant. The warning about "constructive discharge" of employees did not explain the meaning of that complex term or how farfetched it might be to classify nonpayment of the bonuses that way. The referenced cross-defaults only triggered for other defaults exceeding $25 million, and no single employee was entitled to anything close to that.

Nor did the memo discuss the fundamental issues of contract law at stake. Contract law recognizes some dozen legitimate grounds that excuse people from contracts – such as mistake and impossibility. The memo should have identified the leading examples and shown why they do not apply. For instance, the government's takeover of the company could amount to a frustration of the contract's purposes – instead of a team of talented individuals expanding a complex business, an orderly private unwinding of the complex business was now required after government's takeover.

Other recognized excuses from contract obligation the memo should have noted are fraud, misrepresentation, and nondisclosure. These refer to whether AIG employees were honest with AIG during their employment, including their products and risks. If AIG retained employees, agreeing to pay bonuses to those who had deceived it, by engaging in illegal trades, misstating the value of some of the complex transactions or risk levels, or failing to disclose important information about the deals they struck, that would excuse AIG from its obligation to pay. Even though the AIG employees did not necessarily fail in any of these ways, there are standard grounds that excuse duties, and there was evidence that top AIG officials were unaware of punishing provisions employees had included in AIG's contracts with its trading partners.[32]

AIG never hashed out any of these issues. Despite many potential legal avenues to abrogate the AIG bonus contracts, the government never used them either. After the public furor erupted, Congress passed a statute creating a new overseer for pay packages at companies receiving government funds.[33] President Obama named Kenneth R. Feinberg to the post. For AIG, Feinberg was empowered to direct compensation for 2008, 2009, and 2010. He and AIG knew about all these contract law issues and also knew that, under the statute, he could set the next year's compensation at low levels.

Feinberg chose to induce some employees to accept reductions in their bonuses, but said he did not rely on contract law. Feinberg said he instead relied on the statutory leverage he had, which he preferred to the contract excuse approach in the name of the sanctity of contracts. But as Feinberg privately acknowledged, recognizing valid excuses from contractual obligation does not impair the sanctity of contracts one iota. Long-recognized excuses in contract law are a legitimate means of seeking adjustments – perhaps more legitimate than those that the politically charged statute offered.

One year later, in February 2010, the country was no closer to answering the fundamental question of whether contract law required paying the bonuses or, alternatively, recognized an excuse from doing so. Instead, the same company paid the same employees a total of $200 million in cash bonuses in the name of honoring what the company (and the government) continued to call "legally binding" contracts.[34] It remained a mystery whether AIG employees were contractually entitled to the payments and unknown whether they breached any contractual or other duties during the prior two years.

A final revelation came in March 2010. The company for the first time said the contract terms limited the company's obligation to pay bonuses. The company could reduce payments to employees earning outside income by the amount of that income.[35] For bonus payments the company made then, this meant saving $21 million. The company never explained how these indispensible employees had the time to pursue outside income. But, at least and at last, the company did what mattered, disclosed some terms of the contracts and identified a clause limiting its payment duties. Its delay and posturing distracted public discourse into hyperbole for and against the bonuses without regard to the contracts or contract law. Whereas public outrage does not justify getting out of a contract, many legitimate grounds do.[36]

## E. EMBARRASSMENT: THE NEW YORK METS AND CITI FIELD

When a global financial crisis tightened its grip in 2008 and financial institutions were rescued by government bailouts, Citigroup and other banks faced populist rebuke for what many perceived to be a period of lavishness and recklessness that fueled the crisis. Anger percolated over the government's commitment of hundreds of billions of dollars to bail out the banks from their transgressions. The backlash reached Citi's deal with The New York Mets concerning branding rights associated with the team's new stadium, Citi Field, which opened for the 2009 baseball season.

Pressure intensified in January 2009 when members of Congress, including Dennis Kucinich, the Ohio Democrat, and Ted Poe, the Texas Republican, demanded that Citi terminate its Mets contract.[37] Citi promptly quashed speculation that it would do so.[38] Others in Congress supported that decision, emphasizing that the contract and marketing arrangements involve business decisions that are not Congress's job to second-guess or micromanage, despite using billions of public funds to support the bank. A *New York Times* columnist, Richard Sandomir, opined that the money would be better spent retaining workers;[39] some defended the deal on the grounds that it would help the bank's economic position, through improved branding and associated merchandising transactions.

Amid this political blaze, few appreciated that the terms of the contract both governed the relationship and reflected the economic value in exchanges like this. There is a large market for stadium branding rights, of relatively recent vintage.[40] It began as a small market in 1971 (when the New England Patriots signed Schaefer Brewing Company to name its football stadium) through the mid-1990s, when it rocketed.

In the old days, stadiums were named after civic leaders (like John F. or Robert F. Kennedy), families (like Wrigley in Chicago or Busch in St. Louis), features (like Houston's Astrodome), or teams (like the New York Yankees). Since 1997, however, most new big-time sports stadiums have been named for corporations.[41] This phenomenon reflects the corporate financing of new stadium construction in the period, in exchange for corporate investment in brand name and associated merchandising avenues.

The stakes rose accordingly, with the average annual contract price for deals rising from $1 million in 1995 to $5 million in 2002, and terms extending up to twenty or more years. More recent deals reach higher annual prices, like the contract between FedEx and the Washington Redskins involving an $8 million annual price and that between Reliant Energy and the Houston Texans triggering a $10 million annual payment. Bank of America has a contract with the Carolina Panthers football team, paying $7 million annually for marketing and naming rights at that team's stadium.

Smaller deals also exist, such as for collegiate stadiums. Bank of America named University of Washington's basketball arena for $500,000 annually, and Wells Fargo named Arizona State's for a lump fee of $5 million for an indefinite time. Washington Mutual, acquired by JPMorgan Chase amid the financial crisis of 2008–2009, named the Theater at New York's Madison Square Garden on undisclosed financial terms, although undoubtedly much lower than big-time sports team terms.

These naming trends extend to buying the right to give personal names to urban cultural institutions. For example, in 2006, pharmaceutical magnate George Behrakis donated $10 million to Boston's Museum of Fine Arts, which named its "Art of the Ancient World" wing for him in exchange – the first such naming at the museum since 1915.[42] Even municipal school districts nationwide, from Wisconsin to

Texas to California, pursue corporate sponsors to name public school
athletic fields – earning millions in the process.[43]

When the Mets began searching for corporate partners for its new
stadium, the team sought $10 million annually – a price that attracted
many bidders and drove the final cost up significantly. Citi won the
bidding, signing a twenty-year deal in exchange for an annual payment of $20 million. That figure stoked the Congressional fury. But
the price spike for the Mets deal reflects intense interest and compe-
tition among corporations for the opportunity – especially for companies like banks, whose products are difficult to brand. For example,
Barclays, the British bank, signed a contract in 2007 on terms substantially similar to the Citi-Mets deal – twenty years for $20 million per
year – promoting the New York Nets basketball team and naming its
new arena in Brooklyn.

The Citi-Mets contract involves more than a stadium naming in
exchange for cash. The Citi brand is streamed throughout the stadium,
in video programming, and in all Mets publicity materials – print,
radio, television, and Internet. The two businesses develop extensive
joint marketing, event promotions, and merchandising discounts. They
agree to conduct shared community outreach through their respective charitable foundations. As one example, the Citi-Mets contract
requires joint promotion of the Jackie Robinson Foundation Museum
and Education Center to educate children about Robinson's role in
forging social change. A statue at the field's main entrance recognizes
Robinson, the African-American Brooklyn Dodgers baseball player
who in 1947 broke through baseball's "color barrier."

Congressional opponents of the Citi-Mets deal called for its termination, even though they admitted to not having read the contract's
terms.[44] Many stadium-naming and promotion contracts address termination expressly. The only way to make a judgment about whether
Citi or the Mets should withdraw from the contract would be to
examine its terms – which both parties prefer to keep confidential for
competitive reasons. Termination clauses in naming rights contracts
may give either side the right to terminate for given reasons and on
stated terms. Bankruptcy of the corporate partner is a common reason, and one cited for the termination of naming rights contracts
amid a national economic recession of 2000–2002. That ended several

big deals, including between Adelphia and the Tennessee Titans and between Worldcom (MCI) and the Washington Capitals and Wizards.

Some deals adapt the so-called morals clauses appearing in contracts between teams and players or between merchandisers and prominent product spokespeople.[45] Those clauses let teams or merchandisers terminate players or spokespeople if continued association exposes the brand name to embarrassment. The clauses are usually described to include engaging in egregious or obnoxious misbehavior. As an example, the Washington Wizards basketball team invoked a morals clause in 2009–2010 to suspend its star player, Gilbert Arenas, after he brought guns into the stadium. Similarly, some merchandisers suspended their relationship with Tiger Woods in 2010 after the golfer acknowledged marital infidelities.

Companies can engage in misconduct analogous to carrying guns or cheating on spouses and inflict similar costly embarrassment on a team partner. When a company's financial fraud is exposed, for example, that hurts the brand name of any team whose stadium is named for it. Without such clauses, termination may be costly. Consider the case of Enron Corporation and the Houston Astros baseball team. In 1999, the two made a thirty-year deal for total payments of $100 million. After Enron was revealed to be a fraud, the Astros sought to end the contract. But it lacked a termination provision akin to a morals clause. Enron refused to split, and the Astros persuaded it to do so only after agreeing to pay a $2.1 million exit fee.

The Barclays-New York Nets contract gave Barclays the right to terminate its commitment if the team, and its developer-owner, had not assembled the remaining financing for construction of the arena and surrounding area by a stated deadline.[46] Because the condition was unmet, Barclays had the right to walk. It elected not to do so, however, waiving the condition and extending the developer's deadline for financing. Barclay's decision lent support to the reasonableness of Citi's decision not to terminate its Mets contract. Because it involves weighing a number of contending factors, including the terms of the contract, that is a business decision for Citi's board, and officers under its direction, to make.

Termination may not be as easy as some in Congress suggested and may even result in a net cost to the corporate sponsor. Whether the Mets are better off honoring or terminating the Citi contract is likewise a matter of judgment that must be made by the team based on the contract's terms.

Many people still believe that promises must be kept, come hell or high water, and others believe that caveat emptor remains the law of the land. Some people think that extraordinary events justify rewriting the bargains they make just because of their extraordinariness. Others believe that minor children are bound to their deals just as adults are. Yet others appear profoundly mistaken about the role that politics and government power should play in evaluating the validity of private contracts. All such people often rush to judgment about deals they read about without considering the actual terms of a contract or the time-tested principles of contract law. The stories in this chapter show some of the trouble with these beliefs, attitudes, and habits.

Contracts can never perfectly anticipate every potential circumstance. When surprising events arise, it is possible for law to disregard them and insist that people literally keep all enforceable promises they make. Proponents of a formalist approach to contract law would applaud such a stance. That approach would reflect antique beliefs, long ago discarded as flawed, celebrated in doctrines like caveat emptor and pacta sunt servanda: Parties to contracts must beware and their promises must be kept. That increases certainty in contracts and puts parties on high alert to verify the facts underlying their commitments when they make them.

But time has taught us that such a stance is too rigid, unrealistic, and unsympathetic. It fails to appreciate how people make contracts to allocate risks. If everyone is simply held to the technical terms of bargains they manifestly make with no attention to context, many arrangements will result in putting risks on people by happenstance rather than based on intention. There are also other valid policies at stake, such as protecting minors and the mentally ill by allowing them to disaffirm contracts they make.

Yet there is also nothing appealing about a regime that allows escape from contract too readily, whether dealing with mistake owing to forged dimes and fraudulent financial accounts or punishing performance costs owing to crises in the insurance or financial markets.

Make the escape hatches too wide, and people become sloppy. Too many deals would be unwound, impairing the reliability of promises so essential to a society that uses free exchanges to meet needs, build wealth, and enjoy life.

People may take great care to address contingencies, and when they do they are held to the resulting risk allocation. For problems such as mutual mistake, impossibility, and contingencies that terms expressly address, letting parties out of contracts comports with freedom of contract and the ideas of bargain and assent that contracts are based on. When competent parties expressly state what risks are allocated, and list what excuses based on forces majeure they agree on, those terms are enforced.

Political winds or Congressional whims are irrelevant to whether a contract may be excused or should be terminated. Contract law thus takes a pragmatic position – neither being stingy nor lavish with excuses, but providing a tailored set of legitimate exits. Further, even when parties are not excused does not mean that courts order them to perform a specific promise. Most often, it means the breaching party must pay the other side money, as the next chapter reveals.

# 4 PAYING UP

## Remedies

*The duty to keep a contract at common law means a prediction that you must pay damages if you do not keep it – and nothing else.*

– Oliver Wendell Holmes, Jr.

## A.  INTERESTS AND LIMITS: PARIS HILTON AND "PLEDGE THIS!"

Paris Hilton, descendant of the billionaire hotel baron, lives the life of a celebutante, touting products in exchange for fees and royalties. In 2006, she was supposed to promote the sophomoric film, "National Lampoon's Pledge This!" Investors put $8.3 million into the picture, buying the script, hiring talent, shooting, and promoting. It was produced as an independent film, unaffiliated with the major studios that command commercial power in the industry. Investors nevertheless believed it had a good chance of financial success in theaters and on DVD.

Vital to its success was Paris Hilton, as a brand. The film company got Hilton, then twenty four years old, to play the leading role in the film and serve as one of its seven executive producers. Her contract with the Pledge group said she would "perform reasonable promotion and publicity services" for the film, "subject to her professional availability." The contract gave Hilton the right to approve or disapprove specific publicity services but required her to reply to requests within seventy-two hours. Her duties extended to help market the DVD when released. The company paid her $1 million – $65,000 for playing the lead and the rest for these other services.

The film got a credible start after release in late 2006 with a limited run in theaters, followed by the DVD release on December 19, 2006 that investors hoped would generate significant revenue. A big pay-off would require heavy marketing from December into January and February. But Hilton was vacationing with her family in Hawaii that Christmas, then traveled to Japan and Austria to promote products for other clients. The film crew sent her dozens of e-mails during that time to set up promotional interviews. They cited opportunities not only in Austria and Japan, but valued slots in the United States on "The Late Show" with David Letterman, "The Tonight Show" with Jay Leno, and an MTV satellite radio tour.

Hilton acknowledged getting requests, but said she was justified denying or ignoring them because she was "professionally unavailable." She emphasized that she had promoted "Pledge This" before its theatrical release but simply had no time to follow up for the DVD. She and her handlers explained her grueling schedule during that period, adding that it takes Hilton more than three hours a day just to do her hair.

The film flopped and the investors lost money, whether as a result of Hilton's blowing them off, as the company claimed, or the ineptitude of the film's producers, as Hilton contended. The production company, whose sole business was the film, went bankrupt. Its court-appointed trustee sued Hilton.[1] The court determined that Hilton did not breach her contract concerning promotional duties ahead of the theatrical release, but accepted that she breached by failing to promote the DVD. For that, the company could claim one of several different classes of damages potentially available in contract cases.

Expectancy damages are the standard measure in all breach of contract cases. They are intended to compensate the injured party to protect the benefit of the bargain. That means paying the difference between what a party got and what it would have gotten if the promise had been performed. For promotional contracts like the Hilton-Pledge arrangement, that is the difference between the profit the company actually made and what it would have gained had Hilton performed.

This difference is described as "lost profits." In the case of the Pledge film, if it generated $3.3 million in box office revenues plus $5 million from DVD sales, the film broke even, given costs of $8.3 million. So its lost profits were any additional DVD sales it would have earned had Paris promoted as promised.

Hilton stressed a basic principle of contract law, however, which requires the injured party seeking damages for breach to prove the amount of losses with reasonable certainty. Doing that is not always easy, especially for claims like Pledge's of lost profits on a low-budget independent film. In fact, for many years, contract law would not even consider claims of lost profits unless a party had a track record to support a claim. Although that so-called new business rule has evaporated in most states, its replacement is a standard that, while not barring recovery, insists on evidence showing losses with reasonable certainty.


## "Clever Endeavor"

In a well-known case cutting against the Pledge film group,[2] Larry Blackwell, inventor of the adult board game, "Clever Endeavor," had sold 30,000 copies of the game within his first four months of marketing it in late 1989. He then licensed the rights to Western Publishing, distributor of famous games like "Pictionary" and "Trivial Pursuit," getting its promise to promote the game and pay Blackwell a 15 percent royalty on copies sold. Both thought the game could be a hit. It enjoyed first year sales of 165,000 copies, grossing $4 million and netting Blackwell $600,000. But during the next three years, sales plummeted to 58,000, 26,000, and 7,500, respectively.

Blackwell attributed disappointing sales to Western's shoddy marketing, allegedly beneath industry standards, and wanted $40 million for breach. But Blackwell could not prove such losses with the required reasonable certainty. Beside his foray into board games with "Clever Endeavor," he had no track record selling them. He could not offer reliable evidence from other board games that achieved success when marketed properly.

The board game market – part of the entertainment industry – caters to a fickle public. Merchandisers offer huge quantities of games, books, movies, and music, the success of which is impossible to predict reliably. That is so even for those boasting a track record. This does not mean lost profits are not recoverable in the entertainment industry or for new artists or ventures – they are. It is just that they can be difficult to prove with reasonable certainty.

The Pledge film group could point to a relatively successful first stage, in theaters after release, as Hilton promoted the movie. It might have identified other small-budget independent films that were promoted well both for theatrical runs and on DVD to proxy the relationship between box office and DVD sales. Although logical, such proof is hard to come by, and assembling such comparable data involves speculation. After all, most independent films lose money, and box office receipts often exceed DVD sales. Like Blackwell and his board game, this was the Pledge film group's first foray into this fickle field.

People asserting breach of contract against promoters often claim not only direct losses but additional losses from other opportunities that successful ventures create. Had "Clever Endeavor" or "Pledge This" been properly promoted, their creators may have enjoyed new lucrative opportunities to sell other games and movies. But if contract law insists on reliable evidence of lost profits with reasonable certainty, it is even more cautious about recovery for such additional items, called "consequential damages."

## Vanessa Redgrave's Losses

The Pledge film group thus faced a hurdle illustrated by a vintage case involving the actress Vanessa Redgrave.[3] She was to narrate the Boston Symphony Orchestra's performances of Igor Stravinsky's "Oedipus Rex" in New York and Boston. Ahead of those, when global tensions were hot over strife in the Middle East, Redgrave publicized her strong views endorsing the Palestine Liberation Organization, listed by the U.S. government as a terrorist organization.

In America, especially in the liberal enclaves populated by Boston and New York's cultural elite, her views provoked outrage. Would-be opera-goers made their opposing views clear to the orchestra, which felt rattled. Facing the prospect of diminished ticket sales and even disruption of performances, the orchestra terminated Redgrave's contract, which amplified the news story and painted Redgrave in a bad light among other impresarios.

When an irate Redgrave sued the Boston Symphony Orchestra for resulting damages, the Orchestra asserted a right to terminate under the principle of force majeure.[4] A court handily rejected that claim, observing that no wars, famines, or other calamity beset the performance, only political agitation – not a ground for excuse from contractual obligation. So the Orchestra breached the contract.

Redgrave's direct expectancy was easy to identify: The orchestra agreed to pay her $27,500. But Redgrave also claimed the breach caused consequential damages by depriving her of additional professional opportunities. She showed that the roles and compensation in her acting contracts during and after the public controversy were inferior to those she was accustomed to, asserting lower total pay of $100,000.

To recover such consequential damages, Redgrave had not only to prove them with reasonable certainty, but also to show they were the kinds of losses the Orchestra would reasonably expect to follow from its breach. Although the Orchestra reasonably should foresee that its breach would cause Redgrave some lost opportunities, she could not persuade the court these amounted to the full $100,000 claimed. The court was persuaded only to a fraction of that, limiting Redgrave's consequential damages to $12,000.[5]

Given the difficulty the Pledge group faced proving ordinary losses with reasonable certainty, its chances of recovering consequential damages were near zero. It does not mean, however, that it left court empty-handed. As a fallback to the usual claim for expectancy damages, parties unable to meet the hurdles may instead recover out-of-pocket costs incurred in reliance on the contract. The Pledge film company tried this angle against Paris Hilton, but it overplayed its hand. It tried to get the full $8.3 million it said it spent in production costs.

But that amount would give the company vastly more than expected from the deal it made, which was just the profit that would come from revenues greater than its $8.3 million in costs. The fallback remedy of reliance is intended to reimburse injured parties for costs made in direct reliance on a breached promise, not recoup all costs incurred in performance.

## Jack Dempsey's Breached Bout

A classic example of handling reliance damages, favoring Paris Hilton, concerned the Chicago Coliseum's 1926 contract with Jack Dempsey, the heavyweight boxing champion of the world.[6] The Coliseum arranged for the famed pugilist to fight Harry Wills in Chicago to defend the championship title, paying Dempsey $800,000 (about $10 million today) plus half the gate receipts exceeding $2 million (some $24 million today). Dempsey – whose character makes a dozen appearances in the current HBO series, "Boardwalk Empire" – breached and instead fought Gene Tunney in Philadelphia. The Coliseum sought lost profits on the bout, claiming $1.6 million.

However, the Coliseum could not prove these amounts with reasonable certainty because they were the speculative product of multiple variables, including promotional effectiveness, contestants' reputations, publicity, and competing attractions for the public's fussy attention. But the Coliseum could recover costs incurred tied to relying on Dempsey's promise to fight, including costs of special staffing, stadium remodeling, travel, and marketing arrangements. These amounted to a mere fraction of its million-plus of total outlays.

For "Pledge This," anticipating correctly that the court would reject its greedy claim of reliance measured by full costs of production, the company itemized more modest elements incurred in reliance on the specific promise it said Hilton breached. Breaking down its cost structure, it pointed to $137,000 spent rendering post-production work on the film and on the DVD. To recover that, however, the company would still need to show these were incurred in reliance on the breached promise. It was difficult to do this, because the company would have incurred these costs preparing the film for theatrical release anyway. As the film group did not incur those costs in reliance on Hilton's promise to promote the DVD, they were unrecoverable.

## Robert Reed's English Misadventure

The "Pledge This" film company did not claim costs it incurred *before* making the contract with Paris Hilton. But this would have raised a fascinating question about when such pre-contract costs can be recovered.

In a notable English case, after incurring expenses, a film company agreed with the American actor, Robert Reed, that he would perform in a new film.[7] Reed breached. The company was entitled to recover, in addition to its reliance expenses, the expenses it incurred before it made the contract. The rationale: By making the contract, it appeared that Reed, not the company, accepted the risk of loss resulting from his breach. After all, the company could have hired any number of other actors to perform the role, but settled on him.

In contrast, the promoter in Jack Dempsey's case was denied pre-contract expenses. In that case, the making of the contract did not suggest that Dempsey accepted the risk of loss resulting from his breach. After all, the promoter could not have hired anyone other than Jack to defend his heavyweight champion title. Although the "Pledge This" film company did not claim any pre-contract reliance, its right to recover them would depend on whether Paris Hilton's celebutante status makes her more like the one-of-a-kind heavyweight champion of the world or a dime-a-dozen actor.[8]

Running out of recovery options, the "Pledge This" film company turned to the recovery of last resort. When expectancy or reliance damages cannot be obtained, people pursue "restitution." This is a claim to recover damages to prevent the other party from having an undeserved windfall, called "unjust enrichment."[9] The film company argued it was unjust to let Hilton keep $1 million – or at least the $935,000 for non-acting services – after she failed to uphold her end of the bargain concerning promotion. But unjust enrichment usually applies only in cases when someone confers a benefit on someone else without also expressing an agreement about the exchange. It does not apply when people have an express contract and an injured party simply cannot prove the losses as contract law requires.

On the other hand, restitution is known as an "equitable remedy." That means courts tailor vague principles to meet what justice merits in particular cases. In the Pledge-Hilton dispute, the court entertained the film company's restitution claim. But the judge insisted it would have to show exactly what dollar amount was unfair for Hilton to keep – which the company simply could not do. That, ultimately, left it empty-handed. The film, which the judge wryly noted was "never destined for critical acclaim," flopped financially, both in the market and in court.

## B. COMPENSATION: PARIS HILTON AND HAIRTECH

The limits on contract damages tempt many to assert, based on the same facts, not only a contract claim, but a claim for tort. The branch of law addressed to civil wrongs, tort law offers damages not only to compensate, but to punish. This gambit of claiming in both contract and tort was taken by another Paris Hilton client, Hairtech International, Inc., maker of hair-care products. In December 2006, Hilton agreed to endorse Hairtech products exclusively, not touting competing brands, and authorized it to use her images in product promotions. In exchange, Hairtech would pay Hilton $3.5 million plus a 10 percent royalty on sales. Hairtech expected the arrangement to generate $35 million in revenue. Hairtech later sued Hilton for breach of contract and fraud, the latter a tort claim.[10]

The breach-of-contract claim asserted Hilton's failure to appear at promotional events and the endorsement of competing products. The company said Hilton failed to appear at a June 2007 Hairtech product launch party because she was in jail for drunk driving. Hairtech said it spent $130,000 on that event, and expected it to generate $900,000 in direct revenue plus $5.6 million in indirect revenue. The company's fraud claim alleged that Hilton deceived it by making misrepresentations and false promises about her intention to honor the contract.[11] For that, the company claimed tens of millions of dollars in punitive damages (amounts on top of any awards for actual loss, intended to punish).

Hilton handily resisted these claims, starting by showing how the claim for punitive damages was wide of the mark in what amounted merely to a dispute about the performance of a contract. Damages for breach of contract differ sharply from damages for torts. Contract law looks to compensate injured parties by putting them in the position performance would have. This gives them the benefit of their bargain. It precludes damages that would overcompensate and excludes damages for emotional distress, those for pain and suffering, and punitive awards.[12]

Tort law remedies are essentially the opposite. They are intended to restore tort victims to the position they were in before harm occurred. This protects them from an uninvited invasion of their rights. Tort damages are measured as the difference between where the tort put them and where they were beforehand. As a result, tort damages include items that could overcompensate, like for emotional distress and pain and suffering; they also encompass punitive awards intended to deter people from committing torts.

## The Hairy Hand

Fans of John Jay Osborne's book, *Paper Chase*, and of the 1973 Academy Award-winning film based on it, may recognize an illustration from the popular case of *Hawkins v. McGee*.[13] Taught in the film's contracts classroom by Professor Charles W. Kingsfield, Jr. (played by John Houseman), and in most real Contracts classes, the case involved Dr. Edward McGee, who was experimenting with skin grafting in the 1920s. The doctor promised young George Hawkins and his father to render the boy's badly injured hand into a perfect one. But the procedure failed and made the hand worse – deforming it and causing it to grow hair! Hawkins claimed, as Hairtech did, both breach of contract and tort (in this case negligence).

The boy's damages could be measured as the difference in value between the actual result and either the way his hand was before surgery or the way Dr. McGee promised it would become. Tort law's purpose is restoration of the original condition along with potential punishment designed to deter. For George Hawkins, if Dr. McGee was negligent, that means the difference between his hand's post-surgery value and its original value (plus punitive damages). Contract law's purpose is to put party's hurt by contract breach in the position performance would have – and no better. If Dr. McGee was not negligent, George's pure breach of contract claim warranted damages equal to the difference between the hairy hand he got and the perfect hand he was promised (and no punitive damages allowed).

Hairtech's case against Hilton claimed damages measured both ways. Damages to vindicate the breach of contract would be lost profits, but winning these damages requires meeting the requirements of certainty and foreseeability. Recovering lost profits based on the expected $5.4 million in indirect revenue presents the challenges of foreseeability; the claim based on the expected $900,000 in direct revenue presents the challenges of certainty. Those challenges made the claim for $130,000 in out-of-pocket expenses easiest to prove and recover as reliance damages.

The tort avenue, not limited by such rules, opens up an entirely richer possibility, running to many millions in cases such as Hairtech waged against Hilton. This difference between contract and tort remedies reflects how contract is a matter of private freedom, whereas tort is about public duties that law imposes on everyone. Courts deny tort claims for damages that arise solely from breach of contract. But because a single identical action may be both a breach of contract and a tort – a private and a public wrong – the line between these can be indistinct.

## The Beatles' Recordings

Probing this blurred line is a case that the Beatles brought against their long-time producers, EMI and Capitol Records, in 1979.[14] After the companies allegedly distributed Beatles' recordings wrongfully for their own promotional purposes, not to help Beatles' sales, and then lied about their actions, the band charged breach of the contract's payment terms plus fraud. The companies objected to letting the band pursue both claims, saying the fraud allegation was merely a contract claim wrapped in tort clothing to rack up extra damages.

Because contract and tort claims in situations like this are often intertwined, it is more useful to ask whether the alleged tort asserts an invasion of rights that existed apart from contract than to try to separate harms into neat categories of contract and tort. The Beatles persuaded a court that the record companies had both breached the contract by mishandling payments and separately committed a tort by lying about how they distributed the band's music. Such success is rare, however. Most courts analyzing claims arising from a bargain view them as breaches of contract rather than as separate torts. Hairtech's claim for millions against Hilton for fraud fell into that category. There was no indication that Hilton lied when she signed the endorsement contract, nor that she deceived Hairtech while it was in effect.

There was simply no basis for Hairtech to claim that Hilton's conduct amounted to any sort of tort, even assuming that her failure to appear at a product launch or tout competing products was a breach of contract. In fact, the court found most of Hairtech's claims that Hilton breached her contract to be baseless as well, and the company eventually withdrew its lawsuit altogether.[15]


## C.  MARKETS AND MITIGATION: REDSKINS SEASON TICKETS

Americans love sports. They spend millions of dollars on season tickets to root for the home team in baseball, basketball, football, and hockey. Ticket sales provide teams with a steady revenue stream that can be used to finance long-term investment. During the economic boom of the early and mid-2000s, many franchises, like the Washington Redskins football team, built expensive new stadiums. To support long-term construction loans, teams sold season tickets for up to ten years, promising seats in exchange for fan agreements to make annual payments. Amid the late 2000s' economic recession, however, many fans could not afford to maintain the luxury of better times and breached their contracts with the stadiums. In response, some teams sued fans.

One such defendant was Redskins fan Pat Hill, a seventy-two-year-old real estate agent who lived outside Washington, DC.[16] She had held season tickets since the early 1960s and renewed them when the team built its new stadium. But after property values plunged during the recession, her business faltered, and she could no longer afford the $5,300 annual sales price for two seats. Hill asked the team for a grace period, but it declined and sued her for ten years' worth of season tickets. Unable to pay for a lawyer but believing she had a duty to pay her debts, she let the Redskins win a default judgment against her in court for about $60,000.

The *Washington Post* identified Pat Hill as one of 125 similar Redskins' fans the team sued that year, claiming millions of dollars in damages. The team's general counsel, David Donovan, acknowledged the suits, but said they were a last resort and a small fraction of the 20,000 annual team season ticket contracts, most of which were honored or renegotiated. Some fans saw it differently, saying the team's renegotiation proposals often came with stinging penalties. They complained that even as the team was recovering ticket prices from breaching fans, it was reselling the same tickets to other spectators, amounting to double-dipping. The team denied that.

The Redskins would stress that, in the event of breach, contract law lets injured parties like the team recover the financial equivalent of the promised performance. This protects their expectancy by putting them in the position performance would have. For tickets, and other goods, that amount is typically the difference between the agreed contract price and their market value. As examples: if a fan agreed to pay $5,000 for tickets, traded online at the time of breach for $4,000, the team's damages would be $1,000; if a team resold such tickets after breach for $4,500, its damages would be $500.

Fans would respond by explaining how measuring damages using market or resale prices reflects an old and intuitive limit called "mitigation." Injured parties are not entitled to damages they could avoid with reasonable effort. People cannot rack up losses by incurring costs after being told the other side is breaching. They may even have to take steps to reduce losses, like the Redskins reselling tickets to mitigate damages. If a team could resell tickets under a breached contract for more than the contract price, for example, its damages would be zero.

## The Bridge to Nowhere

The Redskins had to acknowledge those basic principles, evident from a landmark case concerning a project to build a vehicle bridge across the Dan River in North Carolina.[17] A county commission initially approved the project by a vote of three-to-two, amid a highly politicized dispute over whether to build a connecting road. The county's contractor began work. Then, one pro-bridge commissioner resigned and an anti-bridge commissioner succeeded him. The county revoked its approval of the project and told the contractor to stop work.

The contractor had by then spent $1,900 on the project. It nevertheless completed the bridge and claimed the contract price of $18,300. The board, still in disarray, at first approved but then rejected the contractor's claim. The court held that the contractor was responsible for mitigating the damages after being told to stop work. The claim for the $18,300 contract price was thus reduced by all costs the contractor could have avoided by stopping when told. It was entitled to the costs it incurred up until that point along with the profits it would have earned on the job, including fixed costs of performance but excluding avoidable costs. (The price in any contract can be broken down into what it costs to perform it plus the resulting profit; so if you exclude avoidable costs, you are left with fixed costs plus the profit.) [18]

The Redskins appreciated that the idea of not compensating for avoidable losses is straightforward in construction contracts. It makes little sense to keep doing what someone told you to stop, like building a bridge to nowhere. But the idea is subtler in cases where the only way to avoid losses, if at all, is to do more than stop work, like reselling tickets. True, mitigating losses is still required if possible. For teams, that is easiest to see for a game that is sold out; reselling a breaching fan's tickets puts other people in those seats, reducing or even eliminating the team's losses.

## Lost Volume Sellers

But consider games that are not sold out: The team could have sold additional tickets whether the fan breached or not. A fan's breach creates no new opportunities to sell tickets and the cost of breach is not avoided. This is equivalent to a commonly seen type of business called "lost volume sellers." Most apt for sellers of standardized goods, like retail dealers, these are businesses with the capacity to make additional sales without regard to whether a particular buyer breaches. [19] For a lost volume seller, the difference between the contract price and any resale or market price does not put it in the position performance would have. To do that requires awarding lost profits.

Whether the Redskins would qualify as a lost volume seller is not obvious, however, because courts restrict the category to a relatively narrow class, as the basketball legend Michael Jordan can attest. He signed an endorsement contract in July 1995 with MCI, the telecommunications company later acquired by Worldcom and later still by Verizon.[20] It was a ten-year contract for Jordan to promote MCI's products. The contract did not bar Jordan from other endorsement deals, except with MCI's competitors. MCI paid Jordan $5 million on signing and agreed to pay another $2 million annually. In exchange, Jordan would be available for ad shoots, four days each year, up to four hours per day. Through 2001, MCI shot several ads featuring Jordan.

When the company went bankrupt in 2002, Jordan claimed MCI owed him $8 million to cover 2002 through 2005. The company conceded it owed Jordan the full amounts for 2002 and 2003 but protested that Jordan had to reduce his damages for 2004 and 2005. Jordan acknowledged skipping substitute endorsement deals that would have mitigated his damages under the MCI contract but argued that he was a lost volume seller not required to do so. Given the modest time commitment endorsement deals entail for star athletes, Jordan said he could have entered into any number of deals, even if still hawking for MCI. The company countered that although in theory that was true, what mattered was whether Jordan would have pursued those other deals in fact. Jordan admitted that a dozen companies had made overtures, but he declined them to avoid diluting his image.

The court agreed with MCI. It contrasted the scenario Jordan portrayed with typical commercial settings where lost volume sellers are recognized. In those, dealers of retail products, such as boats, are seen as lost volume sellers when their ongoing business activities indicate that they would have made additional sales even if the customer had not breached. In effect, they have an infinite capacity to sell. Those outcomes would be different for a dealer in the midst of winding down its business rather than continuing it because there are a finite number of sales left to make. Michael Jordan, curtailing his endorsement portfolio, was equivalent to the seller winding down a business, not to the lost volume seller engaged in an ongoing business. Jordan's recoverable damages were accordingly reduced by the amount he could have earned with reasonable efforts in substitute endorsement deals.

Considering that most Redskins games are sold out, it may be difficult for the Redskins, and other big-time football teams, to be recognized as lost volume sellers. Their reselling of tickets under breached contracts, at least to sold-out games, would count in mitigation of the damages breaching fans owe. For tickets resold at or above the contract price, the Redskins would suffer no damages – and the Pat Hills of the world should not have given up their fight so easily. But the Redskins had one more card to play in their skirmish with breaching fans like Pat Hill.

As a last resort, teams such as the Redskins may distinguish between season and individual tickets. Reducing damages in mitigation is fair and reasonable when a promised performance has a substitute – a contract for a commodity like sugar can be replaced by another contract for sugar, even if at different prices. The mitigation principle applies to such a substituted contract. The mitigation principle does not, however, offset damages by arrangements not qualifying as a substitute, such as gains from replacing a sugar contract with a salt contract. Teams such as the Redskins could contend that when a season ticket contract is breached, they should not be charged with selling individual tickets because the two arrangements are not substitutes.

## Shirley MacLaine's "Bloomer Girl"

The classic case exploring this subject concerned the distinguished actress Shirley MacLaine and a contract with Twentieth Century Fox.[21] Fox promised her the lead in a musical, "Bloomer Girl," to be shot in Los Angeles, and gave her rights to approve the screenplay and director. The studio breached and offered her instead the lead in a dramatic western, "Big Country, Big Man," to be shot in Australia and lacking approval rights.

The studio argued that MacLaine's damages for breach should be reduced by what it offered in the alternative deal, which was an identical $750,000 (about $5 million in today's money). But the mitigation principle only credits alternatives that are "comparable or substantially similar" to a breached bargain. In MacLaine's case, the "Big Country" alternative was both different and inferior to the "Bloomer Girl" deal – in terms of genre, location, and actress control. So MacLaine won full contract damages, unreduced by the value of the alternative.

For the Redskins, the upshot of this analysis is that its duty to mitigate fan breaches probably varies with the type of tickets and games – season or individual and sold-out or not. That variation can make it hard for the team to maintain a uniform policy, which risks creating misunderstanding and resentment among fans who feel they are treated unfairly. Probably for those reasons, the Redskins withdrew most of the lawsuits against fans in the wake of extensive media attention. Even when the law of contracts entitles you to a remedy for a breach of contract, it is not always worth going to court about it. Aside from the contestability of many claims about breach and the remedy, it is often just bad business practice – especially when amplified by bad press. Just ask Pat Hill.

## D. STATED REMEDIES: SPRINT'S EARLY TERMINATION FEES

Cell phones were rare before the early 1990s but a decade later became ubiquitous. The market grew as service providers bought phones from manufacturers and offered them at low rates or free to new customers who agreed to a minimum two years of service. At least one-third of cell phone service customers get a free phone and nearly all get one at a discounted price, meaning cell phone service providers incur significant costs.

To recover costs and earn a profit, providers need assurance of customer continuity. To get it, they used two-year customer contracts, backstopped by an exit fee if a customer terminates early. Until 2008, all major providers charged "early termination fees" (ETFs), or fixed flat fees, of $150 to $200, that did not vary with the time of termination. From the companies' perspective, this was a square deal: Customers get a phone and the company recovers its cost plus a profit. Customers, however, were not so sure. When picking plans, customers often underestimate their likely usage and face extra charges on their invoices for minutes;[22] others dislike the service for other reasons and prefer to switch to competing providers. But ETFs lock them in.

National debate erupted over ETFs in the early 2000s. This prompted numerous class action lawsuits, state attorney general investigations under consumer protection laws, Congressional bills to curtail ETFs, and, finally, Federal Communications Commission hearings. Amid the heat, some companies modified several contracts, including prorating

ETFs according to the point in the term a customer terminates. Verizon led the charge, reducing its ETF from a flat $175 to a variable one of $5 per month remaining on a contract's term when a customer breaches. Not all providers, however, followed Verizon's lead.

The dozens of customer lawsuits against providers claimed that ETFs violated governing principles of contract remedies. The chief claim was that ETFs amounted to punishments for breach of contract, even though it is settled law that contract remedies are meant only to compensate, not to punish. This principle holds even when the contract says what remedy the parties want.


### The Delayed Mausoleum

Supporting the customers' stance is a memorable 1885 case about a mausoleum.[23] A widow named Lynch signed a deal for the Muldoon contracting firm to build a monument to her late husband at his San Francisco gravesite. Lynch agreed to pay $19,000 for the job ($500,000 in today's money) in installments, plus a final payment. The contract set a twelve-month deadline for completion, adding that for every day completion was late, Muldoon would forfeit $10.

The monument was to be carved from a gigantic quantity of Ravaccioni marble quarried in Italy. Muldoon's group promptly ordered the four massive blocks of marble from Italian suppliers. Given its size, the marble could not be transported by rail across the United States and instead had to be shipped from an Italian seaport all the way to San Francisco. There were few ships capable of bearing such a load on that route and, consequently, it took the Muldoons nearly two years to find a vessel, the *Ottilio*, to do it. Once the block arrived, however, the Muldoons completed the job and wanted their final payment of $12,000. But Mrs. Lynch proposed withholding nearly $8,000 under the $10 per day delay clause.

The court emphasized how parties are free to stipulate remedies for breach. There is a lot to be said for holding people to their stipulations, as a matter of freedom of contract, and not rescuing them from improvidently made commitments, including damages for delay. But courts would not enforce clauses that penalize breach, especially where the amount is vastly "disproportionate to any reasonable idea of actual damage."[24] Contract law's insistence on only providing compensation for breach, not punishment, meets that objective, and courts also use it to police the damages clauses people include in their contracts. As the court put it, damages "should be commensurate with the injury, neither more nor less." Although it was difficult to determine Mrs. Lynch's damages with reasonable certainty, meeting the first prong of the standard test, the clause failed because it did not appear calculated to approximate those damages. Instead, it read like a penalty for tardiness.

## Vanderbilt's Traitorous Football Coach

More favorable to Sprint and other cell service providers is a contrasting modern dispute between Vanderbilt University and Gerry DiNardo, its head football coach.[25] In 1990, the school and the coach signed a five-year contract, later extended to seven, with the intention of building the university's football program. DiNardo's starting salary was $100,000, followed by annual raises. The contract stated the remedies for breach: if Vanderbilt breached, it would pay DiNardo his remaining contract salary; if DiNardo breached by taking a job elsewhere, he would pay the university the amount of remaining net salary DiNardo would have received under the contract.

In November 1994, Louisiana State University wooed DiNardo to become its head coach, resulting in DiNardo breaching his Vanderbilt contract with nearly three years left. Vanderbilt requested payment under the contract's formula, which ran to $282,000. DiNardo refused, arguing that the clause was invalid as a penalty. DiNardo pointed out how the damages clause was triggered only if he took a job elsewhere, not if he took a different job within Vanderbilt or retired. That choice would have no bearing on Vanderbilt's damages, suggesting an attempt to coerce DiNardo rather than protect Vanderbilt's expectancy. He also suggested that it was suspicious to make Vanderbilt's damages a function of DiNardo's net salary, a figure that would change according to things unrelated to Vanderbilt's damages, such as DiNardo's income tax exemptions and retirement fund contributions.

The court agreed with Vanderbilt that the clause was a reasonable estimate of its damages, which were difficult to ascertain, as opposed to a penalty designed to coerce or punish. The formula yielded smaller damages toward the contract's end, a sliding scale that tied damages to the importance Vanderbilt attached to the long-term period of the contract. The stipulation was also reciprocal, with agreed damages to be paid by either side on breach. Furthermore, Vanderbilt showed that its actual losses were in line with the clause, even though difficult to prove with certainty: it cost $27,000 more to hire a new head coach, $87,000 in moving expenses to bring on that coach's new staff, and $185,000 in additional compensation for its new staff compared to what it paid DiNardo's staff. Beyond that, it was difficult to calculate damages arising from harms to alumni relations, ticket sales, or public support.

Champions of cell phone customers contended that ETFs penalized them by trapping them with a single provider, more akin to the ancient mausoleum case than the modern football coach dispute. Most of the lawsuits were settled before final resolution, and few judicial opinions addressed the merits. An exception, involving Sprint, held the clauses unenforceable.[26] Both sides agreed that Sprint's damages would be difficult to determine with reasonable certainty, meeting prong one of the traditional test. The fighting issue was whether they were a reasonable forecast of actual damages – and the court found that they were not.

Ordinarily, proponents of stipulated damages clauses meet this test by showing that the forecast was a reasonable one. Following that approach, Sprint argued that the effect was clear: The clause undercompensated Sprint and, accordingly, could not be a penalty to the customer. On this point the two sides offered diametrically opposing expert testimony on how to estimate Sprint's losses upon customer breach by early termination. Experts agreed that the best compensatory measure is the company's lost profits from subscriber breach, which means estimating the company's lost revenue less costs it avoided as a result of the breach. Lost revenues, based on factors like contract price, minutes charged, and usage, are relatively easy to estimate.

In contrast, the cost side is more complex, requiring the perennial challenge of classifying costs as fixed or variable.[27] Fixed costs cannot be avoided after breach, so they are included in compensatory damages; variable costs can be avoided, so they are excluded from compensatory damages. Unsurprisingly, the customers' expert witness testified that nearly all costs varied, and got per-customer lost profits down to below $10. According to the customers, the stipulated sums overcompensated, amounted to a penalty, were unenforceable, and breaching subscribers would owe at most about $10 for any breach. But the company proved that most costs were fixed, not variable, showing that lost profits per customer averaged $525 to $650, vastly more than the stipulated ETFs. Among costs unavoidable as a result of breach were costs companies incurred when subsidizing phones.

The court probed a bit deeper in this case than courts usually do, noting that it involved a standardized ("boilerplate") clause in consumer contracts, not a negotiated term. It stressed that proponents of boilerplate clauses in consumer contracts must show that they made a reasonable attempt to align them with actual damages. Inquiry focuses not solely on the clause's effect, but also on whether the proponent made a reasonable attempt to estimate damages. For the court, the trouble with Sprint's argument was how it made an ex post rationalization substitute for the ex ante focus of the "reasonable attempt" test. The court said it was not enough that a party ends up making no money from a stipulated remedy. Proponents of a stated damages clause must show they made some determination of that sort when they created the clause. Sprint did not do that and could not have because its plan was a marketing device with a deterrent purpose – to lock customers in.

It was insufficient for Sprint to argue that its ETFs benefited customers rather than penalized them. It was not enough that the arrangement enabled Sprint to subsidize handsets and reduce monthly rates. Nor was it enough that applying the usual test – requiring a reasonable attempt – would expose customers to greater liability for higher damages than under the ETF. The purpose of the rule is not necessarily to insulate people from paying higher damages, the court explained. Instead, its purpose is to demand reasonable estimates ahead of time, not enable shifting the focus toward a contest about the effects after the fact.

The rule would be meaningless otherwise, the court reasoned. Applying the test to this case, as in any other, promotes an important function of stipulated damages: reducing uncertainty about damages determinations in litigation. True, Sprint may be right that the ETFs turn out to be a better deal for customers than paying actual damages. But, as the court summed up: "[I]nstitutional intuition is not a substitute for analytical evaluation and retrospective rationalization does not excuse the objective assessment required at the inception of the contract."[28]

## E. SPECIFIC PERFORMANCE: TYSON CHICKENS AND IBP PORK

In 2000, Tyson Foods was the nation's largest purveyor of chickens. It passionately wanted to win control of IBP, the country's number-two pork purveyor, and ardently desired to prevent Smithfield Foods, the number-one pork producer, from doing so. Winning would catapult Tyson to dominance in the meat business. After an intense auction with escalating bids, Tyson finally outbid Smithfield, agreeing to pay more than $3 billion, at $30 per share, to IBP stockholders. It would pay shareholders using a combination of cash and stock in the merged company.

When running the auction, IBP shared extensive confidential business information with both suitors. IBP's meat business was slumping and an important subsidiary business, Foodbrands, had been rocked by an accounting scandal involving at least $30 million of losses to IBP. Its forecasts for the coming year were depressed compared to historical performance. Tyson and Smithfield both learned of these serious business problems that may have deterred other bidders, but they stayed in the fight. Tyson even raised its bid by a full $4 per share despite learning additional bad news about IBP's business.

Upon winning, Tyson and IBP signed a merger agreement on January 1, 2001. The expectation, common in corporate mergers, was for the companies to close their deal within a few months, after doing the paperwork. It is common for merger agreements like that to include mutual promises and conditions that must be met during that period or else the other side can terminate.[29] Here, the contract contained only a generic clause saying Tyson could walk away if a "material adverse change" in IBP's business occurred. Tyson did not insist on any special promises or conditions that IBP's woes may have warranted – like a promise to wrap up the problems at the Foodbrands division or a condition that IBP's performance improve.

After signing the deal, Tyson publicly boasted of defeating Smithfield. It acknowledged that IBP's business was down, but emphasized it was cyclical and set to rebound. During ensuing months, however, severe winter weather degraded livestock nationally, further depressing sales and profits at both IBP and Tyson. Tyson got cold feet about IBP – a case of "buyer's remorse." Tyson claimed a right to get out of the contract, saying IBP's business deterioration was a "material adverse change." Tyson lost that claim.[30] No such change had occurred and the changes that did occur were risks the contract allocated to Tyson, the judge ruled.

That set up the most challenging question of the case: IBP's remedy. IBP was not content with money damages. Instead, it wanted Tyson to be forced to perform the exact promises it made, to merge with IBP, an extraordinary remedy called "specific performance." Tyson preferred to pay cash, the standard remedy for breach of contract. IBP knew that only in rare cases do courts order that a particular promise be performed. Those cases require a finding that money would be inadequate to protect the injured party's interests. Contracts warranting specific performance involve something that is unique, complicating the task of giving it a dollar value. Courts are loath to order people to perform promises when it is impractical to supervise or evaluate compliance. Above all, they balance contending equities in assessing whether to order specific performance.

The precedents span a continuum. At one end are personal services contracts, least likely to yield the remedy of specific performance;[31] at the other are contracts involving interests in real property, most likely to warrant that remedy. Those poles reflect how it is difficult to evaluate personal performances and easy to declare a deed or lease transferred; the real property example reflects a long-standing intuition that most parcels lack commensurable substitutes.

## A Unique Manhattan Billboard

The fine line dividing cases in between, and how to classify the IBP-Tyson merger, can be discerned using the case of a contract to lease billboard space in Manhattan.[32] A real estate owner leased to Van Wagner Advertising the right to erect signs on a billboard on the side of a building facing the Midtown Tunnel, where thousands of vehicles enter Manhattan daily. The owner later sold the building to S&M Enterprises, which planned to develop the surrounding block.

The owner told Van Wagner it was terminating the lease, relying on a contract clause that it felt authorized the termination. However, like Tyson with IBP, the clause did not give the owner the right to terminate.[33] Van Wagner, arguing that the real estate hosting the billboard was unique, sought specific performance to enable it to use the space through the lease term. S&M resisted.

The space was unique in a sense, given its location facing the captive audience driving into Manhattan through the Midtown Tunnel. But every property is unique in some sense, and you could calculate the economic value of Van Wagner's disappointed expectancy in using the billboard for several years. The lease is a market transaction, and there are thousands of them in Manhattan for comparison. In fact, Van Wagner operates hundreds of billboards, as anyone touring Manhattan can see.

New York's Chief Judge Judith Kaye explained that in the law of contract remedies, "uniqueness" is a conclusion and term of art, not a "magic door" to specific performance. Central to the inquiry is whether harm from breach can be measured and compensated in money. Here, it was common to measure damages based on projections, and the large New York billboard market provided reliable benchmarks. Moreover, S&M planned to renovate the surrounding block, so tying the building's sale up for many years merely to use a billboard would be inequitable.

In the Tyson-IBP dispute, the question was thus whether it was possible to translate the value of a breach into money, and IBP made a good case that it was not. If the sole consideration in the merger was cash, that would provide a definitive measure of money damages and preclude specific performance. But this deal gave IBP shareholders both cash and stock in the resulting enterprise. That may be an economic value measurable in money, but the purpose of paying stock in a corporate merger is to give shareholders a stake in the enterprise's potential upside (accepting downside risk). That interest, based on uncertain future prospects of a newly combined venture, does not translate readily into money and may be highly conjectural. A judge could come up with a figure, but it would be unreliable. Specific performance obviates the need for living with such uncertainty.

IBP also overcame a further challenge in weighing specific performance: whether it is practicable to administer. Tyson acknowledged that a merger with IBP remained strategically appealing, although it continued to regret its high bid. That relieved a basic objection to specific performance, putting parties together who ferociously oppose the union. The two would have shared goals. True, senior executives displayed mutual antipathy during the litigation, raising doubt about whether the two teams could work together. But top company officials could address that when consummating the merger by replacing uncooperative executives with team players – a brutal proposition, perhaps, but a reality in the world of corporate takeovers.

So the Tyson-IBP court directed specific performance. Likely a wise decision when made, the judgment was vindicated further after the merger: The combined company's business returned to strong and growing profitability. Synergies from the merger that Tyson earlier perceived were realized. The stock market price of the combined company appreciated in subsequent years.

The result prompts some to wonder whether contract law's normal preference for money damages warrants a second look. That is probably doubtful, because money damages are invariably more reliable and less cumbersome. But having the specific performance remedy available to deal with special situations like this adds to contract law's value and gives it an additional tool to manage disputes between parties.

Many people think that if they breach a promise, courts will order them to perform the promise, despite the difficulties that would entail in many cases, including the extreme ones dramatized by Shakespeare's *Merchant of Venice*. Others think that when money is at stake, those who breach their promises ought to pay the other side's full losses, referencing the proverbial tale that begins "For want of a nail the shoe was lost," which leads ultimately to the loss of a kingdom. Still others think that those who fail to keep their promises are punished, with judges imposing fines on breaching parties. People are convinced that they

know a merchandiser is double-dipping when it claims damages for
one breach even as it makes another deal on identical terms with someone else. Many think that if a contract states what payment is due for
breach, then that amount is due no matter what.

All these views are erroneous for reasons reflected in the stories in
this chapter. Contract law offers a range of remedies for breach. The
primary objective is to protect people's expectations by awarding the
money equivalent of what performance of a breached promise would
have given. But those must be shown with reasonable certainty, have
to be foreseeable to the breaching side, and are reduced by what the
injured party could reasonably avoid. Contract damages are designed
to compensate, not to punish, and that goes equally for damages courts
design as for those parties agree to expressly in their contracts, as the
story of Sprint and early termination fees suggested. Finally, restitution is available to do justice in many settings, such as when bargains
fall apart or when terms cannot be ascertained, as well as the additional
tricky contexts explored in the next chapter.

# 5 REWINDING

## Restitution and Unjust Enrichment

*All sensible people are selfish, and nature is tugging at every contract to make the terms of it fair.*

– Ralph Waldo Emerson

## A. GRATUITY OR EXCHANGE: CARING FOR AUNT FRANCES

Good Samaritans earn their name because they act out of kindness, not seeking pay. But a blurry line divides altruism from profit seeking, nowhere hazier than when people care for distant elderly relatives. Jane Gorden learned this lesson after moving from Houston to Nashville to tend to her octogenarian aunt, Frances Cleveland, at the behest of her aunt's neighbor. Gorden looked after her aunt for five years, placed her in a nursing facility, rented out her home, and paid her bills. In total, she advanced $100,000 to her aunt. Aunt Frances knew of her niece's generosity and once told a companion that Gorden "would get everything she had, if there was anything left." But when Aunt Frances died, she had made no provision in her decades-old will for Gorden, leaving everything – a beautiful home, a classic 1932 Ford – to her hometown church. Her estate denied Gorden's request for reimbursement, asserting the advances were gifts and that the two had made no contract.[1]

Ordinarily, contract law enforces bargains when they are made before performance is rendered. If Aunt Frances had agreed to repay Jane's advances ahead of receiving them, the arrangement would follow the standard pattern and be enforceable. But contract law does not recognize the opposite sequence, performance before bargain, or, in

Jane's case, Jane lending Aunt Frances money followed by the aunt's promise to repay. People conferring benefits without bargains are usually seen to act gratuitously. There is a rationale behind this doctrine: Any other rule would mean that people could impose contract duties on others simply by conferring benefits on them. In such a world, one would expect mail-order companies shipping unordered goods for payment, squeegee windshield washers making enforceable claims for money, and neighbors doing more to each other's homes than anyone would want.

But a principle called "restitution" reflects the limit to the doctrine. In some situations, denying compensation is simply unjust, such as when someone confers benefits on another who either requested them or accepted the benefits. Jane Gorden insisted that described her case with Aunt Frances. Courts construe this exception narrowly, however, to avoid condoning behavior the law calls "officious" under a doctrine that denies such compensation to "officious intermeddlers." People conferring *unwanted* benefits are not entitled to compensation, however valuable or beneficial such actions may be. Gordon and her aunt's estate each could point to an extreme example distinguishing those entitled to compensation in restitution from those deemed officious intermeddlers.

### Bascom's Folly

Favoring the estate is a vintage example from the 1960s involving an unfortunate race horse named Bascom's Folly.[2] Richard West ordered the horse from Belmont Park in New York in the spring of 1962, arranging for the racer to be shipped to Suffolk Downs outside of Boston. On arrival, however, West's trainer declared the horse lame, and West directed that it be returned to Belmont. On return, the seller would not accept the horse. So the driver left Bascom's Folly at the nearby horse farm of Howard Bailey, who boarded him for several years – sending invoices to West, which he returned unpaid, noting on them that he did not own the animal. Because he had merely volunteered to board the horse, Bailey was not entitled to restitution for his costs. West never asked him to do so and even denied owning Bascom's

Folly. Furthermore, West did not receive a benefit and, even if he did, Bailey acted officiously.

## Emergency Surgery

At the other extreme, favoring Jane Gorden, stands 1907's *Cotnam v. Wisdom*.[3] A. M. Harrison was thrown from a street car, suffering serious injuries that rendered him unconscious. A spectator summoned doctors to the scene. The doctors performed a delicate operation, trying to save Harrison's life, but ultimately failed. Harrison died without regaining consciousness. Harrison's estate refused to pay the doctors' bill, claiming that Harrison did not assent to any procedure or payment for it. The court, however, said this did not matter. True, ordinary contracts are founded on mutual assent. But it had long been recognized that, in some circumstances, contract-like duties can arise without mutual assent. The case of doctors performing emergency medical procedures on unconscious accident victims is now the model illustration of this category called "quasi-contracts."

Aunt Frances's estate acknowledged that restitution in quasi-contract is now routinely awarded to health care professionals who supply medical services to protect other people's life or health, when circumstances justify intervening without any prior agreement.[4] But to keep this medical emergency exception within bounds, it applies only to professionals rendering health services. A life-threatening emergency is the ultimate justification for conferring a benefit that warrants enforcing compensation. Professional medical services are an exception because the emergency justifies action without contract, the benefit conferred is unmistakable, and medical professionals expect compensation for their services.[5]

Aunt Frances's estate thus stressed that the law does not entitle Good Samaritans to compensation – whether farmers caring and feeding lame horses or amateurs administering care or food to ailing individuals.[6] The narrow exception encourages the socially desirable result of medical professionals intervening in emergencies; it may be undesirable, however, to encourage emergency medical intervention by lay people.

Further, law does not require that all benefits be reimbursed, and heroic rescues are usually motivated by altruism, not expectation of gain. True, nonprofessionals sometimes do not act selflessly, but in general, people who voluntarily confer benefits on others are not entitled to compensation. This includes people who voluntarily pay other people's debts without being asked. Such behavior is meddlesome and the law does not protect it. Under this doctrine, Aunt Frances's estate contended that Gorden's actions were meddlesome and therefore not entitled to compensation. Because she paid Aunt Frances's debts without being asked, the estate claimed that Gorden could not later re-characterize the advances as loans.

Gorden countered by saying that this general rule does not apply when the payment is made under compulsion of a moral obligation. Those who pay another's debt because of a moral duty are not seen as officious intermeddlers; they act from the bond of human duty, such as those inherent in family relationships. This argument helped Gorden's case that she was not acting officiously when paying her aunt's bills, but it also compelled her to confront a cognate principle. Contract law presumes that family members acting out of moral obligation do so without expecting to be paid, thus precluding recovery for services rendered and benefits provided to kin.

This so-called family member rule is rooted in the traditional rationale that family life is replete with acts of reciprocal kindness and remains a place where law, including contract law and its exchange orientation, should not tread. Perhaps quaint today, the notion, even in its heyday, was a presumption that could be overcome by showing clear intention. In claims for restitution like Gorden's, overcoming the presumption requires showing the beneficiary accepted a benefit that was clearly not intended as a gift.

Ultimately, the court was persuaded that Gorden did not intend a gift. Caring for Aunt Frances was thrust on Gorden. She responded to the call of family duty. Gorden always acted as though she would be repaid, including keeping detailed records. True, she could have made a formal contract with her aunt, but should not be punished for not doing so. Given her condition, Aunt Frances could not repay Gorden's kindness during her lifetime. Yet she knew of her niece's debt and told at least one companion she intended not only to repay her but to leave her everything. The court thus allowed Gorden reimbursement for the $100,000 she advanced as restitution in quasi-contract.

## B. MERE VOLUNTEERS: BATTLING ALASKAN BEETLES

In Alaskan forests during the 1990s, a beetle epidemic was killing spruce trees. In response to the devastation, the state formed an agency to evaluate alternative tactics to contain damage and restore forest health. Many concerned citizens contributed ideas. One such citizen was Terry Brady, an environmentalist and entrepreneur knowledgeable in forestry. Brady proposed to fight the epidemic by harvesting dead trees to salvage timber and then replanting the forests. His plan would involve the state selling timber tracts to people, like him, who would do the work.

In April 1993, a state official suggested to Brady that he apply to the state to buy a tract of timberland and, from there, conduct a model salvage project to demonstrate his plan's utility. In May 1993, Brady offered to buy a large tract near Moose Pass. But the state rejected his offer because it preferred to auction the tract in an open-bidding process rather than negotiate a sale directly to one buyer. Brady then offered to help the state prepare plans for the tract and, by speeding up the process, to benefit his hope of buying it. The state wrote Brady a letter dated July 21, 1993:

> We would like to take you up on your offer to help prepare the site-specific plan. You indicated your willingness to do the research, compile and report the required data, and submit this information to us. Due to our present workload, this assistance would help expedite the sale.

Based on this letter, Brady began collecting data and preparing plans. By September, he submitted draft plans to the state. In mid-October, state officials toured the proposed sale area with Brady and other bidders. Officials praised Brady's plan and eventually used it to formulate the state's battle plan. However, the state's final plan did not include any timber sales, to Brady or anyone else. On October 20, Brady submitted his final report, along with an invoice for his services of

$26,250. The invoice surprised state officials, however, who declined to pay. They wrote: "In all our discussions with you, never at any time was there an indication of our entering into a professional-services contract with you."

In Brady's lawsuit against the state, the court readily accepted the state's argument that Brady's overture and the state's letter did not form a contract.[7] The terms were too indefinite. Even though they roughly defined what Brady would do, they did not specify any amount of compensation or how to measure it. Brady conceded that his oral offer and the state's response may not have formed a binding contract, but contended he was entitled to reasonable compensation for his services, as restitution.

Instead of showing an actual contract, this required Brady to show that he conferred a benefit on the state, without intermeddling, and that it would be unjust for the state to keep the benefit without paying for it. The state argued that it was not unjust for it to keep the benefit of the work, because Brady performed it without expectation of pay. Furthermore, the state argued, Brady's purpose in doing the work was not to earn a fee; rather, it was to gain a business advantage, namely the chance to win a timber-sales contract. Because there was no discussion of compensation, Brady was a mere volunteer.

### The Plagiarism Informant

A helpful precedent for the state of Alaska involved a report on plagiarism.[8] James Martin, a law student, wrote to Bantam Books, saying portions of a paperback edition of one of its books, *How to Buy Stocks*, was plagiarized in *Planning Your Financial Future*. The letter offered to provide a copy of the book, in which Martin highlighted and annotated plagiarized passages. A letter in response, signed by Robin Paris, an editorial assistant of the publisher, invited Martin to send his proffered copy of *Planning Your Financial Future*. His work eventually helped the publisher win a copyright infringement case. The publisher sent Martin an honorarium for $250. Martin wanted more, claiming a one-third share in that recovery.

Martin could not claim that an actual contract had been formed. As with Terry Brady in the Alaska beetle epidemic, the parties mentioned no price or how to measure payment, although they did define what Martin would do. Yet nothing in the correspondence manifested an intention by either side to form a contract. Nor was the publisher's October 21 letter an offer to enter into one. It was merely an expression of willingness to receive Martin's annotated copy. Martin still urged restitution. He argued that a promise to pay the reasonable value of a service is implied in cases like his, where people provide a service that is usually charged for, with the recipient knowing about it and keeping the benefit.

The publisher responded that this principle applies only when circumstances justify the conferring party in expecting to be paid. The benefit must not be given as a gratuity, and the person benefited must do something from which a promise to pay may be inferred. When circumstances suggest something is offered voluntarily, the publisher argued, no intention to pay can be inferred. The court sided with the publisher, finding that Martin was a volunteer, not entitled to restitution.

Terry Brady, the Alaska beetle epidemic battler, was much like James Martin, the battler of plagiarism. Until he submitted his invoice, Brady never indicated that he expected to be paid for developing the plans. Furthermore, his case was weaker than Martin's; both volunteered to provide work, but Brady did so to gain a business advantage, leading him to the timber sale. In business negotiations, whether someone manifested an expectation of payment raises two questions. The first is whether a reasonable person in the recipient's position would have realized from the conferring party's behavior that payment was expected. The second stresses whether allowing retention of the benefits without pay would be inequitable.

It is unlikely that benefits conferred during business negotiations are made with the expectation of payment.[9] Negotiators routinely exchange tentative commitments or incur costs that may be lost if no deal is reached. The costs are usually borne by the party incurring them, even though they benefit the other side. That the other side benefited does not mean it is unjustly enriched. Sometimes those steps help seal a deal, with corresponding gains to the conferring party. Sometimes they do not. Such steps did not help Brady seal an Alaska timberland deal. But that did not make it unjust for the state to keep his plans without paying for them.[10]

## C. TRAILING PROMISES: LENA SAVES LEE'S LIFE

Lee Taylor assaulted his wife, who took refuge in Lena Harrington's neighboring home. The next day, Lee broke into Harrington's home and assaulted his wife again. To defend herself, his wife knocked him down with an axe and was about to decapitate him when Lena intervened. She caught the axe as it fell, mutilating her hand. After saving his life, Lee quickly promised to pay Lena's damages; when he later failed to pay, she sued for breach of contract.[11]

Lee denied his promise was enforceable, because there was no bargain or consideration supporting it. Lena countered that his promise was supported by the benefit she earlier conferred on him. She claimed that her rescue created a moral obligation in Lee to repay her, akin to the moral obligation that nieces may perceive they owe to assist ailing aunts. The actual promise he later made recognized that moral obligation. The making of that later promise was thus supported by the consideration of the benefit she conferred on him, Lena said.

In the eighteenth century, courts often said that kind of moral obligation, followed by a promise to pay money, supported enforcing a trailing promise. People thought of this as "past consideration." But they saw it as valid, equivalent to consideration exchanged presently. The scope of promissory liability seemed to expand unduly, however. It upheld improvidently made voluntary promises – people, like Lee, excitedly promising to pay the hero who just saved their life. So nineteenth-century courts began to restrict moral obligation's validity as consideration.

Lee stressed this restriction, which narrowly limited enforceable trailing promises to those that revived a duty that was invalidated for technical legal reasons. Standard examples were promises to pay debts that had been discharged in bankruptcy, that could not be enforced because a statute of limitations had run, or that had been made when a party lacked capacity because of young age or mental illness.[12] This restriction continues today, validating promises made to reaffirm that kind of discharged debt, but not others. It seems too difficult for law to develop a coherent and reliable account of what constitutes "moral obligation." Such a phrase could run from mere sentimentality to sincere gratitude for life-saving work. The result is that courts enforce trailing promises because of a preexisting legal obligation rather than a preexisting moral obligation.

Lee urged that law need not be squeamish about this. Although moral philosophy, and child-rearing, teach us that promises should be kept (pacta sunt servanda), law has never enforced all promises, moral obligation or not.[13] There is no reason it should enforce moral obligations just because a promise is made to honor them. Doing so would mean that every later promise to honor a previous promise, even previous promises made gratuitously or jokingly, would be legally valid. If promises to attend social dinners or jestingly to sell the Brooklyn Bridge are legally unenforceable, it would be absurd to enforce a later promise for having missed dinner or reneged on the Bridge deal.

Lena could accept all these arguments yet also parry that the law retains enough flexibility so that in "unique circumstances," the doctrine of restitution is used to avoid injustice. Lena could note two classic cases helpful to her claim, although Lee could distinguish them both.

## The Heroic Lumberman

On August 3, 1925, Joe Webb was clearing the upper floor of a lumber mill for W. T. Smith Lumber Company. This work involved dropping a 75-pound pine block from the floor's edge to the ground. As he dropped the block, he spotted his boss, J. Greeley McGowin, on the ground where the block was likely to fall. Its mass would have crushed McGowin and it was too late for Webb to prevent the drop. Webb did the only thing he could to divert its course: He rode the block in order to steer its fall to the ground, away from McGowin. This move saved McGowin's life, but left Webb permanently disabled. One month later, a grateful McGowin promised Webb to pay him biweekly amounts for life of about $200 in today's money, which McGowin paid through his death eight years later. After McGowin died, however, his estate refused to continue the payments.[14]

In court, while Webb argued there was a valid contract, the estate said it lacked consideration. The court identified saving McGowin's life as a clear benefit to him, worth more than money, creating a moral obligation to Webb. Recognizing that, McGowin made the promise of payment – and honored it for eight years. Under those circumstances – including an action undertaken at work and a promise made one month after the heroic moment – the court held that an unrequested benefit conferred can be consideration for a later promise. The estate, therefore, had to pay Webb on McGowin's promise.

### An Escaped Bull

In finding for the lumberman, the court analogized to what has become a famous case concerning a bull that escaped from a pound and wandered onto a stranger's farm.[15] The farmer cared for the escaped bull for half a year while trying to track down its owner. When he finally did, the owner promised to repay the farmer for the bull's care and feeding, but later breached that promise. The court held that the promise to repay the previous caretaking services was supported by consideration, even though the act preceded the promise. In rescuing the bull, the farmer, a total stranger, conferred a material benefit on its owner, and the unique circumstances warrant legal recognition.

Lena's claim against Lee did not meet this unique circumstance test, however. She was not at work when she saved Lee's life, but in her home; she did not tend to a stranger's lost property, but performed an act of neighborly kindness. She was a volunteer, akin to Terry Brady planning Alaska timber policy or James Martin reporting plagiarism. She was unlike Jane Gorden, who owed her Aunt Frances the moral duty of financial assistance, and was therefore no mere volunteer in extending her funds. The court thus denied Lena's claim, citing lack of consideration to support Lee's promise as a contract. It explained, in a remarkably terse opinion of a few sentences: "however much [Lee] should be impelled by common gratitude to alleviate [Lena's] misfortune, a humanitarian act of this kind, voluntarily performed, is not such consideration as would entitle her to recover at law."[16]

## D. NOVEL IDEAS: THE MAKING OF "THE SOPRANOS"

In 2002, Robert Baer, a former municipal judge and county prosecutor from hardscrabble Elizabeth, New Jersey, claimed a right to half the value of the Emmy Award–winning HBO television series, "The

Sopranos," believing he had a deal with writer David Chase to code-velop it.[17] Baer's dream was to write television shows and, eventually, he persuaded a mutual friend to interest Chase in reading one of his scripts. Chase, a native of North Jersey, was already an accomplished figure in television, with several Emmy Awards to his credit, as well as shows such as the "Rockford Files," "Alfred Hitchcock Presents," and "Northern Exposure" under his belt.

The two met in June 1995 in California. At the time, Chase was developing an idea for a television series about a mob boss undergoing psychiatric therapy. In this meeting, Baer suggested that Chase shoot it in North Jersey and the two kicked around some other ideas. In August 1995, Chase submitted a program proposal to Fox Broadcasting, which agreed one month later to finance a pilot for the show. Chase thereafter asked for Baer's help in compiling information about the mafia's inner workings. In response, Baer contacted acquaintances in the local prosecutor's office, including Lieutenant Robert Jones, an organized crime expert. Based on their conversation, Baer prepared notes for Chase profiling some underworld characters and detailing the mob's role in the sanitation business and gambling activities.

In October of that year, the two met again in New Jersey for Chase to do more research. There, Baer regaled Chase with New Jersey true-crime stories during a three-day tour of the region. Baer also introduced Chase to other experts: Detective Thomas Koczur, a homicide specialist, and Antonio Spirito, an Italian waiter and riveting story-teller. Koczur played the tour guide, driving Baer and Chase around to view area landmarks, mob hangouts, and criminal crannies. Some of these later provided the backdrop for the show's regular opening sequence, whereas others appeared in various episodes.

Koczur also arranged for the group to dine with the local mobster, Antonio Spirito, who plied them with personal gangland tales and became the model for the show's protagonist, Tony Soprano. One tidbit Spirito shared referenced two cat-burglar mob brothers called "Little Pussy" and "Big Pussy," the latter a name Chase gave to a character in the series. Jones profiled the Jewish Mafioso, Morris Levy, then in prison, who bore a close resemblance to the role of Hesh Rabkin on "The Sopranos."

After the trip, Chase polished up his pilot and submitted it to Fox, also sending a copy to Baer, who later provided written comments on it. Throughout, there was some discussion of payment between Baer and Chase, but no actual agreement was ever reached and Chase never paid Baer any money. The two had only agreed that Chase would read another of Baer's scripts in return for the help he had given. "The Sopranos" launched in 1999 on HBO, became a popular and critical hit, and ran through 2007. In May 2002, Baer sued, claiming the show and its protagonist were his ideas, entitling him to half the millions in profits Chase had received. Baer asserted breach of contract and quasi-contract, among other claims. The suit sickened Chase's stomach, he sobbed upon learning of it, and five years of litigation followed.[18]

Baer's breach-of-contract claim was readily dismissed. Baer claimed contracts arose during telephone calls in June and August 1995 and during the October trip. He said each time Chase proposed the same deal – "you help me; I pay you" – and each time Baer countered, "I'll take the risk" and if the show succeeds, "you take care of me in an appropriate manner at that time," and Chase said "Fine." Because the two did not agree to any terms, however, such statements were too indefinite to form a binding contract. The parties failed to agree on who was to do what, when or where, in return for how much. Baer accepted this, saying that the profit split, if any, remained to be agreed on later. There was no contract.

So Baer tried to fashion an argument based in quasi-contract, asserting that he conferred a requested benefit on Chase by feeding him ideas for the show, and it would be unjust to deny him a share of the payoff. Chase urged the court to rule that Baer was not entitled to any damages based on the value of the various ideas he conveyed. He said all the ideas were a matter of public record. Chase acknowledged a general rule of quasi-contracts: Recovery is appropriate when a person gives someone else novel ideas of value that the recipient exploits. But the law does *not* recognize any such recovery concerning non-novel ideas. There is nothing unjust about letting someone use ideas already in the public realm, including fact-based stories and identification of known landmarks, Chase argued.

Baer contended that it can be unjust to deny compensation to a person who confers a benefit on another, even if it consists of sharing public information. Baer stressed how he gave Chase ideas for the locations that appeared in the show, the model for the Tony Soprano character, the inspiration for the Hesh Rabkin role, the name "Big Pussy" – and other such ideas that combined to form the plotlines of "The Sopranos." This argument portrayed as novel Bear's assembly and combination of the various ideas, including characters, facts, and locations, into the conceptual singularity that became "The Sopranos."

However, this sort of mosaic theory of novelty had no support in law and little in logic. A non-novel idea does not become novel by being conjoined with another non-novel idea. Some creative difference must arise from the conjoining to warrant recognizing the product as novel. Stringing together a series of mob stories at various locations in North Jersey, based on an assembly of particular facts, did not cut it. Further, none of these ideas belonged to Baer, and many of the stories were actually supplied by others, including Jones, Koczur, and Spirito.

Baer parried that even if his ideas were not novel in general, they were novel to Chase. This argument likewise failed; it is not relevant whether an idea is novel to a particular person. Rather, the issue is whether the idea is available in the public domain. In fact, an important line of cases makes another distinction, between "contract-based" claims to interests in an idea and "property-based" claims. A property-based claim, such as an assertion of copyright or trademark, requires showing absolute novelty – something new under the sun. The standard is relaxed for contract-based claims, which require only that the idea be novel to the buyer.[19] Because Bear's contract claim had failed, and he was making instead a quasi-contract claim, this line of cases hurt his argument.

These losing arguments did not mean Baer had done nothing for Chase – only that he was not an equal partner in the creation of "The Sopranos" and had no claim to value in the ideas. Baer had, however, performed other services and could recover for them. The court called these services "location scout, researcher and consultant." For these, Baer was entitled to a jury's estimate of their reasonable value, a measure called "quantum meruit."

Reasonable value of services can be measured in one of two ways. One method looks at the gain to the recipient – Chase – based on the market value of services rendered – the Hollywood rate for such spadework. That is an especially fair method when the recipient requested services. The other method looks at the loss to the provider – Baer – based on out-of-pocket costs incurred, expenses of riding around town for three days, lunch, and so on. Here, because Chase had requested Baer's services, their market value was the more appropriate measure.

So the two wrangled over what factors determine market value. Baer thought they included the franchise value of "The Sopranos" – a large figure – whereas Chase argued otherwise. Baer offered expert witness testimony that this kind of spadework for a show can earn $5,000 weekly plus bonuses for successful programs, nearing $100,000. Chase countered that it is as common for such work to go unpaid, particularly at the incubation stage where Baer contributed his services.

The trial lasted one week; the jury deliberated for less than ninety minutes. Their verdict: Chase did Baer a favor by reading his first script and Baer did Chase a favor by introducing him to North Jersey mob culture. Baer was entitled to something for his services, which Baer had already done: reading another script. Chase owed Baer nothing more. After hearing the judgment, Chase was relieved: "It is like having a fly in your bathroom for all these years and suddenly getting rid of it with a fly swatter."[20]

## E.  OFF-CONTRACT REMEDIES: ROD STEWART AT THE RIO

Rod Stewart, the British rock-star, signed a written contract to perform a New Year's Eve concert at the Rio Hotel & Casino in Las Vegas at the turn of the millennium, December 31, 1999, in exchange for an advance payment of $2 million. The concert was part of a comeback effort of the aging rocker, then fifty-four, and famous for hit songs like "Maggie May," "Reason to Believe," and "Every Picture Tells a Story." After a career punctuated by ups and downs – love songs, disco, pop – Stewart was still beloved by a shrinking fan base consisting mostly of middle-aged women.

The concert was a success, so the two parties renewed their deal for a repeat performance on the following New Year's Eve, with the Rio paying Stewart another $2 million in advance. In March 2000, however, during a routine CAT scan, doctors diagnosed a cancerous tumor on Stewart's thyroid gland and, two months later, performed a life-saving thyroidectomy. In the procedure, a breathing tube was inserted through Stewart's vocal cords, causing them serious, albeit not irreparable, damage. Stewart's vocal cords did not heal until mid-2001, ruling out the December 2000 show at the Rio.

Although the Rio and Stewart discussed rescheduling the 2000 show for June 2001, the two parties failed to come to an agreement. The Rio chalked the failure up to Stewart's intransigence; Stewart attributed their disagreement to the company's fear that the concerts would lose money. They also took different views of what their bargain required and how to classify the circumstance concerning Stewart's vocal cords.

The original contract for the 1999–2000 millennium concert addressed forces majeure.[21] If either side's performance became impossible due to acts of God, the two sides would both be excused but have to reschedule the concert for a different agreed date. The original contract had a separate clause addressing Stewart's illness or incapacitation. If Stewart was "ill or incapacitated," in his sole judgment, then the show would be canceled and Stewart would return the $2 million advance.

The updated contract, addressing the 2000 show, allowed Stewart to reschedule if, by the end of September 2000, he received an offer to perform for New Year's Eve at a location whose distance from Las Vegas would make it difficult to perform both. In that event, the two would both be excused but have to reschedule the concert for a different agreed date. The updated contract also stated that all other terms of the original remained in effect and applied to the second concert.

After failing to agree on a rescheduled date, the Rio declared the talks over and demanded a refund of its $2 million. Stewart refused, saying the two were required to reschedule or else he could keep the money. The Rio made out a simple case, arguing that the updated contract covering the second concert was clear. The parties were required to reschedule only if the planned concert was canceled because Stewart made a conflicting engagement for that weekend; if the planned concert was canceled for any other reason, including Stewart's illness, the deal was off and Stewart had to return the money. Given that clarity, according to the Rio, there was no need for any trial.

Stewart presented a more nuanced view of the situation. He framed the destruction of his vocal cords not as a result of an "illness" but, rather, as an act of God. For Stewart, then, the original contract's force majeure clause applied and required the two parties to reschedule. Stewart explained that the original contract's illness/incapacitation clause was created solely for the millennium concert, a one-of-a-kind show marking an epoch that could only be held on December 31, 1999.

Both parties thus believed that they were contractually bound to each other, although they disagreed over terms. The judge spotted a more fundamental problem. The two sides had not manifested an agreement on what would happen in these circumstances.

Wounded vocal cords resulting from surgery could be classified either as a force majeure or an illness. Even if clearly an illness, the parties had not been clear about whether the clause would apply to the millennium concert only or to both. True, the parties intended to make a deal, and were clear on the fee of $2 million and a tentative date. But they did not definitely agree on rescheduling after cancelation or what to do with the advance in such situations.

As a result, nothing in the contract governed which side was entitled to the $2 million. This move opened up the case to resolution according to the principles of restitution, to prevent unjust enrichment.[22] Given that the Rio had paid Stewart an advance of $2 million that he had not earned and that no contract entitled him to keep, the Rio was entitled to its return.[23] As the jury foreman explained: "We felt it was only fair, that if Mr. Stewart did not perform the concert that he should give the money back."[24]

The topics covered in this chapter are among the most widely misunderstood by the general public. Many people are surprised to learn that Good Samaritans are not entitled to recover payment for their acts of neighborly kindness. They cannot see why complete strangers, in contrast, are entitled to enforce trailing promises made for benefits received. Views are mixed about cases of distant relatives caring for infirm elders. People understand the law's aversion to officious intermeddlers, but have a hard time explaining the difference between mere volunteers and those entitled to receive pay for services.

Contract law's emphasis on bargain and compensation puts outside its scope many arrangements involving promises and performances. This scope can exclude circumstances where it would be unjust to refuse to recognize a valid claim, such as when abundant evidence shows an expectation of pay, as when a family member lends financial and other aid to an ailing elderly relative. Absent an express contract, however, care must be taken not to require compensation when people act without expecting it, as when they confer benefits to gain advantages during business negotiations.

When unrelated persons work for each other, they usually do so expecting compensation, from self-interest. Law presumes a contract and implies an obligation to pay. A later promise to meet that obligation is enforceable as a contract. Restitution in contract-like settings is confined to those where it is necessary to prevent unjust enrichment, ruling out compensation for pointing to the obvious, as in "The Sopranos" case, but ruling in returning unearned payments when a contract is too indefinite to enforce as written.

The topic of restitution is vast, and is even broader than its overlap with contract, occupying a field unto itself as large as the field of contracts. In its contract setting, restitution provides a surrogate bargain when no actual bargain exists. Despite the vastness of this field and the complexity of the cases, there is a rhythm to restitution and a common sense about it. It provides useful supplements to the consideration doctrine to address the complex notion of moral obligation, a way to evaluate the proposal and use of ideas and an effective tool to rewind exchanges of values made in quasi-contractual settings too indefinite to form a contract. Yet restitution is not the only setting where people's intentions are difficult to determine, which occurs even when people write definite bargains out ahead of time, as the next chapter attests.

# 6     WRITING IT DOWN

## Interpretation, Parol, Frauds

*A verbal contract ain't worth the paper it is written on.*

                  – Samuel Goldwyn

## A. PLAIN MEANING I: EMINEM'S DIGITAL RECORDS

In 1998, the rap artist Eminem, whose real name is Marshal Mathers, and his producer signed an exclusive record contract with Aftermath Records, a record label unit of Vivendi.[1] The rapper's record sales soared throughout the next decade, earning many millions, and filmmakers used his music in movies, yielding millions more. The 1998 contract requires the label to pay the star up to 20 percent of receipts for selling records the old-fashioned way: on vinyl, tape, or disc. It also clearly promises the artist 50 percent of the royalties on licenses of his music marketed in other ways, such as on movie soundtracks.

In 2001, the label began marketing music in a lucrative new way of distributing songs: digitally. The richest deal was a 2002 contract with Apple Computer for distribution on its iTunes products, both in stores and over the Internet. iTunes are permanent downloads of music, consisting of digital copies of recordings that, once downloaded, stay on a user's computer until deleted. Beginning in 2003, the label also formed other profitable contracts with cell phone service providers, which distribute recordings as "mastertones." These include short clips of songs that can be bought to signal incoming calls known as ringtones. In paying Eminem for all these digital deals, the label applied the 1998 contract's 20 percent royalty rate for sales. In 2006, however, Eminem's

126

team objected that, instead, the 50 percent royalty for licenses governed these sales. The difference, which depended on what their written contract meant, added up to many millions of dollars.

The 1998 contract's "Records Sold" provision directs royalties of up to 20 percent of the adjusted retail price of all "full price records sold through normal retail channels." Exactly what percentage applied varied according to how many sales were made, called an "escalation clause" because royalty rates escalate with higher sales. The phrase "normal retail channels" is not defined. Next in the contract is a "Masters Licensed" provision, which directs that: "Notwithstanding the foregoing," royalties of 50 percent of the label's net receipts are due "[o]n masters licensed to others for the manufacture and sale of records or for any other uses." Although the contract does not define the word "license," it defines "masters" as any "recording of sound, without or with visual images, which is used or useful in the recording, production or manufacture of records."

Eminem and the label revised their 1998 agreement twice. In 2003, they increased some royalty rates, but left all other provisions the same, including concerning Records Sold and Masters Licensed. In 2004, they amended the contract to change how quantities are calculated for purposes of royalty escalations. This treated "permanent downloads" as part of sales through "normal retail channels."

Both Eminem and Aftermath Records agreed that, in contract interpretation, the language parties choose governs, at least so long as it is clear and does not yield absurd results. Evidence beyond the four corners of a document, especially evidence that preceded its execution, is admitted only when the writing itself is ambiguous. Judges determine that by asking whether the language is reasonably susceptible to the competing interpretations or whether it shows a single plain meaning.[2] If the language bears one plain meaning, the judge declares the evidence inadmissible and no jury would hear it. But if the judge is persuaded that the language is ambiguous, she declares the evidence admissible. It is then used, along with all other relevant evidence, in a second step, to interpret the contract's meaning and resolve the dispute. That is often done by empaneling a jury and holding a trial.

In Eminem's case, the judge was unable to discern the meaning of the contract as applied to iTunes and ringtones. Accordingly, the judge let both sides present evidence supporting their interpretation. Because the judge found that either side could be right, he empaneled a jury to decide. After a two-week trial, the jury agreed with the label's perspective, finding downloads and ringtones are like all other record sales and not, as Eminem argued, like licenses. On appeal, however, a three-judge panel read the contract and thought its meaning plain as day, and that the jury got that meaning wrong. The label contended that the "Records Sold" provision applied because permanent downloads and mastertones are "records" and iTunes and cell phones are "normal retail channels." Eminem's team stressed how the "Masters Licensed" clause began by negating the scope of the Records Sold clause, opening with the telltale phrase: "Notwithstanding the foregoing."

To Eminem, that put iffy items in the license category rather than the sales category. Even items nominally in the sales category are bumped into the license category when they plausibly fit either, the star argued. Digital works fell in the license category because they are masters that the label lets others use for making and selling records. The appeals court accepted Eminem's argument. It first acknowledged that the license royalty clause was broad but stressed that "[a] contractual term is not ambiguous just because it is broad." It then reported a reading of the "Masters Licensed" provision that portrayed its meaning as plain: it applies to masters, licensed to third parties for use, and "*notwithstanding*" the "Records Sold" clause. The only issue, then, was whether the label "licensed" the "masters" to third parties.

The label resisted classifying its arrangements with Apple and phone companies as licenses. Instead, it said it never thought of its deals in that technical way or described them as such. But the court observed that the deals fit the meaning of the word license in ordinary usage, which merely means permission to act. The label permitted Apple and phone companies to use recordings to sell downloads and mastertones. To the court, that meant they were licenses.

The court likewise found that the arrangements met the second part of the "Licensed Masters" clause, treating the recordings as "masters," in accordance with how the 1998 contract defined the term. The label acknowledged that downloads and mastertones are "records." And it was obvious that they were used or useful to producing downloads and mastertones. So they met the clause's definition.

The appellate judges made a huge leap in their ruling, but possibly correctly. On one hand, it is hard to imagine that a 1998 contract, formed before a technology existed, can have a plain meaning about it. There was nothing to be clear about at the time. On the other hand, the court read the contract as appreciating that technology changes, even in surprising ways. The contract gave the label the right to exploit "masters in any and all forms of media now known and hereinafter developed." The two categories – record sales and licenses – were big enough to hold all new technology, and the contract put a portion in the record sales category and the rest in the license category.

The upshot was to treat downloads and ringtones as licenses, not sales, and to base that choice on what the court saw as the contract's plain meaning. Aftermath Records had to transfer millions to Eminem – the difference between 20 percent and 50 percent of the take on downloads and ringtones. The case does not directly apply to other recording contracts, but would influence the negotiating position of parties to them when fighting over royalties. Newer contracts would be entirely unaffected, however, because the proliferation of iTunes and ringtones after 2005 caused all recording contracts to be explicit about applicable royalty rates.

The issue in Eminem's case is a vexing and recurring problem for courts in many settings. It is also common for people writing contracts that will be performed over many years to appreciate that technological change occurs but in unpredictable ways. Those who drafted the Eminem contract may not have envisioned iTunes, but did include all future forms of masters within the bargain's reach. The case shows that it pays to think through plausible future scenarios and negotiate some parameters for how to handle them. It also shows that failure can be costly: The label's attorneys' fees in its litigation with Eminem exceeded $2.4 million.

Finally, the case underscores the importance of linguistic structure and cues. It is common for contracts with many and complex provisions to include clear attempts at clarifying particularly important deal terms, marked off with such language as "notwithstanding the foregoing." Lawyers use those key terms to cue judges to specific preferences. Judicial ears are attuned to such legal music. Such cues are particularly valuable considering that the limits of language often make it difficult, years later, to determine what people intended when they agreed to a written bargain.[3]

## B. PLAIN MEANING II: DAN RATHER'S LAST BROADCAST

Two months ahead of the 2004 presidential election, on a CBS "60 Minutes" broadcast of September 8, 2004, Dan Rather questioned President George W. Bush's service in the Texas Air National Guard during the Vietnam era. Rather implied that Bush used political influence to avoid that era's military draft by entering the Guard, and then receiving special treatment to skip military duties. A media melee followed Rather's show. Bush supporters challenged its accuracy, the authenticity of documents used, and Rather's journalistic integrity, which many believed was compromised by bias against President Bush. After investigation, CBS disavowed the broadcast and, two weeks later, an emotional Rather apologized for it on national television. But CBS and Rather disagreed on the overall journalistic quality of the broadcast and what to do about it. Rather identified important accurate facts in the broadcast, obscured by the firestorm, and urged a defense of those whose reputations, including his, the broadcast imperiled.

For its part, CBS emphasized the journalistic lapses and wanted to let it go at that. Believing CBS was most interested in the politics of good relations with the White House, as Bush was running for reelection in a heated contest against Senator John Kerry, Rather retracted his apology and claimed CBS fraudulently induced it. The day after President Bush won reelection, CBS told Rather it planned to remove him from his coveted spot as anchor of the CBS Evening News – a stinging rebuke. Rather's last broadcast as anchor was March 9, 2005. During the next fifteen months, through May 2006, CBS kept Rather on its payroll, paying his salary of about $125,000 per week ($6 million annually). CBS gave him irregular appearances on CBS programs covering less significant stories, and his former television profile diminished. He rarely appeared on the network's big-time shows such as "60 Minutes."

Worse, CBS prevented him from pursuing jobs with competing networks or other media. Rather claimed that CBS marginalized him by giving him limited staff and editorial support; rejected most of his story proposals and aired those it accepted at off-peak times; denied him the chance to appear as a guest on other programs; and generally prevented him from refurbishing his reputation. When CBS terminated Rather's contract in May 2006, Rather complained that CBS's treatment breached the contract the two had since 1979 and had amended in 2002. In Rather's interpretation, the 2002 amendment said what CBS had to do if it removed him as News anchor: either appoint him as a regular correspondent on "60 Minutes" or both pay the balance under their contract through its expiration and let him work elsewhere. Rather claimed that CBS breached because it did not appoint him correspondent, maintained his regular weekly payroll status through mid-2006, and barred him from seeking other employment.

In contrast, CBS defended its actions as complying with the contract. It acknowledged the 2002 terms Rather pointed to, but stressed another broader feature of the original 1979 contract, called a "pay-or-play clause." CBS could discharge all obligations under the contract simply by paying Rather the contracted compensation through its expiration date. Nothing required CBS to use Rather's services, whether as News anchor, "60 Minutes" correspondent, or anything else. True, the 2002 additions said if Rather was removed as News anchor, CBS would reassign him to "60 Minutes." But the pay-or-play clause meant that even if CBS removed him and did not reassign him, it was not required to release him from the contract or accelerate that compensation.

The two key contract clauses were thus inharmonious with one another. CBS explained the importance and rationale of the pay-or-play clause in business and editorial terms. It called "absurd" the notion that a network would cede to a reporter editorial authority over who would be on what program, as anchor or correspondent, or what stories would air. Rather emphasized the clauses specifically addressing what would happen if CBS removed him as News anchor and did not reassign him as "60 Minutes" correspondent: the contract would end and he would receive an accelerated salary payout and then could work elsewhere. Meeting CBS's business and editorial accounts of the bargain, this interpretation does not cede network's power to a reporter. Instead, it reflects the elevated status of the person, and ends the bargain if that status is discontinued.

In the end, the court adopted a literal approach, viewed the pay-or-play provision as controlling, and sided with CBS.[4] The pay-or-play provision, paraphrased as follows, was clear and unqualified: Nothing obligates CBS to use Rather's services or broadcast any program, and CBS discharges its obligations by paying Rather's compensation. In contrast, the removal-and-reassignment clause Rather emphasized was qualified, fronted by the provision: "except as otherwise provided in this contract." The court took that as telltale language of intent: that any conflict between the two provisions was to be resolved in favor of the pay-or-play provision.

But it was a close call. The pay-or-play clause dated back to 1979 and is a standard clause in many industries, including broadcast and general entertainment. Whereas it is clearly important to protect networks like CBS from ceding managerial control to staff, employees who accumulate power through notoriety can gain negotiating leverage over their contracts. The 2002 changes were made when Rather personified the network and enjoyed commanding stature – perhaps not on par with his predecessor, Walter Cronkite, but close. It would not be surprising for the network to cede the little that Rather's interpretation of the contract suggested: keep him in high-level posts or let him out and accelerate his pay.

Under the court's and network's interpretation, however, the contract's language, "except as otherwise provided," rendered the whole of that provision meaningless. It is hard to imagine that the two parties took the trouble of writing those clauses with the intention of giving them no meaning. Still, such recurring phrases provide recognizable cues to judges trained to detect certain intent and meaning in them, and people handling contracts are expected to understand that.

## C. PAROL EVIDENCE: THE GOLDEN GLOBES

The Golden Globe Awards are a Hollywood institution, begun amid World War II by a handful of overseas journalists based in Los Angeles.[5] Today, those journalists, members of the Hollywood Foreign Press Association (or HFPA), hail from 55 countries and reach more than 250 million readers. Members annually review several hundred films and individuals to recognize achievements at a fete held in January that is broadcast on television worldwide. The Globes generate millions in annual revenue for HFPA's philanthropic programs that fund arts-related scholarships, educational film programs, and cultural preservation foundations.

Dick Clark, the fabled television personality, became HFPA's producer in 1983. A contract gave him a series of options to produce the show and license its broadcast. Clark exercised these options and produced the show successfully for many years, usually on the NBC network under a separate long-term contract. Throughout that time, Clark would periodically renew his deal with NBC to broadcast the Globes and then exercise his options with HFPA to produce the show. In 2007, however, Daniel Snyder, owner of the Washington Redskins, bought Clark's company (called dick clark productions or dcp), a change that soured relations with HFPA. After several years of bickering about financial aspects of the deal, by 2010, HFPA was growing wary of its relationship with dcp under Snyder. Nevertheless, in February 2010, HFPA started talks with dcp about extending their contract, as the last option dcp had exercised under it would expire after the 2011 show.

For the better part of 2010, the two sides and their advisors negotiated. Then, abruptly, in late October 2010, dcp declared no further need to negotiate, claiming it still had options on further productions of the Globes, so long as it had a deal with NBC to broadcast them. dcp informed HFPA that it had reached a deal extending its NBC broadcast contract through 2018 and was therefore also exercising its claimed options to extend its HFPA contract through that year too. HFPA said it was "blindsided" by this "brazen" and illegal "power grab," denying that dcp had any such right to extend its options or even to negotiate any broadcast contract with NBC

The dispute boiled down to HFPA saying dcp's options on the Golden Globes had expired versus Snyder and dcp claiming options to produce and broadcast the show in perpetuity. For support, dcp cited language from HFPA's contract with Dick Clark, as amended in 1993, which it said sealed its case. In the part where HFPA granted dcp the options, the provision first referenced a finite number of years, but concluded with the following: *"and for any extensions, renewals, substitutions or modifications of the NBC Agreement.*" Snyder's dcp argued that these words literally entitled it to perpetual options to produce the Globes (so long as it had the NBC agreement in place).

HFPA disputed this interpretation, stressing a conversation officials had with Dick Clark limiting the duration of dcp's options. In 1993, Clark made a deal with NBC that envisioned production for many decades based on a series of renewable options. HFPA officials recalled that Clark proposed to HFPA that their deal mirror that one, running so long as the NBC deal was renewed. But they claimed that HFPA declined the open-ended duration, instead getting Clark's verbal assurances that he was proposing a finite term, which had expired in 2011, and that he would always get HFPA's approval of any NBC renewals.

The Golden Globes case reflects a familiar pattern: Oral negotiations lead to a written agreement that is called into question by later disagreements. Snyder's dcp stressed the general point of contract law that the execution of a complete and final written contract supersedes negotiations or stipulations about its subject matter that led up to it. Under this doctrine, written terms that people intended as complete and final cannot be supplemented by evidence of prior agreements or any oral contemporaneous agreements.[6] To dcp, this doctrine – called the "parol evidence rule" – required throwing the HFPA's case out.

The 1993 HFPA-dcp contract, negotiated between two sophisticated parties, appeared complete and final on its face, dcp said. One provision even declared that the contract was the parties' "entire agreement" and that it superseded previous negotiations or agreements – a clause commonly dubbed an "integration clause" or "merger clause" (it "merges" the final deal into the writing). A second provision disclaimed that either party relied on representations of the other not appearing in the writing. Together, dcp urged, these terms and the setting showed that the parties intended and achieved a "fully integrated" contract.[7] That would bar HFPA's evidence asserting that its approval was required for renewals of the NBC deal or extensions of dcp's rights beyond 2011.

To rebut these points, HFPA denied that the parties intended for the agreement to be fully integrated, which would enable it to submit all such evidence. It stressed that there were no arms'-length negotiations over the 1993 amendment or significant involvement of any lawyers for HFPA.[8] HFPA signed the amendment the same day that Dick Clark proposed it. HFPA challenged dcp's characterization of HFPA as a "sophisticated" party, observing that all members are foreign and English is a second language for most. Further, as a matter of context, it observed that dcp drafted this contract, and ambiguous language is construed against the party who drafted it.[9] The upshot: This written agreement did not warrant the respect given to such instruments formed after actual negotiations between experienced enterprises.

The court sided with HFPA on these threshold questions of whether the agreement itself barred hearing evidence about the parties' prior dealings bearing on the meaning of the contract. It was not persuaded that the written agreement contained the final and complete expression of the bargain, despite the boilerplate clauses reciting that intention, and the language dcp relied on could mean different things. One problem with dcp's argument was that it concentrated solely and literally on a few words plucked from a larger sentence and context. Principles of contract interpretation direct attention to those points, including a cardinal rule that agreements should be interpreted as a whole, not isolating discrete words, and by giving effect to each.[10]

The sentence creating the options had two parts: the first granted eight options, followed by a second, referencing the NBC agreement and quoted above, which qualified that grant. dcp's stance that the second clause created an indefinite series of options would negate the point of the express grant of eight. The NBC deal had both a variable start date, depending on what another interested broadcaster elected to do, and variable end dates, depending on whether options were exercised. It was equally plausible that the grant was intended to convey exactly eight options, without regard to when the NBC telecast contract began or ended.

For good measure, HFPA bolstered its position by emphasizing what the parties did in the years after they signed their agreement. In disputes over contractual meaning, it is often helpful to consider how the parties treated it during their course of performance. Evidence about this post-contractual activity is not governed by the parol evidence rule, which only restricts evidence about matters preceding or concurrent with a final writing. HFPA stressed that the parties always acted in accordance with its interpretation: dcp always requested additional enumerated option years ahead of expiration dates and always asked permission before negotiating or signing telecast deals. It followed that practice during the better part of 2010, until its bizarre October turnabout.

In rebuttal to these contentions, dcp contended that the behavior was consistent with its interpretation: It always had the right to proceed unilaterally but, as a courtesy, always sought approval. It added that, even during 2010, dcp never agreed that it needed the HFPA's approval. Turning this evidence back on HFPA's interpretation arguments, dcp noted that if the parties since 1993 intended for HFPA always to have approval rights, it was strange that they had never in all those years said so in their written contract.

HFPA won its day in court over the meaning of this contract. It was entitled to present its story at a trial. Outcomes of such trials hinge on credibility.[11] It is hard to imagine that HFPA would have cut the deal dcp asserted – ceding all power in perpetuity to Clark so long as NBC deigned to continue. dcp's response never met that point, standing instead on the formal written agreement.[12]

## D.  SCRIVENER'S ERROR: WHO OWNS THE L.A. DODGERS?

Language is unruly enough without people making mistakes when drafting, but scrivener's error is nevertheless a fact of life. It played a key role in the divorce case of Frank and Jamie McCourt, who fought over ownership of the Los Angeles Dodgers baseball team in 2010 and 2011.[13] Frank, a businessman and real estate tycoon, claimed sole ownership of the team, whereas Jamie, a trained lawyer, claimed a 50 percent interest.

The fight was a prelude to even more severe problems the Dodgers faced during 2011. These included being put under direct supervision of Major League Baseball, the trade organization the team belongs to, and filing for bankruptcy.[14] Central to the couple's case were accusations of foul play amid some garbled clerical work that occurred when the parties signed a postnuptial agreement.

The prominent Boston lawyer, Larry Silverstein, represented both Frank and Jamie in preparing the agreement years after the two were married. By then, the parties owned many residences and several businesses. They had suffered frightening experiences when the two asset types were commingled. Business creditors threatened foreclosure on a family residence when some of Frank's heavily indebted commercial ventures could not repay loans.

To prevent recurrence, Silverstein drafted the spousal agreement to allocate title to the assets between the couple. The parties intended Jamie to have all residential property and Frank to have all commercial property. This allocation would not give lenders recourse to the residential property if riskier commercial operations, funded with debt, went awry. The two later disputed how they intended to allocate the Dodgers.

In 2004, Silverstein drafted an agreement. The details were spelled out in an attached exhibit that showed which assets belonged to whom. Silverstein initially proposed that the parties sign a total of three original duplicates of the deal, to be held by each of the parties and by him. Late in the process, just before signing, Silverstein elected to double the number to six – out of what he called an "abundance of caution" to have a "set of protective documents."

Both parties signed all six. The exhibits, however, were mismatched in the process so that the final documents said different things: three said Frank alone owned the Dodgers; three said the two shared ownership of the Dodgers equally.

By 2010, the value of the Dodgers had risen to $700 million; meanwhile, the financial crisis that began in 2008 caused the value of the residential property to plummet. Although the property values were never equal, the discrepancy was, by then, acute. Also acute was the acrimony between the McCourts, whose divorce battle, paraded on the front pages of tabloids, traded incendiary allegations of infidelity and power-mongering within the Dodgers organization.

Amid the bitter fight, Jamie wanted a share of the Dodgers. Frank refused. Both argued that the case was simple, albeit for different reasons and yielding opposite results.

Frank explained that Silverstein, the couple's lawyer, made an honest clerical error when preparing the documents. Silverstein accidently created two versions, one declaring the Dodgers to be Frank's alone and another making the Dodgers joint property. Silverstein noticed this error at the last minute and tried to correct it, even though he never explained the error or his correction to either Frank or Jamie.

Despite that clerical error, Frank contended, there was no question what the parties intended: to allocate the Dodgers (and all commercial property) to him and the residences to Jamie. That made sense for both. Although the asset values differ greatly, Jamie was insulated from downside that acquiring the Dodgers – or any commercial property using debt – entails.

Jamie stressed how the value discrepancy suggested something suspicious about the case. She portrayed the clerical garbling skeptically, insinuating that Silverstein and Frank had tricked her into signing documents whose content she had not agreed to.

Jamie laid out a simple case of logic: There were two opposite versions of the contract, it was infeasible to enforce both, and there was no basis to choose which to enforce. Ergo: neither should be enforced. Without an enforceable contract, then, state divorce law applied and prescribed an equitable split of all the couple's assets.


## The Fraudulent Architect

To support her stance, Jamie relied on an impressive precedent involving a contract to build a Turkish bath house on the land of John Ritchie on Carver Street in Suffolk County, Massachusetts, by a builder, Edward Vickery.[15] An architect served as the go-between. He prepared two copies of the contract, identical except for one thing: in the builder's version, the price was $34,000; in the owner's, it was $23,000. Neither knew of the other's figure, of course.

The two discovered the discrepancy only after the bathhouse was nearly done. The builder's labor and materials cost about $33,000. The bathhouse improved the market value of Ritchie's property by $22,000. Given those figures, the architect was a shrewd criminal, as both were in line with what each party was told in their fraudulent versions of the contract. He was indicted for this fraud but fled the state, escaping punishment and leaving these two in a mess.

Vickery and Ritchie were both fraudulently induced by the architect's repeated assurances. Because they were both mutually mistaken about the bargain, neither was more (or less) blameworthy than the other. Rather, each intended a deal at a different price. Thus, no contract was formed.[16] Such a result, however, did not mean the chips were left where they fell.

After all, Vickery did work at Ritchie's request, so it would be an unjust windfall to let him keep the bathhouse without paying the builder. The ruling meant the amount of compensation was set not by the contract but by the reasonable value of the builder's labor and materials – law's standard background principle in such cases.[17]

Jamie portrayed her situation with Frank as akin to the case of the Turkish bath, equating attorney Silverstein to the fraudulent architect. Under that approach, their agreement was invalid and remedies between them would be determined not by its terms but by law's background principles. In the divorce context, that means potentially sharing the marital assets, including the Dodgers, if a judge is convinced that they qualify as "community property."

But that analogy was far from airtight. Silverstein did not commit fraud. He testified to exactly what had happened, hanging his head in shame for his firm's professional sloppiness. In fact, the lawyer's bungling role pointed to an equally impressive precedent cutting the other way, in Frank's favor: scrivener's error.

## The Erroneous Deed

The textbook example of scrivener's error involved a contract dated August 18, 1941, whereby Joseph Hoffman agreed to buy a plot of real estate from William Chapman.[18] The deal was for a 96-foot-by-150-foot parcel of Lot 4, on Edgewood Road in Kensington, Maryland, featuring a single modest bungalow. Before the parcel was surveyed or the deal closed, Chapman gave Hoffman possession.

After the survey, the real estate broker arranged for settlement. On October 20, 1941, Hoffman made final payment and received the deed, which erroneously described all of Lot 4, including another dwelling. When Chapman discovered the error, he requested a deed to the unsold part, but Hoffman refused. The court, siding with Chapman, ordered Hoffman to relinquish the deed that included the remainder of Lot 4.

When evidence leaves no doubt that a mutual mistake was made in producing a written instrument, courts reform it to reflect actual intentions. Law's confidence in written instruments means that courts do not even consider evidence that varies written terms. An exception exists, however, when clear evidence shows convincingly that a written document is the product of mistake or fraud (as in the Turkish bath case).

Without such an exception, the law would undermine rather than promote the reliability of written instruments. Even those mistakenly made or fraudulently induced would be binding, which would nullify, not protect, people's intentions. The court therefore rejected Hoffman's argument that the erroneous deed meant the parties had formed no contract at all. The evidence was abundantly clear that the parties intended to transfer a part of Lot 4 rather than all of it.

Hoffman lived in the single bungalow for two months before settlement. The survey attested to the intention to convey the specific part of Lot 4, not its entirety. This evidence proved that the case was a textbook illustration of scrivener's error: an innocent clerical mistake made by a neutral party helping both sides in a deal. The standard remedy for scrivener's error is "reformation" – to correct the documents and enforce them.

The fight between Frank and Jamie McCourt added a new twist to these old cases. Silverstein had not committed fraud, so the fight was not governed by the Turkish bath case. But nor was it so clear and convincing that Silverstein had merely made a scrivener's error.

Testimony conflicted about whether the couple intended the Dodgers to belong solely to Frank or to be jointly owned. The court found it hard to believe the testimony of either spouse, given their business and legal backgrounds, when they denied that they read or understood the various documents. As a result, the court held that no contract had been formed. Ownership of the Dodgers would be determined not by any deal the parties made, but according to California divorce law governing family property allocation. That did not automatically mean that Jamie owned half the team, however, as the two still had to resolve whether the Dodgers counted as "community prop-erty" under that law. But clarifying these contract issues did pave the way for the former spouses to settle their dispute.

## E. STATUTE OF FRAUDS: CLIFF DUMAS'S PHANTOM RADIO DEAL

Country music personality Cliff Dumas wanted a new job and set his sights on Infinity Broadcasting's Chicago affiliate, US-99.[19] Dumas discussed a five-year contract with US-99's program director, Scott Aurand (aka Justin Case). Talks in 2000 broke down over differences about salary.

When discussions resumed two years later, they still haggled over money. Case e-mailed Dumas several different annual salary ranges, from $125,000 to $250,000, and Dumas replied by e-mail that the range beginning with $175,000 "seems right."

Case followed with further e-mails noting things to discuss, including Dumas's radio personality, the show's format, and the duration of any deal. Dumas recalled ironing out such things in later phone calls. Piecing together various e-mails, Dumas thought terms had emerged: a five-year deal starting August 4, 2002 at $175,000. He also believed they agreed to a deal by phone on May 20, 2002, reinforced by a follow-up e-mail from Case saying the station's rat-ings had fallen and they wanted Dumas to turn things around. On May 30, Dumas quit his job at a station in New Mexico and told Case that a week later.

Case then stressed that a final hiring decision had not been made and was up to station manager Eric Logan. So Dumas followed up with Logan. Although Logan signaled willingness to "move forward," he gave no firm answers, despite many e-mails from Dumas that sum-mer. On July 23, Dumas turned tempestuous, demanding an immedi-ate response and threatening legal action. At that point, station officials stopped returning Dumas's calls or e-mails. A year later, after no response, Dumas sued.

Dumas faced an uphill legal battle. He and the station never reached terms on a binding agreement, for lack of definiteness. Nor was it evident that the station made any promises to Dumas triggering promissory estoppel. Even had there been a bargain or promise plus reliance, the deal was not memorialized by a signed writing as required by the statute of frauds.

That statute, first adopted in England in 1677, remains in place throughout the United States (it was substantially repealed in England in 1954). It requires that certain types of contracts be memorialized in a writing signed by the party charged with enforcement.[20]

The original reasons for the statute sound strange to modern ears. It was adopted in an era when court trials were primitive by today's standards. Juries decided outcomes based on firsthand knowledge of the facts, as opposed to testimony of other witnesses. The result was a spate of frauds and perjuries occurring in court. To address these problems, the statute required signed writings to bind certain deals deemed particularly susceptible to frauds and perjuries.

Although they vary by state, the original English and most of today's statutes apply to contracts for the following types of deals: real property transactions, financial guarantees, many transactions in goods (today, those involving more than $500), and contracts "not to be performed within one year" (known as the "one year clause"). In contracts cases, a threshold issue is whether a contract is within the statute of frauds.

For Cliff Dumas, application of the statute hinged on interpretation of its one-year clause.[21] A vexing question is whether the one-year test should be interpreted literally, so that any period beyond one year falls under the statute, or practically, appreciating how deals can end early, with many nominal multiyear deals not exceeding one year.

When confronting tough questions of statutory meaning, courts often look to a statute's purpose or history. For a statute with origins in seventeenth-century England, however, such tools offer little assistance. Judges rely instead on horse sense. Not surprisingly, judges in different states sometimes give different meanings to identical statutory language.

### Jane Fonda's Luckless Agent

A good illustration involved the actress, Jane Fonda, and her lawyer/ business manager, Richard Rosenthal.[22] Fonda, who lived in California, retained Rosenthal's New York law firm in 1968, for a fee equal to

5 percent of her earnings as a commission. In 1973, after that firm dissolved, Fonda and Rosenthal orally agreed that Rosenthal would continue to represent Fonda, in exchange for 10 percent of her earnings as a commission.

For several years, both parties adhered to that deal. After strains developed concerning her career path, however, Fonda fired Rosenthal in 1980. He sued to recover unpaid commissions.

Fonda denied the two had a contract, citing the one-year clause of the statute of frauds. Rosenthal stressed that the oral agreement he and Fonda made could be terminated by either party at will. In that sense, it had no duration and would not automatically last more than one year. So, he argued, it was not within the statute of frauds and no written memorandum was required.

True, some states, including California, treat the one-year clause narrowly to make it inapplicable to contracts that can be performed within a year. If parties can end a multiyear deal within its first twelve months with impunity, then the contract can be performed within one year. So it is not within the statute, which applies only to deals whose express terms make them incapable of ending within one year.

Other states, including New York, whose law governed the Fonda-Rosenthal contract, take a tougher line on deals involving commission payments. If the paying party can end the contract without a continuing duty to pay, the deal can be ended within one year, but if a payment duty remains, the contract does not end within the year.

In Rosenthal's view, he earned commission fees every time a Fonda project generated revenue. Yet that meant that, once he earned a fee, even if Fonda later terminated, she still owed him the money. Fonda's duty to pay thus depended not on her will, but on the will of others promoting her work and generating revenue for her and fees for Rosenthal. Her duty to pay would thus endure beyond one year. As a result, the court said, the statute of frauds applied to bar his claim to a 10 percent commission on Fonda's earnings.

In the story of Cliff Dumas, the station and host considered a five-year deal, a bargain within the statute of frauds and requiring something in writing. If either side could terminate earlier and have no remaining obligations, that would help Dumas avoid the statute. But Dumas insisted that the parties had a five-year deal and, having so insisted, it was impossible for either to perform fully in any shorter time.

The only way to overcome application of the statute in such set-tings is to stress how the employee's death would terminate it early, ending all obligations. But contracts can end early for many reasons in addition to death, such as mutual mistake or impossibility, and recognizing those as limitations on the one-year clause of the statute of frauds would eviscerate the statute. As a result, such an approach usually applies only to contracts with durations defined in vague terms such as "for life" or "permanent employment."[23]

### Elizabeth Arden's Fortunate Hire

Dumas turned his energy to demonstrating that the writing requirement was satisfied. He pointed to the extensive e-mails between the two parties, which raised an old-fashioned challenge about what type of writing actually counts as the memorandum the statute of frauds requires. The seminal case on this aspect of the statute concerned Elizabeth Arden, the great cosmetics company run by the woman of that pseudonym, whose real name was Florence Nightingale Graham, in her empire's heyday.[24]

In 1947, Nate Crabtree interviewed for sales manager. Arden, with senior executive Robert Johns, offered a two-year contract, paying varying amounts over time. Arden had her secretary type the terms, including the phrase "2 years to make good," on a nearby piece of paper – an order form – but no one ever signed this form.

Crabtree accepted the job. On starting day, Johns signed a payroll order, naming Crabtree and listing salary terms. But a year later, Crabtree did not receive his salary increase, although the company granted an earlier one. Crabtree notified the company's comptroller, who prepared and signed a corrected payroll order.

Arden, however, refused to approve it, so Crabtree sued for breach of contract. Arden said the statute of frauds barred the claim. At issue was whether the signed payroll orders satisfied the statute's requirements. Arden said they did not because they were not prepared with the intention of manifesting a contract and arose only after it was made. Crabtree countered that neither point mattered, so long as they were signed with the intention to validate the information they contained.

Agreeing with Crabtree, the court stressed that the statute of frauds does not require a "memorandum" to be a single document. It can be pieced together from a series. If all are signed, the only problems are assuring that terms can be reconciled. It is trickier when less than all are signed, as with the unsigned order form memo. Some courts insist on cross-references between signed and unsigned writings or refuse to treat the pieces as satisfactory; others recognize a connection so long as the writings address the same subject.

Either way, care must be taken to prevent oral testimony to supplant the writing requirement. Letting people testify about intent based on multiple writings creates risks of fraud and perjury that inspired the statute in the first place. But those risks vanish in cases like Crabtree's where three writings establish that a deal was intended.

The same standards, albeit with opposite result, governed the Dumas case. He could scavenge the e-mails and piece their contents together. They all refer to each other and to the same subject. Dumas thought the April 8 proposal of salary ranges and his reply, about the one starting at $175,000 seeming right, formed a contract to pay at least that. But unlike the Arden case, piecing the e-mails together did not show the conclusion of a bargain, only preliminary negotiations.

That led Dumas to pursue another approach: promissory estoppel. He portrayed that doctrine as belonging to a long list of exceptions to the statute of frauds. There are circumstances where, even though a bargain is of a type the statute governs, courts excuse compliance. Usually that occurs when the circumstances supply protections against the fraud and perjury that the statute targets. Ancient examples are part performance of a contract, where someone has acted in a manner referencing a valid bargain, and admission in court to the existence of a contract.

In recent decades, promissory estoppel has emerged as a possible exception to the statute of frauds, at least in some states.[25] But most courts have rejected this stance. To them, promissory estoppel is simply an alternative route to contractual liability, available when consideration is lacking. In other respects, it follows contract law doctrines, including the statute of frauds. Because Illinois is one of those states, Dumas lost this last-ditch effort.

Even had he won on that point, a final issue in Dumas's case was whether the e-mails satisfied the statute's requirement that the writing be "signed" by the one being charged. This signature requirement is readily satisfied when parties physically inscribe their "John Hancock" with ink on paper.

The signature requirement is also met by a range of sometimes-surprising showings, such as when the artist Jean-Michel Basquiat scrawled a semblance of his name using crayon on a large piece of paper to sell three paintings.[26] Today, this also includes "signatures" affixed to electronic documents, but not the ordinary sign-offs in e-mails such as those Dumas and US-99 exchanged.[27]

Cliff Dumas did not get his dream job at US-99, although he could be heard elsewhere in the country music world. To validate his deal with the station required not only ironing out the final terms of the deal, but putting them in a signed writing. Writings are not required for most contracts to be enforced today, and many claim the statute of frauds is a relic of an ancient age, but it continues to be a valiant supplemental device to sort out which bargains courts enforce as contracts.[28]

Put it in writing, says the common advice, but few people give much thought to problems of interpreting language. Some believe words invariably have a plain meaning, whereas others hold that they are too unruly to provide a clear definition. Hardly anyone thinks about how the scope of a written agreement will be treated in court if disputes arise, although that treatment often will influence what information is used to determine who owes whom what. Many people think that a contract must be in writing to be valid. These are among the most understandable sorts of variations between popular knowledge and actual contract law, although they can also have the most profound practical significance.

Contract law is pragmatic about the significance of people's attempts to write their bargains down. The plain-meaning rule stresses that language can have sufficiently obvious meaning to dispense with jury trials to determine what people meant when they wrote down their deal. Linguistic cues abound, such as the telltale word "notwithstanding," or its opposite, the phrase "except as otherwise provided." Adoption of an elaborate written document manifesting an intention to capture the complete and final terms of a bargain cues readers to accept that the whole deal is set down within the document's four corners. The parol evidence rule kicks in to bar testimony about other agreements the parties may have reached, the parties presumably discharging them during negotiations over the final document.

These principles are not absolute, however. Language is not always free of genuine ambiguity, and many documents that look complete are obviously made in contexts where side deals were possible. In extreme but illuminating instances, a written agreement may be the product of fraud or mutual mistake. Those cases cry out not only for evidence about what the parties really intended, but also for reformation to make the writing reflect the reality. Unsurprisingly, it is hard to find a court that inflexibly adheres to either extreme – of pure literalism or pure contextualism.[29] Both strands influence the analysis and resolution of disputes over the meaning of words and the scope of documents. In addition, the practical difference between the visions is narrower than it sounds: In most cases, language has a plain enough meaning and the scope of a writing can be apprehended from the sense of a deal.

Similarly, some say the statute of frauds is the wisest of laws, others the most foolish. Such extreme stances suggest that it is difficult to be persuaded that either monopolizes the truth. After all, people sometimes treat writings with special significance for good reason – it helps clarify a deal's terms and provides a reference guide as it is performed. But people often intend a deal where a writing has little practical value, such as a one-shot sale of a $500 used couch, that the statute requires to be in writing. The statute thus both hits and misses its legitimate goals, making it neither universally wise nor universally foolish.

Furthermore, for hundreds of years, courts have made the statute of frauds more useful through a network of requirements and exceptions, just as they have with principles of interpretation and the parol evidence rule. Extreme revisions of these tools would be foolish, as they and the problems they address are pervasive, from forming contracts to performing them, as the next chapter reflects.

# 7 PERFORMING

## Duties, Modification, Good Faith

*In a civilized society people must be able to assume that those with whom they deal will act in good faith.*

— Roscoe Pound

## A. IMPLIED TERMS: BUTCH LEWIS AND MAYA ANGELOU

Maya Angelou is a renowned poet and professor at Wake Forest University. Since the 1969 publication of her autobiography, "I Know Why the Caged Bird Sings," her acclaimed poetry had been published widely by Random House and initially reached a distinguished, albeit small, audience. In 1994, Butch Lewis, the former prize fighter and promoter of famous boxers such as Muhammad Ali and Joe Frazier, conceived the idea of popularizing Angelou's poetry by including it in greeting cards and similar media. The idea proved spectacularly successful. Hallmark greeting cards using Angelou's poetry have generated hundreds of millions of dollars in company sales and many millions in author royalties. Lewis and Angelou fought a pitched, eight-year long battle over whether they had a contract to split the take.[1]

Lewis first met Angelou in early 1994 when the scrappy fighter asked the elegant poet to take a trip to Indiana with him to visit his boxing client, Mike Tyson, in prison. During the trip, Angelou and Lewis discussed how she might expand her readership by publishing her works in greeting cards. After negotiations, the two signed an informal letter of agreement on November 22, 1994. Angelou promised to contribute poetry exclusively to Lewis and he promised to promote its publication in greeting cards. The exclusivity feature was important because it meant Angelou could not market her poetry without Lewis and Lewis did not need to fear that his efforts would be undercut by a last-minute switch to a competing promoter.

Aside from exclusivity, the letter recited only basic terms, such as how they would later agree on what poetry to include, that Lewis would fund promotion, and how revenues would be shared – first to reimburse Lewis' investment and expenses, then to split the rest equally. The letter said it would be binding until the two drew up a formal contract. Lewis prepared one in March 1997, but it was never signed. Lewis began marketing efforts immediately, although it took until March 1997 for Lewis and Hallmark to finalize a contract – a three-year deal, covering any new poem Angelou produced during that time. In exchange, Hallmark would pay Angelou and Lewis a $50,000 advance against royalties that would be paid at a flat 9 percent rate of total sales, with a guaranteed minimum of $100,000. Angelou's greeting cards would be administered through Hallmark's Ethnic Business Center, targeted to an African-American audience.

Lewis sent Angelou the proposed Hallmark agreement. By then, however, Angelou's views of Lewis had curdled. For the Hallmark pitch, Lewis prepared sample cards and brought these for Angelou's approval. Angelou found the display of caricatures of African-Americans distasteful and unreflective of her poetry's meaning. Her impression of Lewis worsened when the two crossed paths in Las Vegas in 1997, where Angelou was appalled by Lewis's behavior, which included punctuating his conversations by "grabbing his crotch." After deciding she no longer wanted to be in business with Lewis, Angelou instructed her long-time literary agent, Helen Brann, to "start putting a little cold water on the prospect of this deal with Hallmark." Brann did so by writing to Lewis in May 1997 that Angelou could not accept the proposed Hallmark deal, citing her long relationship with her publisher, Random House. Lewis persisted, urging Angelou to sign the Hallmark deal, but her procrastination finally led him to give up his pleas in February 1998.

But Hallmark's interest survived and the saga took a dramatic turn in June 1999. Angelou was to be in Kansas City, Missouri, location of Hallmark's world headquarters, for a speaking engagement. At the suggestion of a close friend, Amelia Parker, Angelou had lunch with a Hallmark executive with whom Parker was acquainted. Angelou left with the impression that she could make her own deal directly with Hallmark. As a result, Angelou's lawyer promptly wrote Lewis, notifying him that any business relationship created by the November 22, 1994 letter was over.

With Lewis out of the picture, Angelou and Hallmark negotiated directly. Within one year, Angelou and Hallmark signed a contract. It differed greatly from the deal Lewis negotiated: it would cover Angelou's future as well as existing work and include rights to her name and likeness; Hallmark would pay an advance of $1 million against royalties paid at rates up to 9 percent of sales; Hallmark provided a guaranteed minimum payment of $2 million; and product marketing would target a broad general audience. Lewis learned of this new contract by reading a Hallmark press release. He considered it a breach of contract by Angelou, violating his exclusive marketing rights, and triggered the eight-year litigation battle over whether the informal letter of November 22, 1994 created a binding contract.

## Lucy, Lady Duff-Gordon

For support in the battle, Angelou and Lewis both cited a landmark opinion written by Judge Benjamin Cardozo in 1917.[2] That revered case involved Lucy, Lady Duff-Gordon, a fashion plate of the era, who signed an agreement with Otis Wood as a distributor. The detailed writing gave Wood exclusive rights to use and market Duff-Gordon designs. Gains would be shared equally. However, when Duff-Gordon endorsed competing products, Wood argued that she had violated their pact. Duff-Gordon claimed the agreement was not binding because it did not spell out what duties Wood undertook and therefore lacked consideration. She also said it was too indefinite to enforce.

Judge Cardozo disagreed on both points. Even though the contract did not explicitly state Wood's duties, Cardozo saw it as "instinct with an obligation" for Wood to market the brand using reasonable efforts. That implied duty, Cardozo said, provided consideration, and enabled giving meaning to otherwise indefinite terms. Vital to this reasoning was the exclusivity feature: If Wood did not market the goods, they would not be marketed at all. In the ensuing century, Cardozo's insight about "instinct obligations" grew into a general implied duty of good faith that courts use to fill gaps in a wide range of incomplete contracts, including exclusive dealing arrangements.

Angelou used the Duff-Gordon case as a contrast. It featured an elaborate document suggesting it was intended to be final, warranting a modest judicial move to fill the small gaps with such notions of reasonable efforts or good faith. In contrast, she stressed, her letter agreement with Lewis was missing many essential terms, such as exactly which of her works would be included or when or how many she would produce. These were vital, Angelou said, given that her existing contract with Random House covered much of her work. In addition, their letter expressly contemplated a further formal document the two never signed. These terms and that statement could not be turned into a binding contract merely by importing vague gap-fillers such as reasonable efforts or good faith, Angelou said.

Lewis countered that none of the missing terms was so essential to prevent a reasonable person from seeing that the two intended a bargain, and how both parties made commitments that provided consideration. It was a small step to recognize an implied duty to market in good faith or using reasonable efforts – and Lewis had done all that such concepts require. Lewis acknowledged that the letter did not delineate what works of Angelou's were within its scope and instead referred only vaguely to "original literary works" for promotion in greeting cards. But, Lewis argued, the letter recited that the works to be included would be mutually agreed on. And that made the deal definite enough in scope. Although Angelou thought that concession proved her point – that the letter only expressed an agreement to agree, not a commitment to deal – the exclusivity provision indicated an intent to form a bargain. Lewis argued that exclusive marketing contracts like these need not precisely delineate the marketer's duties – any more than it was necessary in the Duff-Gordon case for the contract to spell out Wood's duties.

The court treated the Lewis and Angelou dispute as a modern replay of that between Otis Wood and Lucy, Lady Duff-Gordon. Both involve an exclusive deal with one party creating brands and the other marketing them, a fifty–fifty financial split, and a claim that the creator went behind the marketer's back to do a deal on her own. The features Cardozo identified that justified implying a promise of reasonable efforts also appeared: an exclusive marketing arrangement with the creator's payout strictly a function of the marketer's effort. Unless the marketer exerted effort, the creator would not profit; that implies the creator wanted the marketer to exert effort. That supports an implied bargain, supplying consideration. Any alleged gaps could also be resolved by implication from what the two clearly had agreed about. Lewis could not insist that Angelou write songs instead of poetry and Angelou could not insist Lewis market gibberish, not verse; neither could claim more than 50 percent of the net proceeds.

Angelou may have honestly objected to Lewis's mock-ups for greeting cards and behavior in Las Vegas and regretted jilting her business associates at Random House. But none of that is relevant to whether she and Lewis formed a contract. Instead, these factors indicate that she came to regret the deal, which often occurs after making contracts. One purpose of contracts is to secure arrangements known to be gambles. Some work out favorably, and some do not. In the end, the court thus indicating that Lewis and Angelou formed a binding contract, the two settled their dispute. In January 2006, Angelou agreed to pay Lewis $1 million plus 30.5 percent of royalties under the Hallmark deal from then onward. The Hallmark deal was remarkably lucrative. In its first five years, Hallmark generated $45 million in sales from Maya Angelou greeting cards, paying the poet more than $4 million. Lewis was entitled to a share of that fortune.

## B. EXPRESS TERMS: CLIVE CUSSLER'S MOVIE "SAHARA"

Clive Cussler, prolific writer of best-selling adventure novels, sold the movie rights for several of his books to Crusader Entertainment, a film production company headed by Denver billionaire Philip Anschutz. Following a year of negotiations, the thirty-page agreement, finalized in May 2001, gave Crusader an option to buy rights to two books, including "Sahara," and a third, if the shooting of "Sahara" began within two years. If exercised, Crusader would pay Cussler $20 million over seven years for the two books – plus more for a third. The parties preapproved a screenplay for "Sahara," written by Academy Award–winning screenwriter David Ward. Crusader promised not to change it without Cussler's permission, which he could withhold or grant in his sole and absolute discretion. This discretion was important to Cussler after the professional embarrassment of a 1980 film adaptation of his book, "Raise the Titanic." In exchange, Cussler promised not to discuss the deal or films publicly without Crusader's permission, which Crusader agreed not to withhold unreasonably.

Crusader exercised the option to buy "Sahara" and a second book on November 6, 2001. However, Crusader found the preapproved screenplay unworkable and proposed changes accordingly. Cussler accepted some, rejected others, and, Crusader said, retracted some he had previously accepted. Crusader tried to fashion an approvable screenplay, using a dozen screenwriters who rewrote two dozen versions, but Cussler hated the revisions. As he grew disgruntled, he rejected some screenplays without even reading them. Beginning in April 2003, a disgruntled Cussler took the story to his fans. He broadcast to the press that he did not trust the writers Crusader hired and objected to Crusader's plan to shoot using an unapproved script. Cussler launched a campaign on his Web site urging fans to join the fray, and angry fans responded by flooding Crusader's inbox with protest e-mails.

Cussler gave press interviews disparaging Crusader's version of the script, stating on air that the producer "gutted a lot of the dramatic scenes." He told the Denver Post: "They've sent me seven scripts, and I've inserted each one in the trash can."[3] Cussler's fans, insisting on Cussler's version of the screenplay, mounted an Internet petition saying Crusader's use of an unapproved screenplay breached its contract. Cussler maintained the public disparagement through 2004, and the rage spread virally across the Internet. Shooting of "Sahara" began at the end of 2003, in the midst of the outrage, and the film was released in April 2005. Starring Matthew McConaughey and Penelope Cruz, the film generated $180 million in global revenue, from box offices and DVD. But total costs, including $15 million paid to Cussler, were $160 million, resulting in a net loss for Crusader.

Crusader blamed the financial disappointment on Cussler. His haggling over screenplay approval added millions to production costs and his prolonged public disparagement subtracted millions in revenues. Cussler retorted that the movie's use of an unapproved script hurt his economic interests as an author and screenwriter. Cussler sued Crusader in January 2004, just after shooting began, and the litigation did not end until March 2010.[4] The two parties lodged mirror-image claims: whereas Cussler said Crusader breached by filming an unapproved screenplay, Crusader said Cussler breached by speaking to the press, by acting in bad faith during the approval process, and by publicly disparaging the film. A jury found them both in breach, but said most of the transgressions had not caused the other any damages. The jury did, however, think that Cussler's handling of the screenplay approval process showed bad faith and awarded $5 million in damages to Crusader. Cussler appealed that finding, complaining that the jury wrongly went beyond the contract to reach its verdict. Crusader also appealed, seeking more money.

At issue was the scope of obligation a contract creates. Everyone agreed that Cussler had the right of screenplay approval and promised to avoid public statements about the film and breached the latter duty. Cussler said he met his contract's duties concerning screenplay approval; even though he admitted that he breached his oath of silence, the jury found that caused Crusader no harm. Crusader countered that Cussler's approach to screenplay approval was not in good faith. The fight thus boiled down to the role of good faith in contract performance.

For a century, contract law has instilled in all contracts an implied legal duty to act in good faith, or honestly. As a matter of private autonomy, this duty of good faith is intended to reflect law's sense of what most people forming contracts expect from themselves and others; as a matter of public policy, the good-faith duty encourages people to expect integrity and reliability in legally recognized contractual relations. Despite the seeming simplicity of the good-faith duty, however, this duty has both aided and vexed courts. The concept helps fill in gaps when a contract does not address some contingency that arises later. But an expansive conception of an implied good-faith duty could put courts in the business of rewriting the bargains people make. Courts resist such interventions.

## TSM's Tom Waits Recordings

A pivotal precedent applicable to the Cussler-Crusader dispute involved a company called Third Story Music (or TSM).[5] It had sold Warner Brothers the rights to market recordings by singer/songwriter Tom Waits in exchange for a fixed sum and a percentage of Warner's earnings, with a guaranteed minimum payment. The contract said Warner had the unbridled right not to market the music. Warner opted not to market several recordings to a business that offered to include them in a compilation of Waits' music. TSM sued, saying that such a decision breached Warner's duty of good faith. The claim failed, however, because the contract gave Warner the unbridled right to decline marketing overtures. Good faith's purpose is to protect promises people actually or implicitly make, by instilling a duty to perform such promises honestly. It is not intended to create promises they explicitly did not make.

Crusader tried to show how the TSM precedent differed from its claim against Cussler by distinguishing two types of contracts. In one type, a distributor like Warner can be allowed not to market a product; in the other type, a distributor might be obligated to market but have leeway in exactly how to go about it. Crusader agreed that there is no reason to add a good-faith duty to the first type of contract, when someone is free *not* to do so something. In contrast, Crusader argued, good faith is vital when someone is obliged to act but has leeway in exactly how to do so. In those cases, the leeway has to be exercised in good faith – a distributor could not just go through the motions, but must honestly attempt to market. Crusader portrayed Cussler's duty in this second way. Nothing in their contract said he could ignore proposed screenplays. The contract instead said that if Crusader proposed changes, it had to submit them for Cussler's approval. That meant that Cussler was obliged to read them and give or withhold approval honestly.

Crusader also agreed that Cussler had the right to dismiss a screenplay, so long as that was his honest opinion and even if most people would say he was being unreasonable. But Cussler's actions showed he was being vexatious, not honest, Crusader said. Cussler's behavior was particularly obnoxious when he first approved proposals only later to retract them and when he rejected revisions without reading them. Crusader thought such arbitrary behavior so out of bounds that it amounted to "textbook bad faith."

## Lucy, Again

In rebuttal, Cussler challenged this interpretation of what good faith in contract law requires. It is not that people exercising discretion have to act in a certain way. Rather, "textbook good faith" applies to fill in gaps in exactly what commitments parties made when there is no doubt that they had made some kind of commitment. The textbook example occurs when an exclusive marketer of creative products does not commit to a particular form of marketing plan but is presumed to owe good-faith marketing efforts – as in the famous opinion by Judge Cardozo that the marketer of Lucy, Lady Duff-Gordon's fashions owed reasonable efforts.

This perspective explained the result in the TSM case. It did not hinge on whether Warner could decline marketing overtures or had a duty to market, with leeway in how to go about it. Instead, Warner's unbridled right to decline marketing overtures did not warrant implying a duty of good faith for two other reasons: The contract expressly gave Warner that right, and the parties exchanged many other promises in the bargain, including Warner's promise to make a guaranteed minimum payment.

The Cussler-Crusader contract had characteristics equivalent to those of the TSM-Warner deal. Cussler had the explicit right to withhold or grant screenplay approval in his sole and absolute discretion. And the parties exchanged other promises in the bargain, including their joint preapproval of the screenplay written by David Ward. Crusader could simply have used that screenplay. The contract said Cussler had the right to reject changes, but it did not say that he had to exercise that right honestly, reasonably, in good faith or otherwise, although it easily could have. In glaring contrast, the Cussler-Crusader contract did include those qualifications in other provisions. For example, it gave Crusader the right to veto any requests Cussler might make to speak publicly about the film, providing that Crusader could not withhold approval unreasonably. As the court noted in ruling for Cussler, it may have been unwise for Crusader to give Cussler the unfettered discretion over screenplay approval, but that is the deal it made.[6]

The result of denying Crusader's claims was to leave both parties without any remedy against the other. In other words, both were left exactly where their contract put them, with one caveat. Each party incurred legal fees of approximately $15 million fighting their bitter and protracted lawsuit, a price tag undoubtedly greater than the damages they suffered from the other's transgressions.[7]

The Cussler-Crusader case offers obvious lessons for preparing contracts to anticipate impasses. Less obvious are the case's more valuable lessons to be careful when choosing partners in business ventures and contracts. Cussler and Crusader did not seem to trust one another from the beginning of their relationship. Mistrust is not a good foundation for any deal extending several years. It is particularly problematic in one concerning artistic affairs, such as shooting a film from a popular novel. Also, the cost of litigating resulting disputes can consume vastly more than gains or losses directly at stake – in both money and personal well-being.[8]

## C. UNANTICIPATED CIRCUMSTANCES: DEUTSCHE BUILDING

When the South Tower of the World Trade Center was destroyed on September 11, 2001, debris thrust outward to the north face of the forty-one-story Deutsche Bank building at 130 Liberty Street. The force shattered thousands of windows and gashed a fifteen-story slice in the building's side, opening it up for an invasion of soot, dust, and dirt. The Deutsche Bank building was never reoccupied. A state agency created after 9/11 to rebuild downtown New York, the Lower Manhattan Development Corporation (or LMDC), acquired the building in August 2004 as part of its efforts. The building was so badly damaged and contaminated by the debris that the LMDC decided it had to be demolished. It put the demolition job out for a competitive public bidding process. Construction workers spent much of the next decade dismantling it, while their bosses jousted over who had to pay for it.[9]

The winning bidder was Bovis Lend Lease, a leading project management and construction company. During bidding, LMDC made available its environmental study showing that hazardous materials, especially asbestos, contaminated the building. Both knew the project was perilous. They used an elaborate contract made in October 2005 to allocate the risks. LMDC would pay Bovis a fixed price of $81 million for the agreed work, plus additional payments, at cost plus a profit, for "extra work" the two might agree on. Bovis promised completion by March 2007. The contract allocated to Bovis all risks from project delays caused by government actions or the presence of hazardous materials. The concept of "extra work" was defined meticulously as things beyond the project's initial scope or addressing hazardous materials not known to be in the building. The concept excluded work arising from Bovis's errors or negligence or legal requirements.

As LMDC expected, Bovis subcontracted most of the job to another contractor, John Galt Corporation, a somewhat mysterious firm whose name is reportedly taken from the character in Ayn Rand's 1957 novel, *Atlas Shrugged.* The terms of the Bovis-Galt contract mirrored those of the Bovis-LMDC contract, including a fixed price. As soon as work began, and throughout 2006, Bovis and Galt ran into enormous problems, many of which Bovis claimed were unanticipated and outside its contract with LMDC. Bovis asked for additional payments to cover the extra work, but LMDC declined, stating that all work was within their contract. Slowdowns and manpower reductions followed and continued throughout the project.

To break that impasse, New York City Mayor Michael Bloomberg and New York State Governor Eliot Spitzer intervened. At a meeting in the Mayor's home with all parties in January 2007, Bloomberg and Spitzer directed resolution of the stalemate. This prompted a supplemental agreement between Bovis and LMDC signed a week later. LMDC paid Bovis a nonrefundable $10 million as an extra payment and advanced it a refundable $28 million depending on ultimate resolution of whether these contested claims were "extra work" or not. Bovis and Galt resumed work, but the project was quickly afflicted with a series of safety violations and accidents. Pedestrians were seriously injured by objects falling off the tower, including a pallet jack, a crowbar, and a twenty-two-foot pipe. Such incidents prompted the local construction safety agency to add safety requirements, causing further delays.

The worst incident occurred on Saturday, August 18, 2007, at the end of the cleanup workers' weekend shift. As a result of Galt workers smoking on the seventeenth floor – in violation of law – a seven-alarm fire engulfed the building. The blaze killed two firemen, Joseph Graffagnino, 33, and Robert Beddia, 53, injured many others, and damaged ten floors. The fire was more severe than it would have been because Bovis supervisors had dismantled the fire water supply months earlier, also in violation of law. As a result of the fire, Bovis agreed to pay $5 million to each of the two fireman's families, and accepted new safety protocols, remedial measures, and a monitor. Bovis admitted that its site safety manager falsified records concerning the fire water supply. That manager, Galt, and some supervisors were prosecuted for manslaughter but found not guilty.[10] Ten days after the fire, Bovis terminated its contract with Galt, citing a clause allowing it do so "for cause" without additional payments.

The fire required extensive remediation of the site to enable resuming decontamination, consuming more time. It prompted authorities to increase supervision and tighten enforcement of safety regulations. Amid this disruption, and with Galt off the job, Bovis and LMDC hit another impasse. Bovis considered remediation efforts and regulatory intensity the fire caused to create "extra work," outside the original contract's scope, and sought more money. LMDC balked. It said the fire and other accidents were Bovis's fault, so related costs, including regulatory escalation, were on Bovis, not "extra work." As before, to keep the project moving, Bovis and LMDC signed a peace treaty over this. It reallocated some costs but really represented just a temporary truce, deferring the final battle until all work was done.

Bovis completed all decontamination in September 2009 and demolition in January 2011. By then, LMDC had paid Bovis $150 million – about $70 of the $81 million under the original fixed-price contract plus $80 million under supplemental agreements (including the $28 million refundable advance). The net result: payments nearly twice the fixed price and a project four years late. Still, Bovis claimed another $80 million while LMDC countered that Bovis owed it $100 million, which included the refundable $28 million advance, plus millions more due to the fire, advances paid in the various peace treaties, and damages for delay.

Both sides understood that construction projects often produce surprising conditions during progress, forcing participants to make ongoing adjustments. A contractor may agree to do "extra work" and an
owner to pay for it, forming a binding contract. But a contractor who
agrees to do work already contracted for cannot enforce an owner's
promise to pay more for it. There is no fresh consideration for the promise to pay more – a bar called the "preexisting duty rule." So disputes
commonly arise when an owner later objects to honoring promises for
additional payments by claiming that related work was within the original contract's scope. Contractors respond that the new deal involved
more pay for "extra work," making a valid bargain. Bovis thus asserted
that some work it performed was "extra work," beyond the fixed-price
deal, entitling it to compensation as "extra work." LMDC denied this,
saying all work was within the comprehensive fixed-price contract.

### Unexpected Industrial Detritus

Bovis's position was supported by some commonly cited cases. One
concerned a contractor building a post office in Connecticut in 1978.[11]
It hired an excavating firm to perform, for a fixed price of $104,326
(about $640,000 today), "all" excavation work and "everything" necessary "to finish the entire work properly." Before signing the contract,
the contractor took boring tests and gave the excavator the results. The
excavator began work but discovered extensive debris in a subbasement
from an old factory unrevealed by those tests. The two disagreed about
whether removing it was within the original contract. They compromised with a new exchange of promises – the excavator would remove
it and the contractor would pay cost plus 10 percent. The court held
this to be a separate and valid contract because it addressed work outside the project's original scope caused by circumstances neither party
anticipated.

### Unexpected Landfill Needs

In another precedent favoring Bovis's position, a contractor hired by a
drive-in movie theater owner in Maryland agreed in writing to supply

"all materials" and to perform "all work" to clear the theater site of timber, stumps, and waste, and to grade the site.[12] Once work was underway, it became apparent that substantial additional landfill would be needed. Neither had anticipated this, both relying on a topographical map that proved to be inaccurate. So they orally agreed that the contractor would add more fill for additional pay. Later, the owner claimed that the oral promise lacked consideration because the contractor had agreed to do what it already was required to do. The court held otherwise, saying unanticipated circumstances supported enforcing the oral agreement as a modification of the original.

Bovis had a credible basis for presenting its case as squarely within these precedents. But LMDC emphasized the differences. In the post office and drive-in cases, something unanticipated had arisen: the parties discovered debris deep beneath the post office site despite test borings, or needed additional landfill for the drive-in movie theater despite a topographical survey. In contrast, nothing like that plagued the Deutsche Bank demolition project. Everyone knew exactly what building was to be torn down and knew everything about its condition when they signed the contract. The environmental study furnished by LMDC was accurate. Further, this was a fixed-price contract, a term indicating that the contractor profits when costs are less than estimated and takes losses when they are above that. The contract allocated all risks – fire, delay, regulatory tightening – to Bovis.

In short, LMDC stressed, nothing unanticipated had occurred warranting making it pay more than originally agreed for the agreed work. The post office and drive-in cases were examples of cases in which people modify agreements in the course of performance, in good faith, to meet unanticipated circumstances. But in some cases such midcourse adjustments are the product of one party exerting undue pressure on the other to take advantage of a vulnerable situation. In this rebuttal, LMDC found a venerable line of cases refusing to enforce modifications of bargains that appear to have been coerced in that way, claiming that this was exactly what Bovis did.

## The Salmon Fishermen's Threat

In a classic example favoring LMDC, fishermen agreed to join a vessel plying from San Francisco to Alaska to catch salmon, hundreds of miles away, in a short season.[13] Once the boat reached her destination, the crew demanded increased wages or threatened to stop work. Facing that threat, the skipper knuckled under and agreed to pay more. Back home after the voyage, the vessel operator refused to pay, standing by the original agreement. The court sided with the operator, saying the promise to pay increased wages was unsupported by any fresh consideration. The men gave nothing new, agreeing only to what they already committed to do. The pay raise therefore was unenforceable under the preexisting duty rule. The men's threat to stop fishing was delivered when the boat was in the middle of the ocean, after the short season was underway. It was unjustified because nothing unanticipated had occurred. The threat put the company under duress and it had no choice but to agree to the increased wages.

LMDC stressed that nothing had happened to justify Bovis getting an increase in pay either. The accidents, fire, and resulting regulatory intensity were not innocent matters, and the contract put all responsibility for them on Bovis. Any effort to get more was extortionate and any promise LMDC might have made during the course of performance a product of duress, not free will. Having suffered from duress, LMDC was entitled to recover from Bovis advances it made, plus damages for delay. For the most part, the court agreed with LMDC, relying heavily on the terms of the fixed-price contract and tight definition of extra work that allocated most risks in dispute to Bovis.[14]

## D. ACCORD AND SATISFACTION: LADY GAGA

Lady Gaga catapulted to pop stardom in 2009 at the age of twenty-three. The music phenomenon, whose real name is Stefani Germanotta, took her meteoric path to fame through Rob Fusari, then forty-one, a music producer whose own fame is owed partly to Gaga. Just before her records went white-hot, the two, who worked together and dated for a couple of years, had a falling-out.

In early 2006, Fusari scouted for what he termed a "dynamic female rock-n-roller with garage band chops to front an all-girl version of The Strokes." He hit gold on March 23 when a friend, Wendy Starland, called saying she had just been "blown away" by a young woman named Stefani Germanotta at a New Writers' Showcase in New York's The Cutting Room. Fusari got on the phone with Germanotta and listened to some of her music on her PureVolume Web page, a site where budding musicians post work. Fusari liked what he heard and invited Germanotta to his Parsippany, New Jersey studio for a meeting. Fusari expected a grungy sort, given what he had heard, so was surprised to meet a hip and elegant Italian American.

The two quickly became close, began dating, working together daily, exploring musical genres and shaping a new approach. Fusari encouraged Germanotta to move from rock to dance, adding drums to enrich her music without sacrificing its integrity. Fusari claims coauthorship of the song "Beautiful, Dirty, Rich," a hit from her debut album – and takes co-credit for later hits like "Papparazzi," "Brown Eyes," and "Disco Heaven." Fusari also boasts of minting Germanotta's stage name. Germanotta's looks reminded him of Queen's Freddy Mercury, so he often greeted her with a rendition of that band's hit song, "Radio Ga Ga." When texting Germanotta using that name one day, the phone's spell-check changed *Radio* to *Lady*. The name appealed to Geramnotta, and it stuck – along with such extravagant costumes that she would never be mistaken for Freddy Mercury again.

By May 2006, two months after their initial meeting, the duo had a CD to shop to record labels. Fusari proposed what he always did with new talent: a production and distributorship agreement between his company and the artist. Germanotta would develop material and he would produce it and place it for distribution with record labels. But Germanotta's father, Joe, played a powerful role in his daughter's business activities and preferred a deal between Fusari and a company he co-owned with his daughter, called Mermaid Music. As a compromise, Mermaid and Fusari signed an agreement to create another company, Team Love Child (or TLC), owned 80 percent by Mermaid and 20 percent by Fusari. Germanotta, now Lady Gaga, would make music for TLC to own; Fusari would get it produced and distributed; and all three would share proceeds pro rata.

Fusari took the CD to Island Def Jam records (or IDJ), where top executives L. A. Reid and Joshua Sarubin signed Lady Gaga on the spot to a record deal and set a debut album release date for May 2007. A few months later, however, IDJ pulled out of the deal under a clause in its contract. Germanotta was devastated. Fusari claimed he bucked her up and kept her writing and recording. But Fusari and Germanotta began bickering incessantly and Fusari claimed that Germanotta became verbally abusive to him. The upshot, in January 2007, was to break off their romance.

In Fusari's telling, things turned cold among the team and everyone turned against him. His own manager, Laurent Besencon, now also representing Lady Gaga, paired her with his other clients in music production. Laurent and Joe pushed Fusari to the sidelines. Fusari said this did not deter him, however, and he reached out to his mentor, Vince Herbert, and got him to interest Interscope Records in a record deal. Despite opening that door, Fusari complained that the team froze him out of ensuing negotiations with Interscope as well. Gaga's team had a different view, of course, questioning Fusari's performance and commitment. After proceeding without Fusari, Interscope released a wildly successful Lady Gaga debut album, "The Fame." Four of the album's songs topped the charts and Gaga was on the road to riches.

Gaga paid Fusari $203,000 in June 2009, his share of her recording riches to date. In December 2009, Gaga sent him another check, for $395,000. A curious notation appeared on the reverse side of that one: It said "accord and satisfaction." Fearing a trick, Fusari refused to cash the check and instead sued for several million dollars.[15] Lady Gaga learned that an accord and satisfaction is a valuable tool in contract law designating a deal to resolve a disputed debt. A check with such a notation on it can be a valid offer to settle. The act of cashing the check signals acceptance of the offer. The result is a contract extinguishing the debt, even if the person cashing the check first crosses out the phrase "accord and satisfaction" (or any similar phrase such as "payment in full"). As a matter of public policy, this device desirably promotes compromise rather than litigation.

Checks only work that way, however, if a bona fide dispute exists. People cannot extinguish a debt that is not in dispute just by sending someone a check for a lower amount and writing "accord and satisfaction" on it. The other person can deposit that check, crossing out the words or not, and still recover the balance rightfully due. The explanation for this lies in the doctrine of consideration: Consideration exists in such situations only if both sides give up legitimate claims in a genuine dispute.

Lady Gaga's check containing those words, therefore, would be a valid offer of settlement only if there was a genuine dispute about the debt Fusari claimed. For Fusari, it was not obvious that any such genuine dispute existed. There was little doubt that the parties had entered into valid production and distributorship contracts. There was also little doubt that Fusari had performed his obligations and that nonpayment was a breach. The exact amount due under the contract was yet to be determined. Calculations would involve how many recordings were sold and how proceeds were split. But, for Fusari, it was premature to say there was any particular dispute. To that extent, the act of Fusari cashing the check would not have extinguished his claims.

It was possible, however, to distinguish different roles Fusari played and then identify bona fide disputes concerning some, if not others. In one role, he rendered producer services; in another, he developed and managed distribution arrangements. If multiple roles could mean multiple payment streams, then there could have been genuine disputes that cashing the check might well have settled for good.

## The Disputed Home Improvements

Fusari could find a useful illustration of the general principles and distinctions among payment streams in a case about home improvements. Mark Jensen hired Marton Remodeling to perform home improvement work.[16] After finishing the work, Marton presented Jensen with a bill for $6,538, which Jensen protested, arguing that it listed excessive hours. Jensen offered $5,000, which he considered the renovations to be worth. Marton refused. So Jensen sent Marton a $5,000 check with these words on it: "Endorsement hereof constitutes full and final satisfaction of any and all claims payee may have against Mark S. Jensen."

Marton rejected the proposal and demanded the rest. When Jensen made no further payment, Marton wrote "not full payment" below the notation and cashed the check. He then sued for the $1,538 balance. Marton stressed how he told Jensen, after receiving the $5,000 check, that he did not accept it in settlement. But the court found that merely telling Jensen, on its own, was meaningless. Marton's denial could not invalidate what Jensen made clear in his offer. Actions, like cashing a check, speak louder than words of protest.

Marton countered that there could be no accord because there was not a good-faith dispute about the amount at stake. Because both agreed that the $5,000 tendered via the check was due, the only remaining dispute concerned the excess $1,538. That argument failed, however, because the essence of the $5,000 settlement was, of course, to resolve the dispute about the excess. Under Marton's logic, there could never be a binding accord settling disputes for lower amounts.

Fusari would rightly worry that there are cases involving multiple categories of amounts, such as a sales contract calling for fixed salaries plus variable commissions.[17] Disputes about the fixed portion can be settled without necessarily settling disputes about the variable commissions. In such cases, cashing an accord check proposing to settle a fight over what fixed amount is due does not necessarily resolve disputes about variable amounts.

Although these situations differ from the Jensen-Marton case, which involved a single claim for the final balance under a disputed contract, they may have applied squarely to the deal between Lady Gaga and Rob Fusari. A Lady Gaga check offering to resolve a disputed fee for Fusari's producer services might settle that claim while still leaving open for negotiation the amounts due for Fusari's services in managing distribution arrangements.

Amid this uncertainty, Fusari feared that Lady Gaga's team had set a trap to trick him. Given the millions at stake, Fusari wisely decided not to cash the check. By not cashing it, Fusari preserved all his rights. He then asserted those rights in March 2010 by suing, which Lady Gaga met with a lawsuit of her own. The mutual claims favored Fusari. He asserted breach of contract and claimed entitlement to his share of all recording proceeds under the TLC agreement and payment for producer services.

The former lovers wasted little time and no serious legal wrangling before settling their case in the fall of 2010. Both promised to keep the terms of settlement confidential. What is clear, however, is that Fusari was entitled to contractual payments in the deal. But he was not necessarily right to smell a trap. There is nothing sneaky about this legal route to settlement, which is a common, convenient, and valuable way to resolve disputes informally – a value to society.[18]

## E. ADJUSTMENT: CONAN AND "THE TONIGHT SHOW"

In the early 2000s, Conan O'Brien, a rising talk show host, caught the eye of major television networks, including NBC. In 2004, they entered into a contract, which said that Conan would, starting six years later, host "The Tonight Show," the iconic sixty-year-old program NBC aired at 11:30/11:35 P.M., immediately following the local news. The show had been hosted by the fabled likes of Johnny Carson (from 1962 to 1992) and was then hosted by Jay Leno, who took over in 1992 amid an ugly fight for the coveted spot with his archrival David Letterman. When Leno in 2004 agreed to this orderly transfer of duties to Conan, the show's ratings were at a peak, but he conceded to avoid the bitterness that poisoned his own ascension a decade earlier.

NBC and Conan performed under their contract for seven months in 2009. Then, at year end, NBC decided on a switch. It would air the show at 12:05 A.M., moving to the valued earlier slot a show hosted by none other than Jay Leno! Conan objected, claiming breach of contract, and staging a public campaign, including on the show, to pressure NBC to adhere to the original deal.[19] Eventually, however, Conan and NBC resolved their dispute behind the scenes, never going to court, with a settlement agreement releasing each other from their original contract. NBC paid Conan $45 million in exchange for Conan agreeing not to host any competing television show for one year. NBC reappointed Leno to his old post and the show resumed its impressive run.

Aside from the roles of ego and money in their negotiations, NBC and Conan debated what rights and duties their existing contract created. The deal had several parts that raised a number of different questions. A central question was whether NBC's decision to change time slots was a breach of its contract with Conan. NBC said the contract was silent about when "The Tonight Show" would air. One reason for such silence could be that operational decisions must be left with the network to enable programming management. In that view, NBC had the right to set the time and its decision to change the time slot did not amount to a breach.

A different explanation for the silence is based on common knowledge: for sixty years, "The Tonight Show" aired just after the local news. There may have been no need to say anything in the contract about the starting time. In that view, NBC's time slot switch could be a breach. On the other hand, some local television stations air the local news at 10:00/10:30 P.M., so a time slot of 11:30/11:35 P.M. would not mean the same thing as a time slot right behind the local news. This volley thus suggested that the silence did give NBC discretion regarding the time slot, and its decision to change did not automatically trigger a breach of contract.

Contractual silence, for whatever reason, creates a gap in the contract. The existence of a gap invites the parties to contend that the exercise of related discretion must be done in good faith. That is akin to the situation in landmark cases like Lucy, Lady Duff-Gordon:[20] Silence about an exclusive marketer's duties justified implying that the marketer will use reasonable efforts. However, if NBC had a duty to act in good faith concerning the time slot the contract did not address, then Conan equally had a good-faith duty that would require some flexibility on his part. That could include performing the show at hours NBC elected, so long as these were reasonable. More pernicious NBC decisions, like airing at 2:00 A.M. or only on alternate nights, could appear to comply with technical contract terms but defy the contract's spirit. Such changes would lack good faith and amount to a breach. But the switch NBC proposed was more modest and seemed reasonable.

To play an even bolder game, NBC could add that even if it breached by not keeping Conan in the 11:30/11:35 P.M. slot, it offered Conan a way to reduce his damages by taking the later slot. NBC would remind Conan that contract law says damages to injured parties are reduced by losses they could avoid in mitigation.[21] Any damages NBC caused Conan by breaching the 11:30/11:35 P.M. contract should be reduced by what it offered to pay him in the 12:05 A.M. alternative. Given that NBC did not propose to change what it paid Conan, his damages would be zero. Conan could respond that "The Tonight Show" is a unique franchise, with a sixty-year tradition of airing the minute the local news ends. A later airing is much different and inferior. NBC proposed to fill the traditional slot with archrival Jay Leno in a copycat show. Conan could credibly contend that he would not have accepted a deal on those terms if NBC had offered it six years earlier. The result of this volley would thus depend on the vagaries of a jury assessing the relationship between "The Tonight Show" at 11:30/11:35 P.M. and "The Tonight Show" at 12:05 A.M., with Jay Leno's show preceding it.

Two clauses in the original NBC-Conan contract that reappeared in their settlement sealed the stalemate. As with many contracts for high-profile employment, this one contained a provision stating what damages NBC would owe Conan if it breached: some $40 million. Contract law recognizes such clauses as valid so long as actual damages are difficult to ascertain and the amount is a reasonable attempt to estimate them. Awards of amounts greater than necessary to compensate for a breach are unenforceable as penalties.[22] Damages to talk show hosts from network breaches likely are difficult to ascertain, and that figure for a rising star like Conan may have been a reasonable forecast of actual losses.

Employment agreements like Conan's also often contain covenants not to compete. This refers to a term restricting an employee from engaging in competitive lines of work for a stated period and locale after employment ends. These are important to an employer when an employee's performance generates valuable knowledge or skills at a cost to the employer. Allowing the employee to work elsewhere using that investment undermines its value; it also reduces employer incentives to make such investments. In most states, so long as a covenant is reasonable in terms of time, geographic scope, and activity, it is valid. But California, unusual among states, takes a hard line, banning the covenants except in narrow circumstances. Because the parties were based in California, this presented additional uncertainty: A lawsuit fought under California law would give an advantage to Conan, but one fought elsewhere would give the edge to NBC.

A draw thus resulted from the set of volleys in this legal matchup: the contract's silence about the time slot created uncertainty as to whether NBC breached; the duty of good faith each side owed did not automatically resolve whether either breached; even if NBC breached, its offer of a later slot might count against Conan's damages, although

there was at least an even chance that it would not count because it was
different and inferior; the damages clause was probably valid but not
necessarily; and Conan's covenant not to compete would be upheld in
most states but not in California.

The upshot was a contractual relationship with enough uncertainty, and neutrality, that the parties found it more congenial to settle
their differences outside of court. The contract also made the settlement terms predictable. Ultimately, NBC paid Conan about what the
original contract's damages clause specified and Conan covenanted
not to compete on about the same terms as they originally envisioned.
What appeared to be a tennis match was really an engagement with
a deal that helped the parties resolve their dispute. The contract gave
Conan and NBC guidance, if not ironclad answers. To that extent, the
contract worked, as it enabled a good-faith resolution for the parties
involved, which is also desirable as a matter of public policy.

Many people think that contracts cannot be changed once they are
made or that the typical contract is performed as required and no
changes occur. There does not appear to be a consensus on what
should be done when contracts overlook a problem that the parties
later fight about, and perhaps most people simply do not think about
the problem at all. But many do seem to think that you cannot change
a bargain once you make it, even if unanticipated circumstances occur.
At least a few seem to think that it should be possible to settle a debt at
a discounted price, even if there is no doubt that the full debt is owed.
Too many, alas, seem to think that fighting things out in court is better
than resolving them privately.

Performing contracts almost always presents questions, large and
small, about who is supposed to do what. This often provokes disputes prompting modifications, settlements, or other adjustments.
Freedom of contract means that people make bargains, not courts,
so express terms prevail over implied terms, including legal notions
of good faith. But good faith is sometimes necessary to fill gaps in
incomplete contracts intended as a bargain. The concept of good faith
is elastic, stretching to play many roles in the performance, modification, settlement, and adjustment of deals. It is useful in a broad range
of settings, such as making midcourse modifications, settling disputes

and exercising discretion. Good faith is thus both Protean and modest, of general but limited use, to fill gaps and police abuses while letting people allocate power as they wish.

People should be free to revise their deals during the course of performance, but only when done in good faith based on changed circumstances, not when one side exploits circumstances to induce the other to knuckle under to threats. If duress rather than free will drives a modification, contract law should no more enforce such a bargain than it would enforce those that result from fraud or mutual mistake (as Chapter 3 discussed). Likewise, public policy is served by encouraging people to settle disputes privately, but settlements, such as using an accord and satisfaction, should be recognized as valid only when resolving genuine good-faith disputes.

Contract law's doctrine of good faith may not clarify exactly what duties people owe one another or how discretion must be exercised, leaving parties uncertain about where they stand when performing a contract or adjusting its terms. But that is a necessary cost of the greater value the doctrine yields by reflecting the reality that most people expect their contract partners to act reasonably and honestly, which is all the good-faith doctrine ultimately demands. That uncertainty sometimes facilitates rather than frustrates contract adjustments, an important function, because enough deals require adjustments that contract law is supplemented with a broader array of tools to handle them, which the next chapter presents.

# 8  HEDGING

## Conditions

*The courts should not be the places where resolution of disputes begins. They should be the places where the disputes end after alternative methods of resolving disputes have been considered and tried.*

– Sandra Day O'Connor

## A. INTERPRETATION AND EFFECT: KEVIN COSTNER'S BISON

Kevin Costner cemented his leadership in the Hollywood scene by his production of the heroic 1990 film "Dances With Wolves," in which he starred as Lt. John J. Dunbar. The film, shot in the Black Mountains near Deadwood, South Dakota, inspired Costner's fantasy of developing a luxury resort hotel in the area, where he bought 1,000 acres of land. Despite spending two decades and several of the millions he earned from the film on this dream resort, to be named the Dunbar, it never panned out. For the centerpiece of his plans, Costner commissioned seventeen massive bronze sculptures, assembled as the "Lakota Bison Jump," from the noted local artist Peggy Detmers.[1] The sculptures depict three Native Americans hunting fourteen bison on horseback, at 125 percent of life scale. Costner initially commissioned the sculptures in 1994 under an oral agreement, paying Detmers $250,000. The two agreed to share royalties from sales of reproductions of the sculptures, which they expected would sell for up to $250,000 apiece.

By 2000, however, the resort was not yet underway, and Detmers became anxious about whether her sculptures would be displayed and royalties on sales begin to flow. Costner reassured her in a two-page letter of May 2000. After noting that Costner was paying Detmers another $60,000, this letter outlined how the two would promote fine art reproductions of the sculptures and share royalties on sales. The letter gave Costner sole discretion over displaying the sculptures during the period before the Dunbar was built. Notably, the letter provided what would happen if the Dunbar were not built within a decade: "Although I do not anticipate this will ever arise, if the Dunbar is not built [by 2010] or the sculptures are not agreeably displayed elsewhere, I will give you 50% of the profits from the sale" of the sculptures.

Detmers completed the sculptures in 2002, but the resort was still not under construction. Costner elected to place the sculptures on his 1,000-acre property – intended as the site for construction of the Dunbar. Costner believed that Detmers had approved that location and later developed the site, called Tatanka, at a cost of $6 million, as a stand-alone summertime tourist attraction, with a modest visitor's center, gift shop, and nature trails.[2] Detmers remembered the conversation differently, objecting that the Tatanka was puny compared to the plan of making "Lakota Bison Jump" the showcase of the luxurious Dunbar. Compared to the wealthy patrons of the grand resort Costner envisioned, visitors to the small-scale seasonal site were unlikely to order lucrative reproductions of Detmers' sculptures. She understood that placing the sculptures at Tatanka was temporary, pending completion of the Dunbar.

By 2010, the Dunbar was still not underway, and the two disputed the meaning of the contingency in the agreement. Such a dispute occurs often in contracting: whether Costner made a promise to sell the sculptures or merely a conditional commitment to split the profits from any sale should one occur. The problem recurs because contracts often contain an array of promises coupled with qualifications, called "conditions." The stakes are high. Promises must be performed or else a remedy paid; conditions limit the scope of a promise. If a condition does not occur, then the limited promise never ripens, and, therefore, it need not be performed.

Detmers contended that Costner's letter promised that he would sell the sculptures if the Dunbar was not built by 2010 or the sculptures were not agreeably placed elsewhere. As it was not built and, she argued, the sculptures were not agreeably placed elsewhere, Costner's promise was due. For support, Detmers stressed the economic features of their deal. The sculptures would be valuable as the linchpin of a luxury resort but, without the resort, value could be tapped only by an alternative display or outright sale. She interpreted the letter's pivotal language accordingly. Costner's failure to sell the sculptures was therefore a breach of contract entitling her to damages, Detmers believed.

Costner countered that he had made only a conditional promise – to split the proceeds if he chose to make a sale. He bought and owned the sculptures and decisions about selling them were his alone, he said. He took a literal approach to the language, noting that nowhere did he make any explicit promise to sell. The sentence concerning a sale did not make a commitment, such as that Costner "shall" or "will" sell. Costner's argument took a page from a familiar example used to distinguish promises from conditions. A FedEx shipment contract might say that a package *shall* be transported to Memphis on the next flight or that the package *must* be transported to Memphis on the next flight. Such language suggests a promise in the first case (*shall*) and a condition in the second (*must*). The effects of not shipping on the next flight differ: the first breaches a promise and entitles the customer to damages whereas the second is the non-occurrence of a condition that excuses the customer's duty to pay.[3] Ditto for Costner's letter: It said that he "will" split the profits but made no commitment that he "shall sell" the sculptures.

### An Aborted Vineyard Sale

Costner's stance found support in a well-known case concerning the sale of a vineyard in upstate New York.[4] The contract contained a section labeled "conditions" that stated that the buyer's duty was "subject to" the seller obtaining title insurance. The seller did not get the insurance and the buyer sued, seeking both return of its down payment and damages for breach. But the language and circumstances indicated that obtaining insurance was a condition to the buyer's obligation, not a promise of the seller. Accordingly, its non-occurrence excused the buyer's duty to close, entitling it to its down payment. As the seller was not in breach, the buyer was not entitled to damages. Costner claimed that, like the vineyard seller, he made no promise to sell the sculptures but only a commitment that, if he did, he would split the profits. This equated his conditional commitment to the vineyard seller's conditional commitment: To be bound, he would first have to sell the sculptures, just as the vineyard buyer would be bound only after the seller obtained insurance.

## A Crop Insurance Caper

A contrasting case supported Detmers. It concerned an insurance contract covering a farmer's crops.[5] One clause stated a "condition" to the insurer's duty to pay under the policy that the policyholder *must* establish that a loss occurred. Another said that, when any insured event occurs, the crops "*shall not* be destroyed" before the insurer inspected the damage.[6] After heavy rains damaged some crops, the farmer filed a claim and, using standard farming techniques, plowed the acreage and prepared it for sewing other crops to preserve the soil. Then the insurer's representative inspected the farm and the destroyed crops and denied coverage.

The issue was whether the non-destruction clause was a promise or a condition: if a promise, the farmer breached it, and that entitled the insurer to recover damages while not excusing it from paying under the policy; but if a condition, it did not occur, and the insurer would be excused from paying under the policy. The farmer's first argument was linguistic: the clause about the policyholder establishing loss was called a "condition" and used that telltale word *must*; the non-destruction clause was not classified as a condition and used the formulation *shall not* – the telltale signal of promise, not condition. The farmer's second argument invoked public policy: the importance of protecting people's reliance on contracts and avoiding forfeiture of related costs or advantages. This favors construing ambiguous language as establishing promises, not conditions. If construed as a condition, the farmer would forfeit all premiums paid on the policy. But if construed as a promise, that reliance is protected. The insurer would be entitled to damages for the farmer's breach, measured by the greater difficulty of verifying the claimed crop loss. The farmer thus had the better of the argument.

This argument did not carry the day for Peggy Detmers in her dispute with Kevin Costner, however. The court found the language in Costner's letter to be unambiguous, making the contract rather than any public policy controlling, and the outcome clear. Rather than attempting to classify the contract's language about a sale of the sculptures as a promise or a condition, the court focused on the language about the sculptures being "agreeably displayed elsewhere." The court accepted Costner's version of events, that Detmers in 2002 had approved displaying the sculptures at Tatanka, and this meant that the sculptures were "agreeably placed elsewhere." Detmers objected that "elsewhere" must mean somewhere "other than the Dunbar or the land where it was to be built," and the sculptures were sitting on that land, not displayed "elsewhere." The court rejected that argument, saying that "elsewhere" meant some site other than the Dunbar and, the Dunbar not having been built, any other place would do, including that one. [7]

## B.  ORDER OF PERFORMANCE: CHARLIE SHEEN AND WARNER

A common question in the performance of contracts is: "Who's to blame for breach"? A saga attesting to this point, discussed in this and the next two sections, concerned the hit television show, "Two and a Half Men," produced by Warner Brothers and starring the actor Charlie Sheen.[8] For seven seasons, Sheen successfully played the lead character, with whom he had much in common, both being troubled, well-to-do middle-aged bachelors and having an "easy way with women," as the CBS synopsis of the popular show put it.

Despite Sheen's lurid off-air antics, however, Warner renewed the star in May 2010 for two more seasons. The updated contract, heavily negotiated with extensive provisions, called for Sheen to perform two dozen episodes in each season and Warner to pay him $1.2 million per episode. The relationship had been rocky for a while, owing to Sheen's personal life. He endured a public divorce, culminating in the airing of previous physical and drug abuse charges and an encounter with a prostitute in New York's Plaza Hotel, which involved allegations of substance abuse.

During the last few months of 2010, Sheen lost about twenty pounds, attributed to taking illegal drugs. Even so, Warner went on with the show, creating and airing dozens of episodes starring Sheen. At the same time, the show's creator and producer, Chuck Lorre, began poking fun at Sheen on air about his out-of-control lifestyle. In January 2011, Warner grew worried. Its senior executives confronted Sheen at his home to discuss medical treatment for his addictions. The executives cautioned Sheen that failure to clean up would lead to shuttering the show.

At first, Sheen agreed to enter a rehabilitation facility. Later, however, he reneged, claiming he kicked his bad habits and citing several clean drug tests in early 2011. At that point, the show was to resume taping on February 28, but Lorre had meanwhile decided that, given scheduling requirements, fewer episodes would be made that season. Warner's acquiescence in Lorre's decision, along with Sheen's heightening animosity toward Lorre because of his joke-cracking and episode reduction, brought Sheen to a boiling point. On February 24, Sheen began a media blitz in which he lambasted Lorre and Warner, made bizarre statements disparaging the show, and boasted of superhuman powers to win his battle with drugs and alcohol by blinking his eyes.

In response, Warner announced that it was suspending production of the show. It expressed continuing concern about Sheen's health and stressed that it had demanded assurances that Sheen seek treatment, to no avail. On February 28, Sheen claimed that Warner was in breach of contract for suspending the show without justification. Sheen demanded to be paid for all contract episodes, whether produced or not, citing a so-called "play-or-pay" clause in their contract. In a letter of March 7, Warner responded by terminating its agreement with Sheen, calling his objectionable conduct a breach. Warner cited several promises it said Sheen breached and portrayed his fulfillment of them as conditions to its duties to compensate him.

One such promise authorized Warner to suspend or terminate Sheen's employment based on his incapacity. This included "any physical or mental disabilities" that render Sheen unable to perform essential duties, including significant changes in physical appearance. A similar clause covered any "serious health condition" lasting more than a couple of weeks. Warner said Sheen's appearance, condition, conduct, and statements triggered its rights to suspend or terminate under these clauses. Sheen denied this, claiming he was "clean and sober, and passed every drug test requested." Sheen claimed Warner canceled the series in retaliation for his criticisms of Lorre, as opposed to Sheen's diminished abilities. He argued that nothing he had done in response to Lorre's provocations either breached his contract or prevented a condition to Warner's duties from occurring. To the contrary, Sheen was "ready, willing and able to perform his obligations," and had been from mid-February through late February, as agreed. In Sheen's telling, therefore, Warner was precipitous in alleging Sheen's breach, and its refusal to accept Sheen's performance made it the one in breach.

Sheen asserted, and Warner acknowledged, the clause requiring paying even if episodes are not made. Sheen thought this clause closed the case, but his belief was premature. Even an expansive play-or-pay clause does not automatically mean payment is due without regard to the reasons an episode is not produced. These clauses, common in entertainment contracts, require a producer to pay an entertainer an agreed sum even if the parties do not create art – but they are not unconditional. Like any other promise, they are often subject to conditions, most often the receiving party fulfilling its side of the deal. Warner cited an express limit on Sheen's rights concerning publicity. The contract made Warner officials the exclusive publicists for the show, prohibiting Sheen from publicizing it other than by "normal, incidental, non-derogatory publicity relating solely to" Sheen's role. According to Warner, Sheen's disparaging media rants violated this clause. The clause was not obviously applicable, however, as it restricted publicity, which Sheen did not pursue, and did not squarely bar him from commentary or disparagement. The question remained: Who breached first?

Warner and Sheen were both well aware of recognized principles of contract law used to minimize such impasses, which unfortunately recur in soured relations between contracting parties. Called "constructive conditions" (or "implied conditions"), these principles address the order of performance, or who must go first. In construing a deal, the court attempts to discern what the parties intended, given the context of their deal.[9] Determining whether one side or the other must perform first often hinges on whether either accepted the other's credit risk in choosing to deal with them. If not, it is best to view promises as mutually conditional, so that each side must tender its performance as a condition to the other being bound to perform. People sometimes accept other people's credit risk, of course, such as when employees work for some time before earning their paycheck. In those cases, one party must go first rather than both at the same time. Either way, contract law encourages parties to come together and perform their bargains rather than stand back and declaring that the other has breached.[10]

## The Country Hotel Sale Bust

In Sheen's favor was a venerable case about the sale of a country hotel.[11] The contract called for a down payment, followed by full payment at a closing set for a month later, in exchange for a deed with clear title. Although the contract was not explicit about the order of performance, the court took the naming of a closing date to signal an intention that the performances – property for payments – were due simultaneously. The buyer did not appear at the closing because it learned that the hotel was encumbered by a mortgage made by a previous owner that neither party had known about. The buyer assumed the seller to be in breach.

The court found that the buyer, not the seller, was in breach, much as Sheen portrayed Warner, not him, to be in breach. The seller promised to deliver a deed with clear title, conditional on the buyer tendering payment at closing. The buyer did not do that, so was in breach. The buyer argued that its promise was conditional on the seller being ready, willing, and able to perform; given the mortgage on the hotel, this condition was not met. The court agreed that a seller's inability to perform would excuse a buyer's duty, but said the existence of the mortgage did not prevent the hotel seller from delivering what it promised. It could have discharged the mortgage, for example, and delivered clear title.

Sheen argued that Warner, like the hotel buyer, misconstrued its rights and duties. Warner, like the buyer, had to tender its performance and show readiness, willingness, and ability to perform, not merely assume or declare Sheen's prospective inability. Like the hotel seller with a potentially cloudy title, nothing prevented Sheen from delivering his lines on the set, despite a potentially cloudy mind and body. Warner, in this view, acted precipitously and without justification. Warner, not Sheen, was in breach.

## The Four-Stage Construction

For Warner's part, a contending line of cases stresses the insight about parties not putting themselves at the mercy of the other's credit. This line, generally applicable to employment contracts such as the Sheen-Warner deal, is exemplified by an old chestnut concerning construction.[12] A contractor offered to complete a job in four stages, quoting a price for each or offering the full job for a grand total. Without specifying which payment scheme it preferred, the owner accepted the offer and told the contractor to begin. After completing one-quarter of the project, the contractor sent a bill for the completed work. The owner, refusing to pay, claimed that nothing was due until the entire job was completed.

At that point, much as in the Sheen-Warner case, the contractor claimed the owner wrongly threw him off the work site, whereas the owner claimed the contractor abandoned the job despite requests that he continue. The court sided with the owner, saying that absent express terms about payments being due as work progressed, the contractor had to complete the entire job before the owner owed the price for any part. Warner portrayed Sheen as the contractor and itself as the owner, hiring Sheen to create television programs for stated prices per episode, with Sheen's entire faithful performance a condition to Warner's duty to pay. That made Sheen akin to the contractor, wrongfully abandoning the job.

Warner had the better of the argument on these points. The Sheen-Warner employment setting is more analogous to construction cases than to real estate sales. In employment, as with construction, it is common and practical for services to be rendered before payment is due; in real estate, it is customary and feasible for all documents and payments to be delivered simultaneously at a closing. True, the Sheen-Warner contract specifically addressed the timing of payment by stating separate amounts per episode – a way to distinguish it from construction and employment cases silent about that. But Warner did not commit to pay for episodes that were unproduced because of Sheen's intransigence.

Although Warner had the better of it, the fighting issue boiled down to a question of fact: Was Sheen able or unable to act in "Two and a Half Men"? Determining that is difficult as a substantive matter, involving opinions of artistic taste and judgment.[13] Contract law provides ways to frame issues that help probe the reasonableness of Warner's and Sheen's conflicting opinions about his ability. Analysis so far gives Warner the edge. But this story is so rich that discussion continues into the next section of this chapter.[14]

## C. PARTIAL OR TOTAL BREACH: SHEEN AND WARNER II

In January 2011, after Charlie Sheen's deviant public behavior escalated, Chuck Lorre, the producer of "Two and a Half Men," expressed concern to Warner Brothers about Sheen's ability to perform. Aware of Sheen's erratic personal history and stimulated by Lorre's concern, Warner executives visited Sheen's home and told the actor of their insecurity. They sought assurances that he would straighten up and be prepared to perform his role. At the same time, Warner advised that failure to provide the assurance could lead it to suspend its performance. Warner stressed that these actions followed the lessons of contract law to a tee. When a party has reasonable grounds for insecurity about the prospective performance of the other side, the party must choose to perform its side and risk forfeiting the value of performance, or, alternatively, halt performance and risk being seen to act precipitously in breach of contract.

Contract law offers many ways to reach the middle ground, as Warner's actions suggest. Keeping the deal together is the paramount concern. This reflects a public policy to promote performance and protect expectations rather than let deals crumble, losses scatter, and litigation follow. Tools include encouraging a party worried that the other side will commit a serious breach to ask for assurance of due performance – exactly what Warner did.[15] If assurances are not forthcoming, the nervous party can terminate the contract, halting its own performance without being in breach.

## An Accidental Bulldozing

This practical tool of "self-help" is one of many routes toward keeping a deal together.[16] It and another tool, which classifies breaches as "partial" or "total," appear in a well-known case paralleling the merits of the dispute between Sheen and Warner.[17] A contract required an excavation contractor to perform in a "workmanlike" manner.[18] It authorized the property owner to replace the contractor if delay occurred and called for the contractor to pay replacement costs. The contractor would submit bills at the end of each month (on the twenty-fifth), which the owner would pay by the tenth of the following month. The contractor performed during July, submitting a bill on July 25, due August 10.

But on August 9, its bulldozer damaged a wall on the property. In protest, the owner refused to make the August 10 payment, even though the contractor denied responsibility for the wall damage. Nevertheless, the contractor kept working in August and early September, submitting a bill on August 25, which the owner again refused to pay, prompting the contractor to suspend performance. The owner asked the contractor to resume, and the contractor said it would continue if paid for the completed work. The owner refused, the contractor quit, and the owner hired a replacement to finish the job.

As in the stand-off between Sheen and Warner, both sides claimed the other was first to breach. Each argued that its duties were conditioned on absence of breach, making breach a reason to excuse its remaining obligations. The contractor made the point simply: Each monthly payment was a condition to its duty to render further performance and hence, nonpayment in August and September justified nonperformance. The owner made the point more finely: the bulldozed wall damage was a "partial," albeit material, breach of contract, justifying *suspension*, withholding the owner's usual monthly payment. The contractor's abandonment of the job, on the other hand, became a "total" breach, justifying *termination* and hiring the replacement contractor, at the contractor's expense.

The court agreed with the owner. It found that the bulldozer mishap breached the workmanlike performance commitment and that breach, causing damages twice the amount of the payment then due, was material. The owner, therefore, was justified in withholding payment and the contractor was unjustified in suspending work or quitting. The contractor's suspension was thus a partial breach and quitting was a total breach, justifying the owner not only in suspending performance as it did, but also hiring the replacement contractor.

The hapless bulldozer case offers a helpful analogy to the Sheen-Warner affair. Warner analogized Sheen's misbehavior to the contractor's non-workmanlike behavior – the bulldozer banging the wall. In response, Warner, like the owner, first notified Sheen of this alleged partial breach of contract, seeking assurances that he would cure it. But just as the contractor refused to continue performance in the face of non-payment, Warner claimed that Sheen refused to cure his disability in the face of Warner's cautions that noncompliance would lead it to terminate. In Warner's telling, just as the contractor abandoned work, Sheen, by refusing to seek treatment, effectively abandoned work, as well.

Sheen could deny the analogy on two grounds: first, his behavior was not akin to the bulldozer banging the wall – he did not breach – and, second, Warner's suspension of performance and later termination were both unjustified, precipitous actions putting it in breach. Again, Warner probably had the better of the argument on this point. Its actions, designed to promote performance, not breach, were calibrated to the escalating gravity of the situation. Yet there was one more round to go in the Sheen-Warner case, a drama warranting one final discussion.

## D. WAIVER: SHEEN AND WARNER III

Acting and other personal services contracts, including that between Charlie Sheen and Warner Brothers for "Two and a Half Men," typically contain clauses addressing behavior. Two clauses in Sheen's contract authorized Warner to suspend or terminate if Sheen committed felony offenses involving moral turpitude, or if he engaged in "extra-hazardous activity." Warner asserted that Sheen triggered the felonious/morality

clause by furnishing cocaine to others and engaged in extrahazardous activity by taking extraordinary amounts of cocaine himself. Those
activities interfered with Sheen's ability to perform their contract.

Sheen responded that Warner acquiesced in his felonious and hazardous behavior the previous season, renewing their contract while
drug charges were pending against him:

> While felony charges were pending against Sheen and he was in
> rehab dealing with substance abuse, Warner not only had no objec-
> tion to continuing to work with Sheen on the show, it approached
> Sheen to have him enter into a new contract to perform two addi-
> tional seasons.... Warner even stated that it would not object to
> Sheen entering a guilty plea and having a convicted felon as its
> Monday night star, so long as it would not unnecessarily interfere
> with the production schedule. None of this resulted in Warner sus-
> pending Sheen.[19]

Sheen thus asserted that Warner had waived its right to insist on these
clauses addressing his personal behavior. In technical terms, "waiver"
is a voluntary relinquishment of a known right. It can be effective
absent reliance or consideration, and is usually irrevocable. To be effective, however, the right in question cannot be the material part of an
exchange. Otherwise, the whole idea of consideration would crumble –
people could formally agree to an exchange and later waive rights to
their half. As a result, material promises made in exchanges cannot be
waived and require a bargained-for exchange to change them. Other
terms, like conditions or minor promises, can be waived.

At issue in the Sheen-Warner case, then, was whether the per-
sonal-behavior provisions were material promises Sheen made to
Warner, which could not be waived without consideration, or mere
conditions of Warner's duties, which could be waived without consideration. Naturally, Sheen characterized them as mere conditions that
Warner had waived; Warner claimed they were vital parts of the agreed
exchange and could not be relinquished without getting something in
return, which it had not received.

### The Imbibing Professor

This part of the Sheen-Warner dispute was a modern replay of a
famous century-old case involving an abstinence clause in a book

contract.[20] Professor William Clark, then affiliated with Washington & Lee University, was a prolific writer of law books. He signed a multi-year contract with West Publishing Co., a powerhouse in publishing law books, then and now. The contract stated that Clark would abstain from drinking alcohol during its term and that payment was $2 per page plus $4 per page if Clark so abstained.

Clark imbibed while preparing the manuscript, yet demanded the $4 per page surplus payment anyway. He asserted that West knew he had been drinking while writing and acquiesced in that behavior. West did not dispute knowing that Clark had been drinking, but it did however, urge that Clark's claim of waiver was invalid because it had not gotten anything in exchange for its acquiescence. This move depicted the abstinence provision as a material promise Clark made, so any modification required a bargain, yet it received no consideration. Clark responded that the abstinence provision was not a promise he made as part of the agreed exchange, but a condition to obtaining premium pricing per page. Under long-settled law, Clark observed, anyone can waive a condition without getting consideration in exchange.

The court thus faced an interpretive question: Was the clause a promise, which could not be waived, or a condition, which could? It found that the clause was merely a condition, not a promise. The contract was to get an author to write a book, not a contract to keep Clark sober. The abstinence term was not a material part of the agreed exchange, but an administrative matter, akin to terms about manuscript delivery, proofreading, and citation style. It did not matter that the relative amounts were vastly different – payment of $6 per page instead of $2 per page – because courts do not inquire into the adequacy of consideration.[21]

Which, then, did the clauses in Charlie Sheen's contract resemble? In Sheen's telling, they were merely conditions, nominal, prosaic matter of personal habits that Warner could readily acquiesce in – and did so. In Warner's view, they were the central promises of the agreed exchange, determining Sheen's vital capacity to perform his role. They were not promises it could waive by acquiescing.

Private arbitrators resolved the dispute between Sheen and Warner, following another clause in their contract. Unlike court proceedings, results of arbitration are kept confidential. The public is left to speculate about how the umpires saw the case. Yet Sheen's case closely resembles that of Professor Clark. As in that case, Sheen's commitments to avoid felonious/immoral behavior or extrahazardous activities were not the central part of the bargain. It was not a contract to keep Sheen sober, but one for acting and teleplays. Warner could insist on strict compliance with the conditions and escape its duties if they were unmet. But it could likewise waive the conditions and, having done so, not insist on compliance.

Despite having many contract provisions and contract law on its side, and acting in accord with legal and business standards, Warner probably ended up paying the shattered star something as a result of their falling-out. After all, Warner knew what it was getting with Sheen: a troubled actor playing a troubled character on television. In addition, the entire case boiled down to Sheen's ability to act – a factual matter, not a legal matter, and one on which opinion easily divided.

## E. SUBSTANTIAL PERFORMANCE: SANDRA BULLOCK'S LAKE HOUSE

Sandra Bullock, the Hollywood actress who starred in films such as "Miss Congeniality" and "Blind Side," wanted to build a multimillion-dollar mansion overlooking Lake Austin in the Texas capital, to complement her homes in Los Angeles, New York, and Jackson Hole. In 1997, she contracted with the fashionable local developer, Benny Daneshjou, and his company, The Daneshjou Company, Inc. (or DCI), to serve as architect and general contractor.[22] DCI, along with dozens of subcontractors, was to design and build the lakeside mansion, remodel an existing house on the property, and landscape the grounds. The initial 1997 plan was for a 5,500-square feet spread that DCI estimated would cost around $1 million, but in 1998, the parties amended the plan to call for a 10,000-square feet compound at an estimated cost of $1.5 million, aside from various unspecified items the cost of which would be verified later.

The contract, a relatively short and simple one for a custom home, set a completion date of December 31, 1999. The contract prescribed a "cost-plus" formula. That meant that the contract price to Bullock would be DCI's costs plus a profit set as a stated percentage of that figure. In contrast to a fixed-price contract, in which the builder assumes risks of surprise, in a cost-plus contract, the homeowner assumes such risks. Compared to fixed-price contracts, cost-plus contracts reduce a builder's incentives to cut corners or use shoddy materials, but can create disincentives for builders to control costs. Owners, such as Bullock, typically lean toward cost-plus contracts when quality is more important and fixed-price contracts when price is more important.

After construction on the Bullock compound began, in April 1998, costs escalated. The parties disagreed about the source of the escalation, DCI blaming it on numerous changes that Bullock ordered – 200 by DCI's count – and Bullock on DCI's ineptitude and indifference to cost control under the cost-plus formula. Bullock also claimed extensive defects throughout the job: a leaky roof and windows, faulty wiring, defective masonry, and many others. Bullock and Daneshjou did agree on remediation steps to correct some problems, but success was limited. Eventually, in May 2000, Bullock asked the builders to stop working on the project, but Daneshjou and DCI wished to continue. By then, Bullock had paid DCI $6.5 million in progress payments under the contract.

Unable to work things out, in June 2001, DCI sued Bullock for breach of contract, seeking the balance due under the cost-plus formula. Bullock counterclaimed for breach of contract, seeking the $4 million she claimed it would cost to complete the work in accordance with the contract. She also claimed fraud from allegedly deceptive overbilling and sought the return of most of the progress payments. Daneshjou denied overbilling and, while acknowledging not having performed perfectly, contended that Bullock exaggerated the deviations. DCI said any damages had a much smaller effect on the compound's market value than Bullock suggested.

Following an eight-week trial in the fall of 2004, the jury deliberated for one week. The jury found DCI in breach of contract and that both DCI and Daneshjou had committed fraud by overbilling, saying actual costs were $4 million, rather than the $6 million DCI billed. Its verdict awarded Bullock that difference, plus $2 million to complete the project in accordance with the contract. The jury denied DCI's claims for damages against Bullock. An appeal seemed likely, but DCI persuaded Bullock to negotiate a compromise.

A fundamental issue in the Bullock-DCI negotiations concerned whether DCI, as a party in acknowledged breach of contract, can be entitled to claim any damages against Bullock, either directly or to reduce her recovery. In the early nineteenth century, judges refused to let parties in breach of contract recover anything. In an infamous case, a farm worker breached an employment contract midway through its term yet sought pay for the reasonable value of services rendered. The worker was laughed out of court.[23]

It was then settled that parties to contracts could recover only if they had performed all of their obligations. Courts refused to imagine other possibilities, such as dividing the contract into pairs of corresponding parts. After all, courts reasoned, anything else holds the other party to a bargain they did not make, a "monstrous absurdity."[24] A rule like that would have stopped DCI's case against Bullock in its tracks. There is, however, something inequitable in such results, and courts gradually relaxed this rigid stance.[25] The rule causes forfeiture, when people confer requested benefits on others without being able to claim payment for them. It is based on the highly technical reasoning that sees full performance on one side as a condition to any payment from the other and blindness to imagining a contract as divisible.

The rule also had the odd result of increasing the amount of the forfeiture against those who perform more of their side of the deal. True, contracts should be respected, and a rule requiring perfect performance remains on the books for contracts involving goods, presumably because exactness is expected and nonconforming goods can be rejected so that no forfeiture results.[26] But for contracts where part performance confers a benefit that cannot be returned, as in employment contracts, it is possible to respect the bargain and still require payment of the reasonable value of services rendered, up to the agreed contract price. This is a quasi-contractual remedy, a form of restitution. Thus, employees today are not laughed out of court for trying to recover damages under a contract they admit having breached.

Bullock could accept all this, yet maintain her argument that construction contracts are often more complicated than simple employment contracts. It can be more difficult to determine whether a contractor conferred a benefit on an owner than whether a worker benefited an employer; it is also more likely that a contractor's breach causes an owner damages than a worker's breach causes harm to an employer.

## The Wrong Plumbing Pipes

But DCI would insist that all this means is that for construction contacts, courts require a builder seeking damages to have at least "substantially performed" its side of the bargain. DCI owed this helpful stance to a classic opinion by Benjamin Cardozo, who explained this concept of "substantial performance" in a case involving the construction of a country mansion on Spring Pond in Jericho, New York.[27] Like Bullock's mansion construction contract, it involved custom plans. The contractor built the home, following the plans, and the owner moved in. After nearly one year, the owner discovered that some materials – the plumbing pipes – were not the brand specified but some other brand of identical material and quality. The owner cited this deviation as grounds to avoid paying the balance, akin to the ancient rule that barred a breaching party from any recovery.

Judge Cardozo, however, had little patience with such reverence for "symmetry and logic," stressing instead "practical adaptation" of law to produce just results. After all, the contractor made an innocent mistake, the pipe brands were substantively identical, and any damages the deviation caused the owner could be compensated in money, without imposing forfeiture on the contractor. The test of whether a contractor substantially performed is not mathematical, such as whether a job was two-thirds complete. Rather, the test is contextual and looks to whether the performance meets the contract's essential purpose – here the construction of a home. The test was readily met in the case of the deviant brand of plumbing pipes, because the owner clearly got the mansion, sans the stipulated pipe brand. As a result, this precedent only opened the door for DCI. It remained to determine whether DCI had substantially performed.

## A Misplaced Living Room Wall

A prominent precedent grappling with substantial performance involved building a new home in 1960 on an empty lot using stock architectural drawings.[28] This contract was for a fixed price of $27,000 (about $200,000 today), and the owner paid progress payments of $20,000. Many changes were made during construction, however, and the contractor committed numerous deviations, including misplacing a living room wall, omitting a bench, and furnishing cracked patio tiles. Despite deviations, the owner received a completed home, what it had bargained for, and the damages caused by the deviations could be compensated in money, not preventing the contractor from recovering. Precedents like that supported a credible case to contend that DCI's construction of the Bullock mansion also satisfied this standard of substantial performance, not barring DCI from some recovery. DCI had delivered a completed home, even though many details had not been finalized.

But perhaps the most difficult question in cases of a breaching party claiming damages, and what the Bullock dispute came down to, is how much money to credit the owner for the contractor's deviations. In many cases, there is not a big difference between costs necessary to complete a performance as a contract required and the effect completion would have on the market value of the property. In those cases, the tendency is to use the cost of completion, as it best approximates the owner's expectation. In others, however, such as in the case of the misplaced wall, the cost of completing performance is a large multiple of the difference in value – several thousand dollars to move the wall with minimal effect on the home's market appeal. In those settings, illustrated by the Bullock mansion, choosing the appropriate measure can be vexing. DCI and Bullock would each stress one in a pair of opposing cases illuminating how to address this conundrum.

### The Unrestored Peevyhouse Property

Favoring DCI is a notorious case involving Willie and Lucille Peevyhouse in rural Oklahoma. They owned land under which a mining company speculated coal deposits could be found.[29] The Peevyhouses signed a contract allowing the company to drill in exchange for potential royalties, along with a company promise to restore the land after drilling ceased. The company drilled, found no coal, and left without restoring the land. The Peevyhouses sued to recover for breach of that promise to restore, asking for the cost of completion, some $29,000, although performance would increase the property's market value by less than $300. The court chose the value measure, characterizing the deal as fundamentally commercial and best measured by market values, and classifying the restoration promise as merely incidental to the contract. Under this precedent, DCI would be entitled to recover damages reduced only by the difference in the mansion's value attributable to the deficient work. There was evidence that the difference in value was far less than the $2 million the jury found it would cost to complete.

### The Ungraded Gravel Lot

On Bullock's side stands the equally notorious case involving a property lease whose terms required the tenant to remove gravel from part of the property and then level the land.[30] The tenant removed only the richest gravel and vacated the premises without leveling. The owner claimed as damages the cost of completion, about $60,000, whereas the tenant urged measuring damages by the difference in property value that would result, around $12,000. The court sided with the owner, noting that the tenant had breached deliberately, and citing a famous dictum of Judge Cardozo's in the New York mansion case: "[T]he willful transgressor must accept the penalty of his transgression." The court also stressed that the goal of contract damages is giving the money equivalent of what was promised – the "benefit of the bargain." This case helped Bullock because its reasoning would reduce DCI's recovery by the $2 million that the jury found was the cost to complete the contract to a tee. This amount was considerably higher than the difference in market value between the mansion as delivered and the mansion as promised.

The coal and gravel cases thus pointed in opposite directions for addressing the DCI-Bullock dispute, making it difficult to reconcile the outcomes. At stake is whether market values or personal assessments of contracting parties should determine the measure of damages for breach of contract. That is why the Peevyhouse court stressed the commercial character of that deal, choosing the market value measure, although critics say this overlooked how the owners lived on the property. It is also why the court in the gravel-removal case stressed the terms of the bargain and the expectancy rather than the commercial character of the exchange.

A fruitful way of thinking about these problems is to consider what the injured party likely would do with damages once paid.[31] If the party would complete performance, the cost of completion is eminently warranted, without regard to market values. But if not, it suggests that even that party perceives the payment as closer to a windfall, suggesting market value measures are sufficient. Taking that approach to the Bullock case, is it more likely that the Hollywood star with the proceeds would fix the house or simply take the money and run? As it turned out, despite the massive jury award, the star ultimately decided to tear the nightmarish lake house down.[32]

On the other hand, the jury explicitly found that DCI and Daneshjou had committed fraud in the performance of this contract by overbilling. Judge Cardozo and the gravel case court may overstate the law when suggesting that the "willful transgressor" is subject to a "penalty." Many who willfully breach a contract face no penalty and contract law does not condone awarding punitive damages. But when choosing between two damages measures, the scales tip against the actor whose conduct is deliberate, willful, or fraudulent, in favor of those acting in good faith.[33] Although Bullock and DCI settled on undisclosed terms, there is little doubt that DCI paid Bullock a significant sum, while perhaps winning a small reduction from the amount the jury awarded.

Most people have no idea that there is a big difference between a promise and a condition or how to tell them apart. Many assume that all contracts make clear whether one side has to go first before the other must do anything or whether both sides are supposed to perform at the same time. People tend to think that you either perform a contract or breach it and that a breach warrants going to court. Many people believe that promises must be performed perfectly so that shortcomings forfeit all rights to any promise the other side made.

These misperceptions reflect some of the difficult questions that come up when dealing with the infinite range of deals that people make, including the wide variety of promises that are made and conditions that attach. After all, people are free to determine by contract how their bargains work, including when promises are due and what conditions apply. It is not always easy to interpret contractual expressions, however, although the consequences of classifying an uncertain expression as a promise or a condition are like night and day – finding or excusing liability. A practical appreciation of the sense of a transaction is necessary and encouraging a large dose of self-help by contracting parties is desirable.

## 9 CONSIDERING OTHERS
### Third Parties and Society

*With friends like these, who needs enemies?*

– English proverb

## A. BENEFICIARIES: SUPPLY CHAIN ABUSE AT WAL-MART

Wal-Mart, the world's largest retailer, procures supplies globally, including from factories in such countries as Bangladesh, China, Indonesia, Nicaragua, and Swaziland. The retailer has publicly committed to promoting compliance with local labor laws designed to protect employees against sweatshop working conditions. Such laws address minimum and overtime pay and maximum hours and ban forced labor. Wal-Mart has included terms requiring suppliers to comply with these local laws in its foreign supply agreements. These contracts authorize Wal-Mart to inspect factories for compliance and to terminate suppliers in violation. Wal-Mart also publicly proclaims that in countries with lax law enforcement, the company is the de facto law enforcement agent.

In 2005, employees of foreign suppliers sued Wal-Mart for its failure to enforce its own labor standards.[1] Employees alleged that Wal-Mart does not adequately monitor suppliers and knows of suppliers' routine violation of local labor laws. According to the employees, fewer than 10 percent of Wal-Mart's inspections of its suppliers are unannounced, workers are coached on how to respond, and Wal-Mart's inspectors are pressured to produce positive reports despite factory violations. The employees claimed that Wal-Mart's promise to monitor suppliers' compliance with local labor laws meant that Wal-Mart intended to confer a benefit on employees, even though they are not parties to the contracts. Wal-Mart countered that the employees, strangers to these contracts, had no right to enforce them and, in any event, the company had made no promises of any kind.

The employees saw themselves as being on the right side of history, marking progress in a centuries-long struggle to recognize interests of third parties to contracts. Until the mid-nineteenth century, courts were averse to allowing third parties any enforcement rights in contracts to which they were strangers. Thus, the only people who could enforce contract rights were those who made them.

Resistance to letting strangers enforce contract rights began to weaken with the landmark 1859 case, *Lawrence v. Fox*.[2] Holly owed money to Lawrence and loaned the same amount to Fox, getting Fox's promise to repay that sum to Lawrence. When Fox failed to pay, Lawrence sued Fox directly, on the promise Fox made to Holly. Fox defended by saying he promised Holly, not Lawrence, and therefore Lawrence lacked standing to enforce the promise. Even though this was a good argument at the time, it was also easy to see that both Holly and Fox, when making their deal that Fox would repay Lawrence, intended to benefit Lawrence. New York's highest court decided in an influential opinion that it was therefore both fair and practical to let Lawrence sue Fox directly.

The phrase "third-party beneficiary" today describes people such as Lawrence who are entitled to enforce promises made to others, like Fox's to Holly, when intended for their benefit. After the nineteenth century, this class of cases came to be seen as relatively simple. The person obtaining the promise had a duty to pay money to the person enforcing it – a creditor. The class of creditor beneficiaries readily expanded to include promises bargained for by those owing the third party any other legal obligation, too, beyond money.

The employees in the Wal-Mart case were also spurred on by expansions of this doctrine that occurred in the early twentieth century, when the group of third parties allowed to enforce contracts extended to beneficiaries of promises, even though the person getting the promise did not have any legal obligation to the third party. A paradigm: Aunts could bargain for promises from uncles to transfer assets to nieces, and

nieces could enforce those bargains against uncles.[3] This extension of
the creditor beneficiary rule to include such so-called donee beneficiaries was warranted on analogical grounds. The aunt-niece relationship
showed clear and natural reasons for conferring such benefits. So long
as the uncle-aunt promise was part of a bargain (supported by consideration), letting those beneficiaries sue the promise maker helped
protect and enforce that bargain.

Wal-Mart benefited from historical experience of a backlash against
third-party rights to enforce contracts. During the early twentieth
century, courts flirted with yet further expansion of these third-party
beneficiary rights. Some courts permitted citizens to enforce contracts
against service providers who had contracts with the government. A
common setting involved water supply contracts for municipal fire
hydrants. Citizens harmed by a water company's breach of its government contract could recover damages from the company. This class,
however, was kept narrower than the classes of creditor and donee
beneficiaries. Courts recognized that cities and their suppliers often
do not intend for citizens to have enforcement rights – lest staggering
liability result.[4] Accordingly, although a few cases upheld the rights of
citizens to enforce government contracts, most did not, and the category remains narrow at best.

The Wal-Mart case did not easily fit any of the historical patterns,
making the employees would-be pioneers. The suppliers did not owe
the employees money that Wal-Mart promised to pay for them, nor did
the suppliers make a deal for Wal-Mart to make a donation to them, and
there was no government contract in the picture. But the employees
could validly claim that their employers owed them the duty to comply
with law and they portrayed Wal-Mart as backstopping that obligation
with promises of its own. Their thorniest challenge became how to
characterize what Wal-Mart had agreed to in its supply contracts.

Wal-Mart urged that its contracts said only that Wal-Mart *could*
inspect factories if it wished; if it objected to a supplier's violations, it
*could* terminate the relationship. But those are not promises or duties;
they are rights and options. If Wal-Mart chose not to inspect or terminate, the contracts did not give the suppliers any right to sue Wal-Mart.
Wal-Mart contended it would be hard to imagine it promising suppliers anything about assuring their compliance that the suppliers could

enforce. However far-fetched that may seem, the employees pointed to language in the contracts suggesting Wal-Mart had committed to do just that. Wal-Mart's standards said Wal-Mart "*will* undertake affirmative measures" to assure compliance (emphasis added). The employees stressed how the context and Wal-Mart's public stances could explain why Wal-Mart would have made such a commitment.

Known supplier violations prompted Wal-Mart to adopt its standards in 1992; Wal-Mart represents to the public its commitment to performing rigorous inspections; since 2003, its standards have stated that "the conduct of its suppliers can be attributed to Wal-Mart and affect its reputation," and Wal-Mart acknowledged that labor laws in many countries are not enforced by authorities, rendering its inspections "the main law enforcement mechanism for" factories it buys from.

## A Sweatshop in Brooklyn

For legal support, the employees relied on a sweatshop case arising in the United States, where the Department of Labor (DOL) enforces federal labor laws, including governing minimum wages and overtime. For years, the sportswear manufacturer, Street Beat, had farmed out garment making to factories located in Brooklyn, New York, known to violate those laws, making workers toil day and night, year-long, without paying overtime or minimum wages.

To settle charges that it violated federal labor laws, Street Beat signed a contract with the DOL promising to monitor the factories for compliance and not buy from violators. Despite that, employees of some factories claimed ongoing violations and sued Street Beat as third-party beneficiaries of its DOL contract. A court allowed the suit, because the contract manifested DOL's and Street Beat's intention to benefit employees.[5] The sole purpose of the requirement that Street Beat would monitor labor standards was to benefit employees.

Although not frivolous, the employees' case against Wal-Mart failed. The court held that the contract's provisions did not amount to Wal-Mart promising anything and did not create any duty of Wal-Mart to monitor suppliers. The language and design of the agreements showed that Wal-Mart reserved the right to inspect suppliers but did not require it to do so. After stating Wal-Mart's intention to enforce the standards by monitoring, the contract's language elaborates potential consequences of a supplier's noncompliance: Wal-Mart can cancel orders and cease business with that supplier. But the contract stated no comparable adverse consequence to Wal-Mart for not monitoring.

The Street Beat case, although persuasive, missed the employees' mark. Street Beat expressly promised the DOL that it would monitor its suppliers' factories. That promise's purpose was to assure that factories complied with laws, including overtime and minimum wage laws. A factory's noncompliance, along with Street Beat's continued dealing with them, would entitle the DOL to sue Street Beat for damages. That showed an intention to generate money to pay employees for shortfalls in what noncompliant factories paid. The DOL bargained for Street Beat's monitoring duty along with damages for breach, intended to benefit employees.

The legal commitment Wal-Mart makes in its supply contracts is merely to buy goods – nothing else. Wal-Mart could, of course, make promises that it intends to have third parties enforce – just as any other party can. But there are limits to allowing strangers to enforce promises not made to them. Those must be respected to protect not only freedom of contract – letting people deal on terms they wish – but also freedom from contract – not imposing duties that people did not agree to.[6]


## B. ASSIGNMENT: JP MORGAN'S CABLEVISIÓN LOAN

In the global financial crisis of 2009, many large banks such as JP Morgan Chase (or JP), were forced to take drastic measures to manage their exposure to the risky credit quality of their corporate loan customers. An acute case involved a $225 million loan JP had made in 2009 to Cablevisión, a Mexican telecom company.[7] Borrowers like Cablevisión always share top secret information with lenders and lenders promise to keep this information confidential. Also typical for commercial loans, the JP-Cablevisión agreement reduced JP's risk exposure by Cablevisión promising to limit its operations in particular ways. This power gives lenders the ability to control expansion of a borrower's business and thus manage the lender's risk exposure.

Given a lender's power over a borrower, commercial loan agreements commonly limit how the lender can transfer its interests to other banks. Agreements usually let banks hive off small parts of loans to other banks, such as 2–3 percent, called "participations," where the other lenders are passive, getting no rights over the borrower. But agreements usually restrict bolder steps, requiring the borrower's permission before a bank can transfer the whole loan, called an "assignment," because all lender rights and duties are transferred. The JP-Cablevisión agreement followed suit. JP could sell participations in its loan to other lenders without Cablevisión's consent, but was forbidden to assign the loan without it.

The financial crisis dried up interest among most lenders to share participations or take assignments, but JP found a taker in Banco Inbursa, a Mexican bank controlled by the billionaire Carlos Slim Helú, owner of Telmex, Cablevisión's archrival. JP officials sought Cablevisión's consent to assign the loan to Inbursa but, of course, Cablevisión refused. JP persisted, even threatening that it could structure a deal with Inbursa as a participation, not an assignment, to avoid needing Cablevisión's consent. Despite Cablevisión's refusal, JP went forward anyway with what it labeled a "participation" – of 90 percent of the loan to Inbursa. It was due to that betrayal that Cablevisión sued JP to stop the deal.

Common law through the nineteenth century was suspicious about transfers of contract rights, but modern contract law is supportive. There is value in freely transferable contract rights, because people sometimes need to relieve themselves of contractual obligations and others find it valuable to be in on a deal. One way to enable that is a transfer. So long as performance quality under a contract does not vary with the performing party's identity, the other party should not care. That is how JP characterized its loan agreement with Cablevisión. But when performance quality could vary, the other side would care, and law protects them. Cablevisión took that stance, a challenge typical of recurring fights concerning contracts transferred to a direct competitor.

## Sally Beauty

Cablevisión found support in a well-known case from the early 1980s concerning Nexxus Products,[8] a company that markets hair care products sold using distributors for resale to salons. It agreed with Best Barber & Beauty Supply that Best would be the exclusive distributor of Nexxus products in Texas. The agreement was memorialized in a letter from Best's president to Nexxus's vice-president, which both signed. It spelled out cooperation in promotion and rules about canceling the contract (each side could cancel by giving four months' notice). The agreement said nothing about either side assigning their rights.

Two years later, Sally Beauty Co., a subsidiary of Alberto-Culver Co., a large manufacturer of hair care products and Nexxus competitor, bought Best. Sally took over all of Best's contracts, including the one with Nexxus. In protest, Nexxus promptly canceled its agreement with Best. Its president explained to Sally officials that Nexxus could not keep as its distributor a company owned by a direct competitor. When Sally sued Nexxus for breach of contract, Nexxus denied that the assignment by Best to Sally was valid.

Nexxus contended that a distributorship contract involves personal services. It said it chose Best based on distinctive qualities that Sally could not match. If true, that would be a compelling argument, because courts accept objections to assignments when the other side's performance is personal and distinctive. But this contract did not involve personal services or special skills. It concerned the marketing and sale of commercial hair products. It was between two commercial enterprises, Nexxus and Best, not the two executives who signed the letter.

Nexxus had a stronger argument when contending the agreement was not assignable to a direct competitor without its consent. Nexxus bargained with Best for an exclusive distributorship. Therefore, Best's interests would be aligned with those of Nexxus. In exclusive dealing arrangements like this, distributors use reasonable efforts to market goods. Nexxus had reasonable doubts that Sally, a direct competitor, would meet that standard in the same way that Best would. In addition, the contract, a short formal letter, was silent on assignment. The court interpreted this silence as implying that transfers of rights should be made only in good faith; a transfer to a competitor does not show good faith.

Anticipating arguments that JP would amplify in its feud with Cablevisión, Sally objected that preventing such assignments would wreak havoc in the national economy by obstructing the legitimate transfer of contract rights. Sally argued it could fulfill the obligations of the contract on par with Best. Furthermore, there is nothing wrong with a competitor selling its competitor's products – car manufacturers often allow other car makers to distribute their cars. But the court was not persuaded. After all, Sally's parent could change its corporate policy at any time and direct Sally to perform in ways markedly inferior to how Best was performing. Nexxus had not accepted that sort of risk in the bargain.

Such precedents made a strong case for Cablevisión when protesting JP's attempted assignment of its loan agreement to the company's archrival. There was an important difference between its contract and the Nexxus-Best contract, however, which JP could exploit. The Nexxus-Best contract was silent about assignment, leaving a gap in the contract that justified the implication that assignments be made only in good faith. In contrast, the JP-Cablevisión loan agreement addressed assignments and participations directly: Assignments required consent and participations did not. JP contended that the deal it struck with Inbursa was a participation, not an assignment; accordingly, no consent was required.

JP's argument was too technical for the stomach of Judge Jed Rakoff of New York's federal district court, however. True, JP designed the arrangement to look like a participation and drew up the terms to comply with the rules about participations in its loan agreement with Cablevisión. Those addressed details about how both lenders would share loan fees, split the loan further with other banks, and keep information confidential from third parties. But these were narrow points of technical compliance. They did not meet the thrust of Cablevisión's claim, that JP used a disguise to achieve what was substantively restricted. JP gave Inbursa wide-ranging rights, including access to Cablevisión's confidential business information. Those rights were broader than what JP usually gives other banks in participation deals, Judge Rakoff observed. For example, Inbursa would have broader-than-usual rights against Cablevisión if it failed to repay the loan when due. That is sensitive, because those rights would be of great value to a competitor at a time when a rival faced financial difficulties.

These types of unusual provisions stoked Judge Rakoff's skepticism about the deal, prompting him to issue a temporary order halting it until JP could provide better explanations to justify the loan transfer. That ruling induced JP to throw in the towel and settle the dispute. It reversed its loan sale to Inbursa and even barred some JP employees from working on Cablevisión matters.

### Haagen-Dazs Ice Cream

An even easier precedent helped settle the dispute. Pillsbury marketed its Haagen-Dazs Ice Cream using an exclusive distributor called Berliner. Breyer's Ice Cream, a direct competitor, bought Berliner, prompting Pillsbury to terminate the distributorship contract. A court readily found the termination valid. The court explained: To insist that a producer stay in a contract to distribute its products when the distributor transfers its interest to a direct competitor "defies common sense."[9]

## C. INTERFERENCE: NEW ENGLAND PATRIOTS AND STUBHUB

Internet ticket brokers, such as StubHub, facilitate buying and selling tickets to events across the world, from Bruce Springsteen concerts in your hometown to hockey games at the Vancouver Olympics. StubHub seemed like a great boon for consumers but caused problems for venues. In sales through these ticket brokers, the venues lose control over who holds tickets and who attends events, particularly important to big-time sports franchises from the Miami Dolphins to the Seattle Seahawks. Sports franchises require this sort of control and reserve the right to eject fans for inappropriate behavior and to cancel their season ticket subscriptions.

That is why sports stadium tickets say they are a "revocable license," meaning the team reserves the right to revoke tickets from any holder and refund the purchase price. Each ticket has a unique bar code that is scanned on entering the stadium. When any ticket is canceled, the bar code is voided and the ticket and any related season tickets made invalid. Teams usually resell canceled tickets with new bar codes to fans on their wait-lists.

Using StubHub's service, some of these ejected fans began selling their canceled tickets on the site at a profit. Buyers would appear at the stadium only to be denied admission. That caused the venue and team intangible costs from dealing with upset holders turned away. It also increased the team's administrative expenses. One team, the New England Patriots, pointed out to StubHub that the tickets it sells have a restriction on transferring printed on them. People selling tickets online therefore breach that contract and, the Patriots claimed, that meant that StubHub committed the tort of "interference with contract" when promoting sales of Patriots tickets online. On this basis, the Patriots sued StubHub in November 2006.[10]

The team stressed that people have a valid expectancy interest in the economic value of their contracts. Strangers who impair that interest make an invasion that law protects against when the interferer knows about the relation, intends to interfere with it in a legally improper way, disrupts it, and causes economic harm. There is no doubt that football teams, and stadiums, have contractual relations with ticket holders and that StubHub knows that. So the dispute in the Patriots-StubHub case hinged on whether StubHub's actions were legally improper and, if so, whether that caused the Patriots economic harm. The Patriots asserted that StubHub's actions were legally improper because they facilitated violating state anti-scalping laws. These laws make it a crime for people "in the business" of reselling tickets to sell at premium prices (more than $2 above face value in Massachusetts, where the Patriots play).

Most fans are not barred from such reselling because they are not "in the business" of ticket selling.[11] But StubHub's program for "Large Sellers," people who used the site to sell a large number of tickets to multiple shows, are in that business, so the statute applies. True, StubHub does not sell tickets itself, serving instead as a broker. But the Patriots contended that aiding others in violating the statute was unlawful. StubHub objected to this contention by equating its business to old-fashioned newspaper classified ads, which match sellers to buyers just as its online ticket site does. Newspaper publishers are not held to interfere with associated contracts. Similarly, StubHub argued, it was akin to Craigslist, a digital version of traditional print ads, which is likewise treated as old-fashioned newspapers for similar reasons.

The Patriots distinguished these enterprises by observing that both newspapers and Craigslist charge fixed prices for ad space and have no interest in whether resulting transactions close at a high or low price. In contrast, StubHub takes a percentage of the resale price. Buyers acquire tickets by clicking a *Buy Now* link. StubHub gets a 25 percent commission: 15 percent of the price from sellers plus a 10 percent surcharge on buyers. That gives it a clear incentive favoring higher prices, which tends to increase the likelihood of criminal violations of anti-scalping laws.

StubHub parried by pointing to the prominent disclosure on its Web site about anti-scalping laws and its rules requiring users to comply. The Patriots objected that these steps did not exonerate StubHub from knowingly abetting violations. Because the site does not require sellers to disclose a ticket's face value, neither the company nor buyers could determine compliance. Illegal scalping was easy on the StubHub site and made the company's see-no-evil defense specious: "[W]illful blindness is certainly not a defense to this crime," the Patriots said.

The court agreed with the Patriots, holding that StubHub's participation in statutory violations was enough to make its conduct legally improper against the Patriots. So the case turned to whether the Patriots could show that StubHub's conduct caused the Patriots economic harm.

StubHub observed that the Patriots get paid by the team's original ticket buyers regardless of StubHub's actions. The tickets are bought and paid for before they enter the StubHub market. Revocations do not cause losses because the Patriots promptly resell revoked tickets to wait-list fans for the same price as refunded. The Patriots conceded those points but claimed that StubHub damaged its economic goodwill by threatening its capacity to maintain a safe stadium. Those who buy tickets directly from the Patriots, especially long-term season ticket holders, are more likely to promote safety. They have much to lose if the team revokes their tickets based on fan misbehavior in the stadium. In contrast, StubHub ticket buyers often are fans of archrivals like the Philadelphia Eagles or New York Jets. They may attend Patriots games purposefully to disrupt the stadium and may be indifferent to being ejected from a game or barred from the stadium for life. Some hooligans may even make ejection a point of pride.

Although plausible, the court accepted StubHub's objection that this claimed at most a speculative economic loss. The kind of harm the Patriots portrayed seemed more in the nature of irritation and vexation than tangible pecuniary injury. The team had not shown that StubHub buyers were less mannerly than others or that sales via StubHub increased trouble at games. There had not been any change in demand for season tickets since StubHub opened. And even serious decreased demand would likely be trivial, given the lengthy wait list to get Patriots' season tickets – some 20,000 strong.

The court was more receptive to the Patriots' claim for losses based on direct administrative costs from StubHub sales. Workers at the ticket window faced complaints and fielded questions from those turned away when presenting canceled tickets. Others spent time verifying dishonored tickets for disappointed fans to submit to StubHub for refunds under a StubHub program that guaranteed that. This meant expanding the workforce by staff or hours at related cost. Although not overwhelming in amount, these costs were real and could be quantified. That was enough to show economic harm.

Sustaining a thin but valid claim for interference with contract, the Patriots persuaded the court to order StubHub to share the identities of those buying and selling Patriots tickets. That improved the team's ability to gauge whether buyers were more likely true Patriots fans or hooligans from competing towns out to cause trouble at the stadium – and whether any sellers were actively conspiring to support such disruptive elements. That greater ability to control eased the team's objections.

Fans today can buy Patriots tickets using StubHub, just as they can for other teams allied with StubHub, including the Indianapolis Colts, Chicago Bears, and Washington Redskins. People now spend billions trading tickets on StubHub, part of e-Bay since 2007. It contributes a secure and transparent ticket resale market – vastly better than the often shady practice of scalping tickets in the parking lot just before kickoff.

## D. TORTS: KATIE JANEWAY'S TRAGIC ACCIDENT

In the summer of 2002, Maureen Janeway enrolled her fourteen-year-old daughter, Katie, in a summer camp run by the City of Santa Barbara.[12] The camp was for children with disabilities and offered many activities, including arts and crafts, group games, sports, field trips, and swimming. Katie, who attended the camp every summer for several years, had cerebral palsy and epilepsy. Each year when Katie's mother, Maureen, enrolled her, the camp had her sign a one-page application form saying that the Janeways legally released the camp and its workers from "any negligent act." Each year, Maureen explained to camp officials Katie's developmental capabilities and limits, noting she was prone to seizures when swimming and required close supervision.

In 2002, the camp's precautions for helping Katie included assigning her a special counselor, Veronica Malong, to provide close supervision during swimming sessions. Veronica was a college student with one year of experience as a special education aide at Katie's school, where she knew Katie and had seen her suffer seizures. Veronica had instruction in handling seizures from that school's nurse and from the camp. During the second day of swimming sessions in 2002, while waiting to enter the pool's locker room, Veronica witnessed Katie having a mild seizure. Even though Veronica told another counselor to report this to a supervisor, the supervisor never got the report. Forty-five minutes later, Veronica had not heard from the supervisor and judged it safe for Katie to swim, as the seizure seemed to have passed.

At the pool, Veronica sat poolside near a lifeguard, watching the deep end. Besides camp participants, 300 other children were in the area. Veronica watched Katie jump off a diving board and swim back to the pool's edge. At Veronica's behest, Katie exited the pool and rested for a few minutes. Veronica then asked Katie whether she wished to dive again, and Katie said yes. Katie dove into the water, bobbed to its surface, and began swimming toward the pool's edge. As she did, Veronica turned her attention from Katie for some 15 seconds. When Veronica looked back, Katie had disappeared. She and others futilely searched several minutes for Katie, then blew an air horn and evacuated the pool. Lifeguards rescued Katie from its bottom, but she died the next day.

Naturally bereft, Katie's parents, Maureen and Terral Janeway, were also wounded by what they considered the camp's and Veronica's gross negligence in caring for their daughter, knowing her condition yet failing to supervise her closely. The behavior seemed, at minimum, to depart from the care that reasonable people in similar settings would usually provide, and also showed a more serious lapse during their daughter's fatal dive. The camp, in defense, pointed to the one-page form Maureen Janeway signed when enrolling Katie in camp, creating amnesty from liability for "any negligent act." The Janeways objected that such a contract should be invalid, as it would release people from their ordinary negligence, and, more importantly, shelter them from the more serious "gross negligence."

History was on the Janeways' side, although contemporary attitudes enabled the camp to mount a valient defense. Historically, law hesitated to enforce contracts that prospectively released liability for torts, whether unintentional torts like negligence or intentional torts like fraud, assault, or battery. But this judicial reluctance represents a clash between two fundamental bodies of law: contracts and torts.

Freedom of contract is contract law's central value and supports enforcing party choice about what standards of obligation parties owe each other. On the other hand, promoting adherence to civil obligation – tort law's aspiration – points to resisting enforcement of amnesty clauses. Traditionally, law tended to give tort law the priority by invalidating amnesty contracts. That stance was codified in some state statutes and expounded in many judicial opinions, although judges during the twentieth century began to relax the stricture.

## Amnesty for Ordinary Negligence

In 1963, California's Supreme Court handed down a seminal case, *Tunkl v. The Regents of the University of California*.[13] It assimilated these contending principles, but in a way helpful to both sides in the dispute over Katie Janeway's death. In *Tunkl*, a patient signed a contract releasing a University of California hospital from liability for negligence. After medical treatment, the patient sued, claiming two doctors committed ordinary negligence during treatment.

The court unanimously declared the release invalid, reconciling the precedents to stand for the idea that amnesty clauses can be valid only if they do not impair the "public interest." The court identified several ways of characterizing the public interest in contract amnesty settings. In a widely quoted passage, the distinguished judge, Matthew Tobriner, wrote:

> The social forces that have led to such characterization are volatile and dynamic. No definition of the concept of public interest can be contained within the four corners of a formula. The concept, always the subject of great debate, has ranged over the whole course of the common law; rather than attempt to prescribe its nature, we can only designate the situations in which it has been applied. We can determine whether the instant contract does or does not manifest the characteristics which have been held to stamp a contract as one affected with a public interest.

With that dynamism in mind, Justice Tobriner identified a "rough outline" of transaction types where amnesty is invalid, which helped focus resolution of Katie Janeway's case. These are characterized by: settings subject to government regulation; released parties who provide something of great public importance; released parties who enjoy strong bargaining power; contracts formed using take-it-or-leave-it terms, without offering to charge different prices that corresponded with different liability risk allocations; and arrangements that put control over risk in the released party.

Under this test, followed in most states, amnesty clauses for ordinary negligence are not automatically valid or invalid. The space for freedom of contract remains vast, and people are entitled to bargain for whatever consideration and terms they wish. At stake, however, is contract law's insistence on voluntary mutual assent. The factors in this public-interest test identify those casting doubt on whether the manifested assent was indeed voluntary. The test probes whether a tool to shift risk is really something the releasing party intended. Although the public-interest test is not a bright-line rule, courts find its flexibility appealing when evaluating the validity of contracts relieving people from ordinary negligence.

The results of the cases seem roughly in line with what most people would expect and did not favor the Janeways. Invalid in most states are clauses releasing the following from liability: residential landlords, child care service providers, harbor boat berth operators, auto repair shops, banks, and public high schools sponsoring athletic teams and cheerleading squads. In contrast, amnesty clauses for ordinary negligence are valid in some states in cases involving: gyms and fitness clubs; bicycle, car, and motorcycle racing; ski resorts and equipment; skydiving and aviation; horseback riding; white-water rafting; and scuba diving. Not all states line up equally in sorting out these varied arrangements, with some endorsing what others reject and vice versa, but all struggle to balance identical principles. To that extent, the camp's position in Katie Janeway's case was strong, supporting the disclaimer of liability for negligence at a recreational summer camp.

## A Misleading Authorization

The camp's stance was fortified by the clarity of the document Mrs. Janeway signed releasing the camp from negligence liability. In an illustrative case, Jerilyn Richards wanted to ride as a passenger with her husband, Leo, a truck driver, on trips of his employer, Monkem Co.[14] As a condition to allowing her to ride, the company required Jerilyn to sign a form labeled "Passenger Authorization." The form authorized riding and also contained a broadly worded clause releasing the company from liability for virtually anything imaginable, not limited to riding in the truck. When she claimed damages against the company arising from an accident while she rode in the truck, the company pointed to that release.

The court held it invalid. The document's principal purpose and heading, authorizing passenger riding, obscured the release's substance, which concerned amnesty. True, people have a duty to read the contracts they sign, but that does not justify holding people liable to terms that are inconspicuous. That is especially so when terms are nonnegotiable, as in this case. Further, the clause's scope was essentially infinite, not limited to riding in the truck. Although none of these points alone was fatal, taken together, they warranted invalidating the clause. The release Mrs. Janeway signed was free of such defects.

But the Janeways had one more arrow in their quiver: challenging the camp's attempt to disclaim its liability for *gross* negligence. This raised the more profound issue of just how free people should be to make contracts relieving them from legal liability for their harmful actions. At the outer edge, law has long and universally held invalid a contract to immunize people from liability for criminal behavior, such as murder, drug smuggling, and tax evasion. It severely restricts contracts relieving people from liability for intentional torts. (There has long been, however, an essential qualification for consensual violent sports, including punches between prize fighters and tackles in football, and similar activity in hard-contact athletic contests, although this does not give participants carte blanche.[15])

Trickier are clauses addressing behavior between the two extremes of ordinary haplessness and intentional infliction of injury. Amid these polarities lies the hazy zone called "gross negligence" and its cousins, described in equally hazy terms like "wanton," "willful," or "reckless" behavior. Katie's family drew on a large body of literature and string of precedents showing both legal experts' and courts' long-held aversion to immunizing people from misbehavior beyond ordinary negligence. This literature and law contends that allowing such behavior would shelter aggravated misconduct from legal review and stimulate the "moral hazard" that yields such undesirable behavior.

The Santa Barbara camp, joined by six interested parties that filed their own formal papers with the court, claimed that impairing contractual freedom by invalidating the contract would be disastrous public policy. Proponents of amnesty included the stock car racing association (NASCAR), the Sierra Club, two fitness center chains (Bally and 24 Hour Fitness), a group of national sports clubs, and municipal associations. The camp and these parties interpreted the law as settled, by scores of cases, that recreational and sporting activities, including swimming at camps, were unaffected by a public interest. Therefore, the clause releasing the camp from liability for any negligent act, whether ordinary or gross, should be validated.

But the court found the camp's argument unpersuasive. The public interest balancing test cedes some territory of torts to contracts, letting people's own bargains change social rules embedded in tort law. Yet that test was developed in the narrow context of ordinary negligence and does not mean such a balancing should apply to more serious violations such as gross negligence. Furthermore, the cases refusing to enforce contracts immunizing gross negligence do not vary according to whether an arrangement is affected by a public interest or not. They depend on deciding how much deference to give contracts that change social rules.

The camp and its fellow proponents of amnesty thought public policy dictated enforcing rather than invalidating these clauses. Stressing that gross negligence is a hazy concept, they warned that providers will be exposed to unwarranted liability, real and threatened, and that providers will stop or reduce offering affected programs as a result. This hazards-of-liability argument was unpersuasive too, however, because law distinguishes between ordinary and gross negligence in many contexts. While hazy, the doctrines do not systematically propagate lawsuits or excessive liability. Courts are good at filtering out cases lacking merit.

Nor is there evidence that invalidating amnesty for aggravated conduct discourages recreational programs. Several states have long declared amnesty clauses for ordinary negligence invalid in particular settings with no reported evaporation of programs. As examples:

- Vermont makes release of liability for ordinary negligence at ski resorts invalid and remains a flourishing skiing destination.
- Connecticut voids them for horseback riding lessons and is known as horse country.
- West Virginia invalidates them for university rugby teams, but the sport remains popular there.

A New York statute invalidates release from ordinary negligence by gyms, recreational, or amusement companies, which courts interpret to encompass horseback riding, parachuting, skydiving, country club tennis, and riding mechanical bulls in bars – yet those activities thrive in New York. Protective laws may even be a draw for some customers.

What the proponents of amnesty failed to emphasize was how such clauses can also create incentives for programs and employees to be careless – the problem called moral hazard. It has long been a purpose of tort law, including the law of negligence, to encourage people to take reasonable care – a policy threatened by amnesty for serious misbehavior. The court allowed Katie Janeway's parents to proceed with their case against the camp, which was later settled on undisclosed terms.

Many people think that no one but the parties to a contract can have any rights or duties under it. Others think that any interference with another party's contracts is verboten. The reality is necessarily more subtle. After all, contracts radiate benefits to many people beside those who make them. Exchanges between buyers and manufacturers of goods help workers who make the products and consumers who eventually buy them.

A contract's value can increase when one party transfers it to another for a premium, as when an entrepreneur sells a business along with all its contracts. That value can attract interest of other strangers, sometimes leading them to interfere in the deal. Contracts can also radiate negative effects too, including by relaxing the standards of behavior people in society otherwise live with.

These radiating benefits, and the possibility of negative effects, mean third parties sometimes have stakes in a contract to which they are strangers, and contract law takes a middle ground in balancing resulting tensions. On one hand, freedom of contract and freedom from contract usually mean that only parties to the contract can participate in its performance and enforcement. On the other hand, people sometimes intend to let third parties perform and enforce contracts, and contract law accommodates that. Freedom of contract is promoted by limiting the rights of third parties to obtain assignment of contracts or to interfere with contracts others have formed, even though that limits a contract party's flexibility to deal with others.

Regarding the standards of behavior society expects of all citizens, contract law likewise accommodates a middle ground. It generally recognizes private bargains to eliminate responsibility for ordinary negligence. But it more jealously guards law's prerogative to police against more serious lapses such as gross negligence. That raises profound issues concerning the relationship between contract law and tort law – issues that are beyond this book's scope.

# CONCLUSION

Take the following quiz to compare common beliefs about contracts with the reality. Consider whether the statements are true or false.

1. Promises to make gifts are legally enforceable.
2. Advertisements create offers that can be accepted to make a binding contract.
3. Clicking "yes" on a terms-of-use icon does not create a binding contract.
4. An airline ticket's confidentiality clause prevents the airline from sharing personal data.
5. Employees can only be fired for "cause."
6. Contracts must be fair to be legally valid.
7. A celebrity's payment to a gadfly to hush up about a private affair creates a valid contract.
8. Gambling contracts are invalid.
9. Promises must be kept, come hell or high water.
10. Caveat emptor ("let the buyer beware") rules.
11. Children are responsible for their contracts just as adults are.
12. When someone breaches a contract, courts most often order them to perform it.
13. When courts award money for a breach of contract, the amount includes all losses the breaching party caused.
14. Courts punish people who breach contracts by requiring them to pay punitive damages.
15. If a contract says what money should be paid upon breach, courts award that amount.
16. Good Samaritans are legally entitled to compensation for the benefits they confer on others.
17. To be valid, a contract must be in writing and signed or notarized.

18. Contracts cannot be changed once they are made.
19. Promises must be performed to a tee so that shortcomings forfeit all rights to any promise the other side made.
20. No one but the parties to a contract can have any rights or duties under it.

If you chose true for any of these, you are most likely reading this conclusion before reading the book. All the statements are false, and this book has explored why.

The correct answers are the product of centuries of ongoing refinements that give contract law unmatched pedigree, with an amazing constancy in which classic cases from scores or hundreds of years ago remain pivotal to resolving disputes today. Modern contract law – from the founding of the United States until today – has never been extreme but tended always towards a sensible, practical center. Yes, there was, in the nineteenth century, a greater emphasis on writings, bargains, and pure freedom of contract and during the twentieth century a conscious appreciation of the limits of language, the possibility of defects in bargains and the appeal of the notion of freedom from contract. But although these hypothetical extremes could be stated, actual contract law did not appear extreme. The cases, as contrasted with some theories and many prescriptions, were consistent with the wealth of ancient precedents drawn on in this book's modern stories.[1] Contract law has eschewed the fringes.

Visionaries remain enamored of a world of pure freedom of contract on the (political) right hand or a world of pure social justice on the left hand. But the actual practice of contract law is neither such world. Rather, contracts in the real world reflect broader and longer-standing truisms of democratic capitalist society, where endless balancing of contending values occurs. Freedom of contract remains vital, but is not unlimited; written instruments carry considerable but not absolute weight; bargain remains the essence of contract, but there are other ways to make a binding commitment, and not all bargains are lawful.

Although contract law is dynamic, today's contract law concepts are so basic and finite that there is little in it that only lawyers find accessible. Everyone can understand the law of contracts from stories that happen every day. That is important because contract law is repeatedly put to new tests each generation. Contract law's powerful old tools adapt admirably, if imperfectly, across centuries and settings to resolve innumerable disputes concerning rights and duties arising from promissory exchange. Endlessly elastic, contract law rises to meet challenges from what seem like new problems using time-tested principles of consideration, bargain, assent, and compensation for breach. Today's challenges may warrant different responses, but each invites a clear role for applying ancient contract law principles to novel settings. Lighting the way are the even more numerous examples in this book showing how those venerable tools remain vibrant despite enormous economic, social, and technological change. All the examples reveal the beauty of contract law and how appeals to drive it hard to the left or the right would, in effect, threaten to derail its sensible center.

# NOTES

## Introduction

1. *Facto v. Pantagis*, 915 A.2d 59 (N.J. Super. 2007).
2. *E.g.*, David Segal, What They Don't Teach Law Students: Lawyering, *N.Y. Times* (Nov. 19, 2011) (criticizing the continued teaching of *Hadley v. Baxendale*, an ancient case noted in Section A of Chapter 4).
3. David A. Hoffman & Tess Wilkensen-Ryan, Breach Is for Suckers, *Vanderbilt Law Review* 63 (2010): 1003.
4. Cynthia Estlund, How Wrong Are Employees about Their Rights, and Why Does It Matter?, *New York University Law Review* 77 (2002): 6; Pauline T. Kim, Bargaining with Imperfect Information: A Study of Worker Perceptions of Legal Protection in an At-Will World, *Cornell Law Review* 83 (1997): 105.
5. Seana Valentine Shiffrin, The Divergence of Contract and Promise, *Harvard Law Review* 120 (2007): 708; Seana Valentine Shiffrin, Could Breach of Contract Be Immoral?, *Michigan Law Review* 107 (2009): 1551; Daniel D. Barnhizer, Context as Power: Defining the Field of Battle for Advantage in Contractual Interactions, *Wake Forest Law Review* 45 (2010): 607.
6. Alan Schwartz & Robert E. Scott, Contract Theory and the Limits of Contract Law, *Yale Law Journal* 113 (2003): 541; Robert E. Scott, Rethinking the Default Rule Project, *Virginia Journal* 6 (2003): 84; Joshua Fairfield, The Cost of Consent: Optimal Standardization in the Law of Contract, *Emory Law Journal* 58 (2009): 1401.
7. C. C. Langdell, *A Selection of Cases on the Law of Contracts* (Boston: Little, Brown & Co., 1879).
8. Today's American law of contracts generally remains common law in the sense that it is the product of judicial decisions resolving disputes one by one, as distinguished from statutory law passed by legislatures. Within contract law, however, special bodies of statutory law may apply to particular transaction types. The most pervasive example concerns transactions in goods,

governed by the Uniform Commercial Code (UCC). Given the particular setting and needs of merchants and others dealing in goods, the UCC sometimes sets out principles or rules that differ from the common law of contracts. As with the common law, however, the UCC takes a highly practical approach.

9. Stare decisis reflects the idea that "what has been already decided should remain settled." *See* Orin Kerr, How to Read a Legal Opinion, *The Green Bag 2d* 11 (2007): 52.

10. That does not always stop people from suing for breached dinner dates. *See* Les Ledbetter, Jilted California Accountant Sues His Date for $38 in Expenses, *N.Y. Times* (July 26, 1978).

11. For an amusingly absurd variation on this point that gained national attention, see *Pearson v. Chung*, 961 A.2d 1067 (D.C. 2008). A dry cleaner shop allegedly lost a customer's pants and otherwise failed to honor a posted sign guaranteeing customer satisfaction, for which the customer sought millions in damages – and was properly laughed out of court.

12. Section A of Chapter 5 illustrates, giving the case of *Cotnam v. Wisdom*, 104 S.W. 164 (Ark. 1907).

13. *See* John Mueller, *Capitalism, Democracy and Ralph's Pretty Good Grocery* (Princeton, NJ: Princeton University Press 1999).

14. Nathan Isaacs, The Standardizing of Contracts, *Yale Law Journal* 27 (1917): 665.

15. Contemporary successors to these treatises are Professor Richard A. Lord of Campbell University on the Williston treatise and Professor Joseph M. Perrillo of Fordham University on the Corbin treatise. From 1994 to 2001, I served as an editor of Corbin's treatise.

16. *Allegheny College v. National Chautauqua County Bank*, 156 N.E. 173 (N.Y. 1927) (Cardozo, C.J.); *see* Alfred S. Konefsky, How to Read, or at Least Not Misread, Cardozo in the Allegheny College Case, *Buffalo Law Review* 36 (1987): 645.

17. The concept of "estoppel" is a general tool in Anglo-American law, the word having roots in the old French word, *estopper*, meaning "to stop" or "to bar." The term "promissory estoppel" is relatively young, apparently minted by Samuel Williston in about 1920. *See* Benjamin Boyer, Promissory Estoppel: Requirements and Limitations of the Doctrine, *U. Pennsylvania Law Review* 98 (1950): 459.

18. *See* Lon L. Fuller & William R. Perdue, Jr., The Reliance Interest in Contract Damages, *Yale Law Journal* 46 (1936): 52.

19. *Mitchill v. Lath*, 160 N.E.2d 646 (N.Y. 1928).

20. It is common for commentators to misspell the plaintiff's name in the case; it is Mitchill, not Mitchell.

21. Charles Fried, *Contract as Promise* (Cambridge, MA: Harvard University Press, 1982).

22. Randy E. Barnett, A Consent Theory of Contract, *Columbia Law Review* 86 (1986): 269.

23. *See* Melvin A. Eisenberg, The Bargain Principle and Its Limits, *Harvard Law Review* 95 (1982): 741.

24. *See* Anthony T. Kronman & Richard A. Posner, *The Economics of Contract Law* (Boston, MA: Little Brown & Co. 1979); Eric A. Posner, Economic Analysis of Contract Law after Three Decades: Success or Failure?, *Yale Law Journal* 112 (2003): 829.

25. *See* Nate B. Oman, A Pragmatic Defense of Contract Law, *Georgetown Law Journal* 98 (2009): 77.

26. Grant Gilmore, *The Death of Contract* (New Haven, CT: Yale University Press, 1970).

27. *See* Stewart Macaulay, An Empirical View of Contract, *Wisconsin Law Review* (1985): 465.

28. Lawrence Friedman, *Contract Law in America: A Social and Economic Case Study* (Palo Alto, CA: Stanford University Press 1965).

## 1. Getting In: Contract Formation

1. *See* Brenda Goodman, King Papers, Back in Atlanta, Will Be Placed on Display, *N.Y. Times* (October 10, 2006).

2. *King v. Boston University*, 647 N.E.2d 1196 (Mass. 1995). This discussion is based on both the court's opinion in the case and the briefs filed by the parties.

3. Charles Fried, *Contract as Promise* (Cambridge, MA: Harvard University Press, 1982).

4. During the Middle Ages, the seal was a particularly valiant device, made using heated wax impressed with a mark, like a signet ring, a finger, or a bite of tooth. If affixed to a document that was also signed and delivered to another party, the seal signified the formation of an enforceable contract (New York Law Revision Commission Report [1941]). However, many ordinary people lacked resources to use these devices. European law seized on the device of a notary to determine the legality of a bargain. Although no general principle of contract law requires this in the United States or England, special statutes require certain kinds of documents to be notarized to be legally effective.

5. Lon Fuller, Consideration and Form, *Columbia Law Review* 41 (1941): 799.

6. Restatement (Second) of Contracts, Sections 90(1) & 90(2) (1982).

7. *Congregation Kadimah Toras-Moshe v. DeLeo*, 540 N.E.2d 691 (Mass. 1989).

8. One of the rare cases enforcing a charitable pledge without regard to consideration or reliance is *Salsbury v. Northwestern Bell Telephone Co.*, 221 N.W.2d 609 (Iowa 1974).

9. *Elvin Associates v. Franklin*, 735 F.Supp. 1177 (S.D.N.Y. 1990).

10. *Leonard v. Pepsico, Inc.*, 88 F.Supp.2d 116, *aff'd*, 210 F.3d 88 (2nd Cir. 2000). This discussion is based on both the court's opinion in the case and the briefs filed by the parties.

11. *Lefkowitz v. Great Minneapolis Surplus Store*, 86 N.W.2d 689 (Minn. 1957).

12. *Mesaros v. United States*, 845 F.2d 1576 (Fed. Cir. 1988).

13. *National Bank v. Louisville Trust Co.*, 67 F.2d 7, 102–103 (6th Cir. 1933), *cert. denied*, 291 U.S. 665 (1934).

14. *Keller v. Holderrman*, 11 Mich. 248 (1863).

15. *Lucy v. Zehmer*, 84 S.E.2d 516 (Va. 1954).

16. For examples and analysis, see *Pizza Hut, Inc. v. Papa John's Intern., Inc.*, 227 F. 3d 489 (5th Cir. 2000) and *Castrol Inc. v. Pennzoil Co.*, 987 F. 2d 939, 946 (3d Cir. 1993). For more on the subject of puffery, see David A. Hoffman, The Best Puffery Article Ever, *Iowa Law Review* 91 (2006): 1395.

17. *Leonard v. Pepsico, Inc.*, 88 F.Supp.2d 116, *aff'd*, 210 F.3d 88 (2nd Cir. 2000). For more on this topic, see Keith A. Rowley, You Asked for It, You Got It … Toy Yoda: Practical Jokes, Prizes and Contract Law, *Nevada Law Journal* 3 (2003): 526; Jay M. Friedman & Stephen R. Brill, Is an Advertisement an Offer? Why It Is, and Why It Matters, *Hastings Law Journal* 58 (2006): 61.

18. This discussion is based on the complaint and other filings of the parties in the case of *Kolodziej v. Mason*, Civil Action No. 1:10-CV-2012-JEC (N. D. Ga. 2010). On May 20, 2011, the Georgia federal court, while accepting that it had the power to hear the case, transferred it to the Florida federal court in the interests of convenience.

19. *Carlill v. Carbolic Smoke Ball Co.*, 1 Q.B. 256 (Court of Appeal, England 1893).

20. A. W. Brian Simpson, Quackery and Contract Law: The Case of the Carbolic Smoke Ad, *Journal of Legal Studies* 14 (1985): 345.

21. *Newman v. Schiff*, 778 F.2d 460 (8th Cir. 1985).

22. *Barnes v. Treece*, 549 P.2d 1152 (Wash. 1976).

23. *James v. Turilli*, 473 S.W.2d 757 (Mo. App. 1971).

24. *Cobaugh v. Klick-Lewis, Inc.*, 561 A.2d 1248 (Pa. Super. 1989).

25. Bill Torpy, Law Student Moves Fast for $1 Million, *Atlanta-Journal Constitution* (July 11, 2010).

26. Electronic Communications Privacy Act, 18 U.S.C. §§ 2510 et seq. and Computer Fraud and Abuse Act, 18 U.S.C. § 1030.

27. *Specht v. Netscape Communications, Corp.*, 306 F.2d 17 (2nd Cir. 2002) (Sotomayor, J.). This discussion is based on both the court's opinion in the case and the briefs filed by the parties.

28. *Raffles v. Wichelhaus*, 2 Hurl. & C. 906, 159 Eng. Rep. 375 (English Court of Exchequer 1864).

29. A. W. Brian Simpson, Contracts for Cotton to Arrive, *Cardozo Law Review* 11 (1989): 287.

30. *Kabil Development Corp. v. Mignot*, 566 P.2d 505 (Oregon 1977); *see Hotchkiss v. National City Bank*, 200 F. 287 (S.D.N.Y. 1911).

31. *ProCD v. Zeidenberg*, 86 F.3d 1447 (7th Cir. 1996) (Easterbrook, J.); *see* Eric A. Posner, ProCD v. Zeidenberg and Cognitive Overload in Contractual Bargaining, *U. Chicago Law Review* 77 (2010): 1181. The same court adopted similar reasoning in *Hill v. Gateway 2000 Inc.*, 105 F.3d 1147 (7th Cir. 1997). A lower court in a different federal circuit challenged the reasoning to reach the opposite result; *Kloceck v. Gateway 2000 Inc.*, 104 F. Supp. 2d 1332 (D. Kan. 2000).

32. For more on this topic, including practical recommendations for handling such contracts, see Stephen E. Friedman, Improving the Rolling Contract, *American U. Law Review* 56 (2006): 1.

33. Richard Pérez-Peña, News Sites Rethink Anonymous Online Comments, *N.Y. Times* (April 11, 2010).

34. *See* Richard A. Epstein, In Defense of the Contract at Will, *U. Chicago Law Review* 51 (1984): 947.

35. *McDonald v. Mobil Coal Producing Inc.*, 820 P.2d 986 (Wyo. 1991).

36. *See Pine River State Bank v. Mettille*, 333 N.W.2d 622 (Minn. 1983).

37. Woodrow Hartzog, Promises and Privacy: Promissory Estoppel and Confidential Disclosure in Online Communities, *Temple Law Review* 82 (2010): 891; Allyson W. Haynes, Online Privacy Policies: Contracting Away Control Over Personal Information? *Penn State Law Review* 111 (2007): 587.

38. *Smith v. Trusted Universal Standards in Electronics Transactions Inc.*, 2010 WL 1799456 (D. N.J. 2010); *Cherny v. Emigrant Bank*, 604 F.Supp.2d 605 (S.D.N.Y. 2009); *In re Jetblue Airways Corp. Privacy Litig.*, 379 F.Supp.2d 299, 325 (E.D.N.Y. 2005).

39. *Meyer v. Christie*, No. 07–2230, 2007 WL 3120695 (D. Kan. 2007).

40. *Johnson v. National Beef Packing Co.*, 551 P.2d 779 (Kan. 1976).

41. *Dyer v. Northwest Airlines Corp.*, 334 F.Supp.2d 1196 (D. N.D. 2004).

## 2.  Facing Limits: Unenforceable Bargains

1. *Waters v. Min Ltd.*, 587 N.E.2d 231 (Mass. 1992).

2. *Sturlyn v. Albany* (1587) Cro Eliz 67 ("when a thing is to be done by [a contract party], be it never so small, this is sufficient consideration to ground an action").

3. *Mandel v. Liebman*, 100 N.E.2d 149 (N.Y. 1951); *see Weiner v. McGraw-Hill, Inc.*, 443 N.E.2d 441 (N.Y. 1982) ("courts have not hesitated to find consideration not only in what is now the proverbial peppercorn … but in 'a horse or a canary or a tomtit'").

4. *Embola v. Tuppela*, 220 P. 789 (Wash. 1923).

5. *Batsakis v. Demotsis*, 226 S.W.2d 673 (Tex. App. 1949).

6. Mark Mazzower, *Inside Hitler's Greece: The Experience of Occupation 1941–44* (New Haven, CT: Yale University Press, 1993).

7. *Batsakis*, cited above.
8. *Wilton v. Eaton*, 127 Mass. 174 (Mass. 1879); *Judy v. Louderman*, 29 N.E. 181 (Ohio 1891).
9. *Fischer v. Union Trust*, 101 N.W. 852 (Mich. 1904).
10. A final famous case illuminating this terrain is *Schnell v. Nell*, 17 Ind. 29 (Ind. 1861). Zacharias Schnell, a widower, wrote, signed, and sealed an agreement to give effect to his late wife Theresa's will. She intended to bequeath money to their children, but her will failed to do this, all property passing to the husband. The agreement promised $200 to each of three kids (at least $5,000 in today's money), saying this was in consideration of love and respect for his wife and that he had received 1 cent consideration from the children. After the husband failed to pay, they sued to enforce their contract. The claim failed. True, the general rule is that courts do not inquire into the adequacy of consideration. But there is an exception when exchange is for unequal sums of money. The court found the bargain of $600 in exchange for 1 cent to be an "unconscionable" contract and void. What motivated it was love and affection, impulses of morality. That is not enough to make a promise legally binding. And everyone can objectively compare 1 cent with $600.
11. This discussion is based on the opinions in *Jordan v. Knafel*, 823 N.E.2d 1113 (Ill. App. 2005) (reversing holding that the contract was extortionate and therefore unenforceable); and *Jordan v. Knafel*, 880 N.E.2d 1061 (Ill. App. 2007) (affirming holding that the contract was unenforceable because of both fraudulent inducement and mutual mistake).
12. Bill Carter & Brian Stelter, Letterman Extortion Raises Questions for CBS, *N.Y. Times* (Oct. 2, 2009).
13. Federal statutes declare it illegal to threaten to harm a person's reputation unless money is paid. 18 U.S.C. §§ 875(d). The law does not stop people from trying, as Bill Cosby can also tell you. In January 1997, a twenty-two-year-old woman named Autumn Jackson claimed Cosby was her father and eventually demanded that he pay her $40 million in exchange for not making this claim public. She was arrested, prosecuted, convicted, and landed in jail on federal criminal charges of threatening reputation harm unless money is paid. *See United States v. Jackson*, 180 F.3d 55 (2d Cir. 1999).
14. Another comparable case is *In re Yao*, 661 N.Y.S.2d 199 (1997).
15. *See* Juliet P. Kostritsky, Illegal Contracts and Efficient Deterrence: A Study in Modern Contract Theory, *Iowa Law Review* 74 (1988): 115.
16. *Fiege v. Boehm*, 123 A.2d 316 (Md. App. 1956).
17. *Harte v. Stahl*, 27 Md. 157 (Md. App. 1867).
18. *Duncan v. Black*, 324 S.W.2d 483 (Mo. App. 1959). This case involved a farm sale when federal law regulated cotton by authorizing production on specific acreage and banning production elsewhere. In a sale of several hundred acres, the seller promised the buyer a "65 acre cotton allotment." When

authorities allotted that farm only 50 acres the following year, the seller let the buyer use another 15 he kept. The buyer asked the seller to make up the shortfall in the next year's allotment too, but the seller refused. After the buyer threatened suit, the seller settled by promising payment of money. The buyer later sued to enforce that promise, but the court found that it lacked consideration. Giving up a right to sue when federal law barred the basis for the claim did not "make a mountain out of a molehill" – the ban covering the acreage meant there was no "molehill" of a dispute to settle.

19. For more on this topic and the Knafel-Jordan case, see Michelle Oberman, Sex, Lies, and the Duty to Disclose, *Arizona Law Review* 47 (2005): 871.

20. *Tompkins v. Jackson*, 2009 WL 513858 (N.Y. Sup. Ct. Feb. 3, 2009, Civil Action No. 104745/2008).

21. *Id.*

22. Section A of Chapter 6 tells a story concerning the rap artist Eminem, whose real name is Marshal Mathers.

23. *Marvin v. Marvin*, 18 Cal. 3d 660 (Cal. 1966).

24. *Marone v. Marone*, 413 N.E.2d 1154 (N.Y. 1980).

25. For more on this topic, see Henry G. Prince, Public Policy Limitations in Cohabitation Agreements: Unruly Horse or Circus Pony? *Minnesota Law Review* 70 (1985): 163.

26. What once was considered immoral and prohibited by statute is often viewed differently generations later. Through the twentieth century, statutes made adultery criminal. Promises surrounding those affairs were not legally binding either. But those statutes have either been repealed or fallen into disuse, presenting challenges to judges when asked to enforce related bargains. Courts could overtly declare that the bargains are valid, but many judges remain squeamish about the subject. That sometimes leads them to avoid declaring an arrangement illegal and instead to find it unenforceable on more traditional contract law grounds. For two examples of courts using consideration doctrine to deny enforcement to such contracts, see *In re Greene*, 45 F.2d 428 (S.D.N.Y. 1930) and *Whitten v. Greeley-Shaw*, 520 A.2d 1307 (Maine 1987).

27. Note, Judicial Enforcement of Agreements to Share Winning Lottery Tickets, *Duke Law Journal* 44 (1995): 1000.

28. *Sokaitis v. Bakaysa*, 975 A.2d 51 (Conn. 2009).

29. *Sokaitis v. Bakaysa*, 2010 WL 2383902, 49 Connecticut Law Reporter 812 (Conn. Super. May 11, 2010).

30. Terry's letter is modified to correct a few grammatical and spelling mistakes.

31. *Matter of Baby M*, 537 A.2d 1227 (N.J. 1988); *see* Carol Sanger, (Baby) M is for Many Things: Why I Start with Baby M, *St. Louis University Law Journal* 44 (2000): 1443.

32. *Johnson v. Calvert*, 851 P.2d 776 (Cal.), *cert denied*, 510 U.S. 874 (1993).

33. *USA Today*, Lives of Indelible Impact (May 29, 2007), *www.usatoday.com/news/top25-people.htm*. The newspaper noted that Melissa Stern was then a junior at The George Washington University, where I teach.

## 3. Getting Out: Excuses and Termination

1. Diana B. Henriques & Al Baker, A Madoff Son Hangs Himself on Father's Arrest Anniversary, *N.Y. Times* (Dec. 11, 2010).
2. *Simkin v. Blank*, 80 A.D. 3d 401, 915 N.Y.S.2d 47 (N.Y. App. Div. 2011), *appeal pending*, N.Y. County Clerk's Index No. 101501/09 (N.Y. 2012). This discussion is based primarily on the briefs of the parties, as well as the opinion of the court. For a journalistic account of the case, see Peter Lattman, Madoff Victim Seeks Divorce Do-Over, *N.Y. Times* (May 30, 2011).
3. When only one party to a contract is mistaken, excuse is rarely recognized – only if the mistake concerns a matter objectively determinable, such as a mathematical calculation or scientific operation, and then subject to the other party's detrimental reliance. For examples, see *Elsinore Union Elementary School District v. Kastorff*, 353 P.2d 713 (Cal. 1960); *S.T.S. Transport Services v. Volvo White Truck Corp.*, 766 F.2d 1089 (7th Cir. 1985).
4. *Beachcomber Coins, Inc. v. Boskett*, 400 A.2d 78 (N.J. 1979). For an older analogous case, see *Wood v. Boynton*, 25 N.W. 42 (Wis. 1885).
5. *Sherwood v. Walker*, 33 N.W. 919 (Michigan 1887); *see* Robert L. Birmingham, A Rose by Any Other Word: Mutual Mistake in Sherwood v. Walker, *U.C. Davis Law Review* 21 (1987): 197.
6. *Smith v. Zimbalist*, 38 P.2d 170 (Cal. App. 1934).
7. A related famous case announces that neither buyers nor sellers have special disclosure duties in arm's-length commercial dealings. Parties signed a contract to trade commercial tobacco for cash during the War of 1812 when naval blockades barred the crop's export and the price was accordingly depressed. The buyer knew that a peace treaty had been signed that would end the blockade and raise the price but did not disclose that to the seller. The U.S. Supreme Court agreed with the buyer, Hector Organ, that he had no duty to inform the seller of such public information. *Laidlaw v. Organ*, 15 U.S. 178 (1817). Mr. Organ was represented in the case by Francis Scott Key, whose "Star Spangled Banner" was inspired by events during that war. Ian Ayres & Richard E. Speidel, *Studies in Contract Law* (New York: Foundation Press 7th ed. 2008): 525.
8. For more on this topic, see E. Allan Farnsworth, *Alleviating Mistake: Reversal and Forgiveness for Flawed Perceptions* (New York: Oxford University Press 2004); Keith A. Rowley, To Err is Human, *Michigan Law Review* 104 (2006): 1407 (reviewing Farnsworth, *Alleviating Mistake*); James A. Gordley, Mistake in Contract Formation, *American Journal of Comparative Law* 52 (2004): 433; Lon L. Fuller, Mistake and Error in the Law of Contracts, *Emory Law Review* 33 (1984): 41.

9. The briefs of both parties in the appeal cited my analysis of the case as posted on the blog, Concurring Opinions.

10. *Trump v. Deutsche Bank*, Index No. 403012/09 (Supreme Court of the State of New York).

11. This is akin to the case of *Facto v. Pantagis*, 915 A.2d 59 (N.J. Super. 2007), mentioned in the Introduction.

12. *Taylor v. Caldwell*, 3 B. & S. 826, 122 Eng. Rep. 309 (King's Bench, England, 1863); *see* Robert L. Birmingham, Why Is There Taylor v. Caldwell? Three Propositions About Impracticability, *U. San Francisco Law Review* 23 (1989): 379.

13. *Krell v. Henry*, [1903] 2 K.B. 740 (Court of Appeal, England, 1903). This case involved cancellation of a coronation parade for King Edward VII because of his illness; an American parallel occurred when the inauguration parade for President Ronald Reagan was canceled because of inclement weather. Francis X. Clines, Reagan Sworn for 2d Term; Inaugural Parade Dropped as Bitter Cold Hits Capital, *N.Y. Times* (Jan. 21, 1985).

14. *Lloyd v. Murphy*, 153 P.2d 47 (Cal. 1944) (Traynor, J.).

15. *American Trading and Production Co. v. Shell International Marine, Ltd.*, 453 F.2d 939 (2d Cir. 1972).

16. *See* Malcolm Sharp, Pacta Sunt Servanda, *Columbia Law Review* 41 (1941): 783.

17. *Paradine v. Jane*, Aleyn 26, 82 Eng. Rep. 897 (King's Bench, England, 1647).

18. An American case appeared during the American Revolution, when the Pennsylvania Supreme Court followed the ancient case of *Paradine v. Jane* by holding a tenant obliged to pay rent even though the premises were occupied by the British Army. *Pollard v. Sha*affer, 1 U.S. (1 Dall.) 210 (Pa. 1787).

19. *Kel-Kim Corp. v. Central Markets, Inc.*, 519 N.E.2d 295 (N.Y. 1987).

20. Floyd Norris, Trump Sees Act of God in Recession, *N.Y. Times* (Dec. 5, 2008).

21. *Berg v. Traylor*, 148 Cal. App. 4th 809 (Cal. App. 2 Dist. 2007).

22. *See Ortelere v. Teachers' Retirement Board*, 250 N.E.2d 460 (N.Y. 1969).

23. *Halbman v. Lemke*, 298 N.W.2d 562 (Wis. 1980); *Kiefer v. Fred Howe Motors, Inc.*, 158 N.W.2d 288 (Wis. 1968).

24. Contracts made by minors and the mentally impaired were once held invalid rather than, following the modern approach, making them voidable at the election of the minor or mentally impaired person.

25. *Sharon v. City of Newton*, 769 N.E.2d 738 (Mass. 2002).

26. *Webster Street Partnership v. Sheridan*, 368 N.W.2d 439 (Neb. 1985).

27. For more on this topic, see Alexander M. Meiklejohn, Contractual and Donative Capacity, *Case Western Reserve Law Review* 39 (1988–1989): 307.

28. Other statutes in various states likewise dissolve the infancy doctrine for particular contract types, ranging from enlistment in the military to borrowing funds for college. *See generally* Thomas A. Jacobs, *Children and the Law: Rights and Obligations* (St. Paul, MN: West Group 2007).

29. Helene Cooper, Obama Orders Treasury Chief to Try to Block AIG Bonuses, *N.Y. Times* (March 16, 2009).

30. I wrote an op-ed trying to help lower the temperature. Lawrence A. Cunningham, A.I.G.'s Bonus Blackmail, *N.Y. Times* (March 18, 2009).

31. AIGFP Employee Retention Plan.

32. Many AIG contracts, ensuring against default on other people's debts, required AIG to post increasing amounts of collateral with trading partners when the value of those debts fell or AIG's credit quality was downgraded. Those provisions proved to be the company's ultimate downfall. *See Financial Crisis Inquiry Commission, The Financial Crisis Inquiry Report* (New York: Public Affairs 2011), pp. 201, 243.

33. Emergency Economic Stabilization Act (2008), Section 11, amended by American Recovery & Reinvestment Act (2009); TARP Standards for Compensation and Corporate Governance, 31 C.F.R. § 30.1 et seq.

34. Brady Dennis, AIG Plans to Pay $100 Million in Another Round of Bonuses, *Wash. Post* (Feb. 3, 2010).

35. Mary Williams Walsh, A.I.G. May Cut Bonuses by About 30%, *N.Y. Times* (March 14, 2010).

36. For more on this topic, see Richard E. Speidel, *Contracts in Crises: Excuse Doctrine and Retrospective Government Acts* (Durham, NC: Carolina Academic Press, 2007).

37. David Enrich, Citi Explores Breaking Mets Deal, *Wall Street Journal* (Feb. 3, 2009).

38. Jim Baumbach, King Says Citi's Deal Good Business, *Newsday* (Feb. 10, 2009).

39. Richard Sandomir, Citigroup Puts Its Money Where Its Name Will Be, *N.Y. Times* (July 20, 2008).

40. Dennis R. Howard & John L. Crompton, *Financing Sport* (Fitness Information Technology, 2nd ed. 2004).

41. Marc Edelman, A Primer on Property-Rights Theory in Professional Sports, *Fordham Intellectual Property, Media and Entertainment Law Journal* 18 (2008): 891.

42. Geoff Edgers, $10 Million Donor to MFA Drops His Anonymity, *Boston Globe* (Sept. 19, 2006).

43. Jennifer Medina, Los Angeles Schools, Facing Budget Cuts, Decide to Seek Corporate Sponsors, *N.Y. Times* (Dec. 16, 2010).

44. This admission came in e-mail correspondence to me.

45. Daniel Auerbach, Morals Clauses as Corporate Protection in Athlete Endorsement Contracts, *DePaul Journal of Sports Law and Contemporary Problems* 3 (2005): 1.

46. Rich Calder, Bank: We Won't Bail Out on Nets Arena, *N.Y. Post* (Nov. 14, 2008).

## 4. Paying Up: Remedies

1. *Goldberg v. Paris Hilton Entertainment*, 2009 WL 2525482 (S.D. Fla. Aug. 17, 2009).

2. *Western Pub. Co., Inc. v. MindGames, Inc.*, 944 F.Supp. 754 (E.D. Wis. 1996), *aff'd*, 218 F.3d 652 (7th Cir. 2000).

3. *Redgrave v. Boston Symphony Orchestra*, 855 F.2d 888 (1st Cir. 1988).

4. Section C of Chapter 3 discusses forces majeure.

5. The classic 1854 English case of *Hadley v. Baxendale* stated this now-canonical limitation on contract damages. A miller sued a carrier for lost profits incurred when its mill closed as a result of the carrier's delay in shipping a part essential to its operation. The evidence suggested clerks of the miller and carrier may have discussed some aspects of the mill's operations and need for swift shipment and return, but not necessarily that the mill would be stopped without it or lost profits would result. The court announced two rules regarding remedies for breach of contract: (1) damages include those that arise naturally, in the usual course of things, from breach; and (2) damage beyond those must have been in the contemplation of the parties, at the time they made the contract, as the probable result of breach. For the latter, "consequential damages," circumstances must be communicated to the party who later breaches, in order for it to liable. After all, a contract price includes, in effect, an insurance premium for the cost of breach: damages payable. The promise maker needs a way to gauge probable damages, especially information that distinguishes between ordinary circumstances flowing from a breach and special circumstances needed to adjust the usual price. Contract law's limitation on consequential damages induces "special" people to reveal information about their special needs at the time of making a contract.

6. *Chicago Coliseum Club v. Dempsey*, 265 Ill.App. 542, 1932 WL 2782 (Ill. App. 1st Dist. 1932).

7. *Anglia Television Ltd. v. Reed*, 1 Queen's Bench 60 (1972).

8. For more on this topic, see Mitchell L. Engler & Susan B. Heyman, Rethinking Contract Damages, *Temple Law Review* 83 (2011) 119.

9. Chapter 5 is devoted to restitution and an additional example appears in Section D of Chapter 6 (the case of the fraudulent architect and Turkish bath, *Vickery v. Richie*).

10. *Hairtech v. Hilton* (complaint filed August 2010). As a tort, remedying a fraud can mean an award of damages, including punitive amounts, or provide a basis for excusing a contract, as noted in discussions elsewhere in this book, such as those involving the case of Michael Jordan's paternity (in Section B of Chapter 2) and AIG's bonuses (in Section D of Chapter 3).

11. For more on this topic, see Ian Ayres & Gregory Klass, *Insincere Promises* (New Haven, CT: Yale University Press 2005).

12. To paraphrase a famous line uttered by Tom Hanks's character in the 1992 film, "A League of Their Own": "There's no crying in contracts."

13. *Hawkins v. McGee*, 146 A. 641 (N.H. 1929); *see* Jorie Roberts, Hawkins Case: A Hair-Raising Experience, *Harvard Law Record* 66 (No. 6 1978): 1.

14. *Apple Records, Inc. v. Capitol Records, Inc.*, 529 N.Y.S.2d 279 (N.Y. 1st Dept. 1988).

15. *See* Paris Brushes Off Hair Suit, *N.Y. Post* (March 9, 2011). For more on the question of tort-like remedies for contract breaches, see Timothy J. Sullivan, Punitive Damages in the Law of Contract: The Reality and the Illusion of Legal Change, *Minnesota Law Review* 61 (1977): 207; Douglas J. Whaley, Paying for the Agony: The Recovery of Emotional Distress Damages in Contract Actions, *Suffolk U. Law Review* 26 (1992): 935.

16. James V. Grimaldi, Redskins Take Hard Line on Seating Contracts, *Washington Post* (Sept. 3, 2009).

17. *Rockingham County v. Luten Bridge Co.*, 35 F.2d 301 (4th Cir. 1929).

18. To make this vivid, think of the relationship as *Contract Price* equals *Costs* plus *Profit*, and abbreviate those words in a formula: $CP = C + P$. When distinguishing between avoidable/variable costs (AVC) and fixed/overhead costs (FOC), modify it as: $CP = AVC + FOC + P$. Subtracting avoidable/variable costs from the contract price results in $CP - AVC = FOC + P$.

19. *Neri v. Retail Marine Corp.*, 285 N.E.2d 311 (N.Y. 1972); *see* Mark Pettit, Jr., Exercising with Neri v. Retail Marine Corp., *St. Louis University Law Journal* 44 (2000): 1487.

20. *In re Worldcom, Inc.*, 361 Bankr. Rep. 675 (S.D.N.Y. 2007). For more on the subject of the lost-volume seller, see Daniel W. Matthews, Should the Doctrine of Lost Volume Seller Be Maintained? A Response to Professor Breen, *U. Miami Law Review* 51 (1997): 1195; Victor Goldberg, An Economic Analysis of the Lost-Volume Retail Seller, *S. California Law Review* 57 (1984): 283.

21. *Parker v. Twentieth Century Fox*, 474 P.2d 689 (Cal. 1970). Another way to view the studio's contract was a version of a pay-or-play clause. The studio agreed to pay $750,000 for the right to use MacLaine for the "Bloomer Girl" film and to pay that amount whether it did or not. It was an option and the payment its price. From that viewpoint, the actress was entitled to the money without regard to any other factor, including anything about any alternative movie. In that view, mitigation was not an issue. *See* Victor Goldberg, *Framing Contract Law* (Cambridge, MA: Harvard University Press, 2006).

22. Oren Bar-Gill & Rebecca Stone, Mobile Misperceptions, *Harvard Journal of Law and Technology* 23 (2009): 49.

23. *Muldoon v. Lynch*, 6 P. 417 (Cal. 1885).

24. *Id.*, at 418.

25. *Vanderbilt University v. DiNardo*, 174 F.3d 751 (6th Cir. 1999).

26. *In re Cellphone Fee Termination Cases*, 193 Cal. App. 4th 298, 2011 WL 743462 (Cal. App. 1 Dist. March 4, 2011), *cert. denied*, 2011 WL 4344574 (U.S. Nov. 7, 2011).

27. *E.g.*, *Leingang v. City of Mandan Weed Board*, 468 N.W.2d 397 (N.D. 1991); *Kearsarge Computer, Inc. v. Acme Staple Co.*, 366 A.2d 467 (N.H. 1976); *Hallmark Ins. v. Colonial Penn Life*, 990 F.2d 984, 990 (7th Cir. 1993).

28. The appellate court's decision in the *Sprint* case could be justified in yet another way. A principal reason the trial court had invalidated the clauses was not that they charged subscribers too much, but rather too little – the company's losses from breach by early termination were greater. As the old mausoleum case suggests, contract law's primary concern with stipulated remedies concerns punishment. It invalidates clauses that spur rather than compensate. This doctrine flags terms fixing unreasonably large, rather than unreasonably small, sums. There have been few cases invalidating clauses for undercompensating rather than overcompensating and they are usually accompanied by other factors, like a party acting negligently. *E.g.*, *Samson Sales, Inc. v. Honeywell, Inc.*, 465 N.E.2d 392 (Ohio 1984). But the court in the mausoleum case also noted that, like porridge that should not be too hot or too cold, damages for breach of contract should compensate breach, neither more nor less.

29. Chapter 8 discusses such conditions more fully.

30. *In re IBP, Inc. Shareholders Litigation*, 789 A.2d 14 (Del. Ch. 2001).

31. *E.g.*, *American Broadcasting Companies v. Wolf*, 420 N.E.2d 363 (N.Y. 1981); *Fitzpatrick v. Michael*, 9 A.2d 639 (Md. 1939).

32. *Van Wagner Advertising Corp. v. S&M Enterprises*, 492 N.E.2d 756 (N.Y. 1986).

33. The clause's wording was vague. S&M thought it authorized the original owner and itself to terminate the lease any time after the building was sold; Van Wagner and the court read it narrowly to allow termination only if done as part of a deal to sell the building.

## 5. Rewinding: Restitution and Unjust Enrichment

1. *Estate of Cleveland v. Gorden*, 837 S.W. 2d 68 (Tenn. App. 1992).

2. *Bailey v. West*, 249 A. 2d 414 (R. I. 1969).

3. *Cotnam v. Wisdom*, 104 S.W. 164 (Ark. 1907).

4. *Nursing Care Services, Inc. v. Dobos*, 380 So.2d 516 (Fla. Dist. Ct. App. 1980).

5. Restatement (Third) of Restitution and Unjust Enrichment, § 20 (Tentative Draft No. 2) (2002).

6. Except in a handful of states, there is no general law in the United States requiring people to act as Good Samaritans, whereas such laws are common in European countries.

7. *Brady v. Alaska*, 965 P.2d 1 (Alaska 1998).

8. *Martin v. Little, Brown & Co*, 450 A.2d 984 (Pa. Super. 1981).

9. *Songbird Jet Ltd. v. Amax, Inc.* 581 F. Supp. 912 (S.D.N.Y. 1984).

10. For a classic discussion of the officious intermeddler or mere volunteer, see John P. Dawson, Negotiorum Gestio: The Altruistic Intermeddler, *Harvard Law Review* 74 (1961): 1.

11. *Harrington v. Taylor*, 36 S.E.2d 227 (N.C. 1945).

12. Section C of Chapter 3 discusses lack of capacity owing to young age or mental illness.

13. Section A of Chapter 1 discusses this point.

14. *Webb v. McGowin*, 168 S.E. 196 (Ala. App.), *cert. denied* 168 S. E. 199 (Ala. 1935). For interesting discussion of this case, as well as an equally famous one with which it is commonly contrasted, see Geoffrey R. Watson, In the Tribunal of Conscience: Mills v. Wyman Reconsidered, *Tulane Law Review* 71 (1997): 1749.

15. *Boothe v. Fitzpatrick*, 36 Vt. 681, 1864 WL 2408 (Vermont 1864).

16. For more on this topic, see Stanley Henderson, Promises Grounded in the Past: The Idea of Unjust Enrichment and the Law of Contracts, *Virginia Law Review* 57 (1971): 1115.

17. This discussion is based on all of the opinions and some of the filings in the case, especially the final opinion *Baer v. Chase*, WL 1237850 (D.N.J. April 27, 2007). Others include *Baer v. Chase*, 2005 WL 1106487 (D.N.J. April 29, 2005); *Baer v. Chase*, 2004 WL 350050 (D.N.J. Feb. 20, 2004); *Baer v. Chase*, 392 F.3d 609 (3d Cir. 2004).

18. Robert Straus, Jury Rejects Man's Bid For Share of 'Sopranos,' *N. Y. Times* (Dec. 20, 2007).

19. *See Apfel v. Prudential-Bache Securities, Inc.*, 616 N.E.2d 1095 (N.Y. 1993).

20. Robert Straus, Jury Rejects Man's Bid For Share of 'Sopranos,' *N. Y. Times* (Dec. 20, 2007).

21. Section C of Chapter 3 discusses forces majeure.

22. Section D of Chapter 6 describes a similar example in the case of the fraudulent architect and Turkish bath, *Vickery v. Richie*.

23. The saga of Rod Stewart and the Rio did not end with that jury verdict. Stewart again appealed the case, objecting that the lower court was wrong to instruct the jury that it could find absence of a contract because the parties had never disputed that. The appellate court agreed, telling the lower court to hold a new trial. Skirmishes in the lower court renewed. Rio asked for another summary ruling in its favor, renewing all its old arguments, but the court denied it. From there, no record of the case appears, suggesting that the two continue to wrangle a decade after the fallout. The two appellate opinions are *Rio Properties v. Armstrong Hirsch*, 94 Fed. Appx. 519 (9th Cir. 2004) and 254 Fed. Appx. 600 (9th Cir. 2007).

24. For more on this topic, see Richard R. W. Brooks & Alexander Stremitzer, Remedies On and Off Contract, *Yale Law Journal* 120 (2011): 690; Robert A.

Hillman, An Analysis of the Cessation of Contractual Relations, *Cornell Law Review* 68 (1983): 617; Andrew Kull, Rescission and Restitution, *Business Lawyer* 61 (2006): 569.

## 6. Writing It Down: Interpretation, Parol, Frauds

1. *F.B.T. Productions, LLC v. Aftermath Records*, 621 F.3d 958 (9th Cir. 2010), *cert. denied*, ___ U.S. ___, 131 S. Ct. 1677 (March 21, 2011). For a journalistic account of the case, see Ben Sisario, Eminem Lawsuit May Raise Pay for Older Artists, *N.Y. Times* (March 27, 2011).
2. *Pacific Gas & Elec. Co. v. G.W. Thomas Drayage & Rigging Co.*, 442 P.2d 641 (Cal. 1968) (Traynor, C.J.); *W.W.W. Associates, Inc. v. Giancontieri*, 566 N.E.2d 639 (N.Y. 1990) (Kaye, later Chief Judge); *Taylor v. State Farm Mutual Automobile Ins. Co.*, 854 P.2d 1134 (Ariz. 1993).
3. For more on the topic of contract interpretation, including some examples of judicial error and suggestions for improvement, see E. Allan Farnsworth, 'Meaning' in the Law of Contracts, *Yale Law Journal* 76 (1967): 939.
4. *Rather v. CBS Corp.*, 68 A.D.3d 49, 886 N.Y.S.2d 121 (N.Y. App. Div. 2009). This discussion is based on both the court's opinion in the case and the briefs filed by the parties.
5. *Hollywood Foreign Press Association v Dick Clark Productions* (filed Nov. 2010).
6. *Thompson v. Libby*, 26 N.W. 1 (Minn. 1885); *Mitchill v. Laith*, 160 N.E. 646 (N.Y. 1928); *see* John D. Calamari & Joseph M. Perillo, A Plea for a Uniform Parol Evidence Rule and Principles of Contract Interpretation, *Indiana Law Journal* 42 (1967): 333.
7. *LaFazia v. Howe*, 575 A.2d 182 (R.I. 1990); *Sabo v. Delman*, 143 N.E.2d 906 (N.Y. 1957); *Sherrod, Inc. v. Morrison-Knudsen Co.*, 815 P.2d 1135 (Mont. 1991).
8. *See Hatley v. Stafford*, 588 P.2d 603 (Oregon 1978) (addressing handwritten instrument prepared by unsophisticated party not represented by counsel and other circumstances suggesting absence of intention that writing should be a complete and final integration of the bargain, citing *Masterson v. Sine*, 436 P.2d 561 (Cal, 1968) (Roger Traynor, Chief Justice)).
9. Often called by its Latin name "contra proferendum," this principle to resolve uncertain meaning against the party responsible for drafting it diminishes incentives to finesse the writing process and encourages the drafting party, with greater control, to communicate clearly to the other side. This is not exactly a principle of *interpretation* because it is not strictly about meaning; courts often refer to it instead as a principle of *construction* because it is about the legal effect of a contract. It helps only when there is an ambiguity. It does not add weight to the scale when deciding whether ambiguity exists. *See Joyner v. Adams*, 361 S.E.2d 901 (N.C. App. 1987).

10. *Skookum Oil Co. v. Thomas*, 162 Cal. 539 (Cal. 1912); *see* also Larry A. DiMatteo, Reason and Context: A Dual Track Theory of Interpretation, *Penn State Law Review* 109 (2004): 397.

11. *See* Lawrence A. Cunningham, Toward a Prudential and Credibility-Centered Parol Evidence Rule, *U. Cincinnati Law Review* 68 (2000): 269; Mark P. Gergen, The Jury's Role in Deciding Normative Issues in the American Common Law, *Fordham Law Review* 68 (1999): 407.

12. The trial was scheduled for January 2012, just as this book was going into final production.

13. *In re the Marriage of McCourt*, Case No. BD514309 (L.A. Superior Court, Dec. 7, 2010). This discussion is based on both the court's opinion in the case and the briefs filed by the parties. For a journalistic thumbnail sketch of the case, see Jennifer Steinhauer, Dodgers' Fate Hinges on Owners' Divorce, *N.Y. Times* (July 9, 2010).

14. Associated Press, Los Angeles Dodgers File for Bankruptcy Protection, *N.Y. Times* (June 28, 2011).

15. *Vickery v. Ritchie*, 88 N.E. 835 (Mass. 1909).

16. Section A of Chapter 3 discusses excuse based on mutual mistake.

17. Chapter 5 and Section E of Chapter 8 discuss such remedies.

18. *Hoffman v. Chapman*, 34 A.2d 438 (Md. 1943).

19. *Dumas v. Infinity Broadcasting Corp.*, 416 F.3d 671 (7th Cir. 2005) (applying Illinois state law).

20. The relevant section of the Illinois statute of frauds applicable to the Dumas case said: "No action shall be brought … upon any agreement that is not to be performed within the space of one year from the making thereof, unless the promise or agreement upon which such action shall be brought, or some memorandum or note thereof, shall be in writing, and signed by the party to be charged therewith, or some other person thereunto by him lawfully authorized."

21. Another example is *Snyder v. Bronfman*, 13 N.Y.3d 504 (2009) (exploring distinctive clause in New York's statute of frauds involving contracts to act as business-sales broker in exchange for a commission).

22. *Rosenthal v. Fonda*, 862 F.2d 1398 (Cal. 1988).

23. *See Fitzpatrick v. Michael*, 9 A.2d 639 (Md. 1939).

24. *Crabtree v. Elizabeth Arden Sales Corp.*, 110 N.E.2d 551 (N.Y. 1953).

25. Restatement (Second) of Contracts § 139 (1982); *Alaska Democratic Party v. Rice*, 934 P.2d 1313 (Alaska 1997) (presenting what amounts to a multifactor inquiry suggesting that the facts of a case, and especially remedies available, may warrant embracing or rejecting a promissory estoppel exception rather than seeing the decision as an either-or test that varies by state).

26. *Rosenfeld v. Basquiat*, 78 F.3d 84 (2d Cir. 1996) (signature requirement satisfied by scrawl of artist in crayon in short memo on larger piece of paper exchanging three paintings for $12,000, later valued at $350,000).

27. Electronic Signatures in Global and National Commerce Act of 2000, 15 U.S.C. 7001 (2000). To similar effect is the Uniform Electronic Transactions Act, adopted in the vast majority of states. For more on this topic, see Margaret Jane Radin, Online Standardization and the Integrating of Text and Machine, *Fordham Law Review* 70 (2002): 1125.

28. Opinions about the statute of frauds have long been sharply divided, called variously the wisest and the most mischievous law ever. *Compare* Hugh F. Willis, The Statute of Frauds: A Legal Anachronism, *Indiana Law Journal* 3 (1928): 427 *with* Karl N. Llewellyn, What Price Contract? An Essay in Perspective, *Yale Law Journal* 40 (1931): 704.

29. *Interform Co. v. Mitchell*, 575 F.2d 1270 (9th Cir. 1978).

## 7. Performing: Duties, Modification, Good Faith

1. *B. Lewis Productions, Inc. v. Angelou*, 2008 WL 1826486 (S.D.N.Y. 2008). That final opinion in the case followed five other full judicial opinions resolving various aspects of the case over its long history. Those opinions are as follows: *B. Lewis Productions, Inc. v. Angelou*, 2001 WL 727022 (S.D.N.Y. 2001) (initial opinion agreeing to hear the case); *B. Lewis Productions, Inc. v. Angelou*, 2003 WL 21709465 (S.D.N.Y. 2003) (initial opinion denying claims); *B. Lewis Productions, Inc. v. Angelou*, 99 Fed. Appx. 294, 2004 WL 1147071 (2d Cir. 2004) (appellate court reviving the case on Lewis's claim for breach of contract, directing the trial court to consider it); *B. Lewis Productions, Inc. v. Angelou*, 2005 WL 11384474 (S.D.N.Y. 2005) (recognizing potential breach of contract claim); and *B. Lewis Productions, Inc. v. Angelou*, 2007 WL 2295971 (S.D.N.Y. 2007) (terms of settlement and further dispute about whether it included certain amounts Hallmark paid Angelou).

2. *Wood v. Lucy, Lady Duff-Gordon*, 118 N.E. 214 (N.Y. 1917) (Cardozo, J.).

3. Linda Castrone, Ornery as Ever, Clive Cussler Lives Life as One Big Adventure, *Denver Post* (Dec. 4, 2003).

4. *Cussler v. Crusader Entertainment, LLC*, 2010 WL 718007 (Cal. App. 2nd Dist. March 29, 2010). This discussion is based on both the court's opinion in the case and the briefs filed by the parties.

5. *Three Story Music v. Waits*, 48 Cal. Rptr. 2d 747 (Cal. App. 2nd Dist. 1995).

6. Another great example of the appeal and boundaries of good faith concerns the discretion that standardized test services have in canceling scores. *Dalton v. Educational Testing Service*, 663 N.E.2d 289 (N.Y. 1995). One test taker, Brian Dalton, improved his SAT score by 410 points between tests taken in May and November. The jump triggered automatic review by the Educational Testing Service (ETS), which, based on a finding of disparate handwriting, determined the tests were taken by different people, and so canceled the November score.

The two had signed a contract giving ETS the right to cancel scores if ETS found reason to question their validity. Dalton had the right to challenge that finding by supplying additional information. Dalton supplied such information, including records showing that he had mononucleosis during the earlier test, proof that he took a preparatory test before the later but not the earlier test, and statements from the November test proctor and other test takers vouching for his presence then.

ETS upheld its decision to cancel but without even a rudimentary effort to evaluate the additional information Dalton supplied, relying again solely on the handwriting comparison. That breached ETS's obligation to perform its contract in good faith, the court ruled. When a contract envisions exercising discretion, good faith requires exercising it without being arbitrary or irrational.

True, the good-faith duty is limited and imposes no duties that are inconsistent with those a contract expressly creates. This contract expressly authorized ETS to cancel if it had reason to question a score's validity. The contract did not require it to prove invalidity, nor did its invitation to let test takers supply additional information translate into a requirement that it conduct any particular investigation. That said, the contract did require ETS to consider relevant additional information Dalton supplied. Its failure to do so put it in breach of contract.

7. *Cussler v. Crusader Entertainment, LLC*, 2010 WL 3491513 (Cal. App. 2nd Dist. Sept. 8, 2010).

8. For more on the topic of good faith in contracts, see Steven J. Burton & Eric G. Andersen, *Contractual Good Faith: Formation, Performance, Breach, Enforcement* (Boston: Little, Brown & Co., 1995); Teri J. Dobbins, Losing Faith: Extracting the Implied Covenant of Good Faith from (Some) Contracts, *Oregon Law Review* 84 (2005): 227; Harold Dubroff, The Implied Covenant of Good Faith in Contract Interpretation and Gap-Filling: Reviling a Revered Relic, *St. John's Law Review* 80 (2006): 559; Michael P. Van Alstine, Of Textualism, Party Autonomy and Good Faith, *William & Mary Law Review* 40 (1999): 1223.

9. *Bovis Lend Lease (LMB) Inc. v. Lower Manhattan Development Corp.*, Index No. 2009–603243 (N.Y. Sup. Ct. May 9, 2011). This discussion is based on examination of extensive documents involved in the case, including the original contract, briefs, and other filings of the parties and judicial opinions in the case. For a journalistic account of aspects of the case, see Charles V. Bagli, As Deutsche Bank Tower Shrinks, Dispute Rages on Costs, *N.Y. Times* (July 6, 2010).

10. *See* John Eligon, Final Defendant Acquitted in Deutsche Bank Fire, *N.Y. Times* (July 6, 2011).

11. *Brian Construction & Development Co. v. Brighenti*, 405 A.2d 72 (Conn. 1978).

12. *Evergreen Amusement Corp. v. Milstead*, 112 A. 901 (Md. 1955).

13. *Alaska Packers' Association v. Domenico*, 117 F. 99 (9th Cir. 1902); *see* Debora L. Threedy, A Fish Story: Alaska Packers' Ass'n v. Domenico, *Utah Law Review* (2000): 185.

14. For more on this topic, see Robert Hillman, Contract Modification under the Restatement (Second) of Contracts, *Cornell Law Review* 67 (1982): 680; Henry Mather, Contract Modification under Duress, *South Carolina Law Review* 33 (1982): 615.

15. *Fusari v. Team Love Child LLC*, Index No. 2010–650179 (N.Y. Sup. Ct. filed March 17, 2010); *Germanotta v. Fusari*, Index No. 2010–650183 (N.Y. Sup. Ct. filed March 18, 2010). This discussion is based on the complaints each party filed in their lawsuits against the other. The case settled before the parties filed other documents, and no judicial opinion was rendered.

16. *Marton Remodeling v. Jensen*, 706 P.2d 607 (Utah 1985).

17. *E.g., Bennett v. Robinson's Medical Mart, Inc.*, 417 P.2d 761 (Utah 1966).

18. For more on the topic of accord and satisfaction, including legislative incursions into the common law, see Bryan D. Hull & Aalok Sharma, Satisfaction Not Guaranteed: California's Conflicting Law on the Use of Accord and Satisfaction Checks, *Loyola L.A. Law Review* 33 (1999): 1; Michael D. Floyd, How Much Satisfaction Should You Expect from an Accord? *Loyola U. Chicago Law Journal* 26 (1994): 1.

19. This discussion is derived from the author's blog posts on the subject as the story developed and related news sources cited there. Lawrence A. Cunningham, Contract Law Issues in the Conan-NBC Affair, Concurring Opinions Blog (Jan. 12, 2010); Lawrence A. Cunningham, Conan-NBC Contract Issues II, Concurring Opinions Blog (Jan. 15, 2010). For a journalistic account of the case and its settlement, see Bill Carter, Fingers Still Pointing, NBC and O'Brien Reach a Deal, *N.Y. Times* (Jan. 21, 2010).

20. *Wood v. Lucy, Lady Duff-Gordon*, 118 N.E. 214 (N.Y. 1917) (Cardozo, J.).

21. Section C of Chapter 4 discusses mitigation of damages for breach of contract.

22. Section D of Chapter 4 provides examples of this in discussing early termination fees in cell phone service contracts.


## 8. Hedging: Conditions

1. *Detmers v. Costner*, Civ. 09–60 (4th Cir. Ct. South Dakota, Dec. 17, 2010); *Detmers v. Costner*, Civ. 09–60 (4th Cir. Ct. South Dakota, June 28, 2011). This discussion is based on both the court's two opinions in the case and the briefs filed by the parties.

2. The Tantanka Web site is http://storyofthebison.com

3. The FedEx example is adapted from the classic English cases of *Constable v. Cloberie*, 81 Eng. Rep. 1141 (King's Bench 1626) and *Glaholm v. Hays*,

*Irvine & Anderson*, 133 Eng. Rep. 743 (Court of Common Pleas 1841), often used in contracts courses to illustrate the distinction between promises and conditions.

4. *Merritt Hill Vineyards Inc. v. Windy Heights Vineyard, Inc.*, 460 N.E.2d 1077 (N.Y. 1984).

5. *Howard v. Federal Crop Insurance Corp.*, 540 F.2d 695 (4th Cir. 1976).

6. *Id.* (emphasis added).

7. Detmers appealed to the Supreme Court of South Dakota, where the case was pending when this book went into final production in January 2012.

8. Discussion of the case of Charlie Sheen and Warner Brothers is based on letters of lawyers representing the parties in the dispute and a complaint Sheen filed in court; further proceedings, however, were conducted in private arbitration without producing any public record. The principal letters are those written by Sheen's lawyer, Martin D. Singer (Feb. 28, 2011), and by Warner's lawyer, John W. Spiegel (March 7, 2011). The complaint is captioned *Sheen v. Lorre*, Case No. SC111794, 2011 WL 817781 (Cal. Superior Court March 10, 2011).

9. In the seventeenth century, many saw promises made in contracts as independent of each other. That meant both parties could sue the other for nonperformance, even if they had not performed their side of the bargain. *Nichols v. Raynbred*, 80 Eng. Rep. 238 (King's Bench 1615) (exchange of cash for a cow in which, if neither side performed, both were entitled to sue the other); *Pordage v. Cole*, 85 Eng. Rep. (1669) (cash for real property). Such a regime discourages performance and encourages lawsuits – neither an appealing public policy. People could state their intention differently by using terms of art signaling that the performance of one was a condition to the duty of the other. This practice was exemplified by such magic words as "for the same cause" that experienced contracting parties understood to make promises mutually conditional. *Fineux, C.J., in Anon.*, Y.B. 15 Hen. VII (1500). But contract law's default rule establishing constructive (or implied) conditions was not crystalized until a famous 1773 opinion of Lord Mansfield, in *Kingston v. Preston*, 99 Eng. Rep. 437 (King's Bench 1773).

The case involved a deal to sell a master's silk business to an apprentice in the trade at fair value. The buyer would pay a monthly purchase price, with the balance secured by a financial guarantee. The buyer claimed to be prepared to close the deal, but the seller refused. The seller's defense was that the buyer had not offered to give the required financial guarantee. The buyer responded that the exchanged promises were "independent" so that, even had he not performed, he was entitled to sue. The seller portrayed the promises as "dependent," making the buyer's performance (or at least tender of it) a condition to the seller's duty. Given that the buyer had not obtained the guarantee, it would be unreasonable to expect the seller to transfer its business to the buyer on the strength of the buyer's unsecured credit alone.

Lord Mansfield agreed with the seller, identifying the "evident sense and meaning of the parties" as consistent with his position. In doing so, Mansfield delineated types of contract provisions still used today to regulate the timing and manner of performance – and to encourage performance rather than lawsuits. These are *promises* (which he called "mutual and independent"), the basic expression of duty whose breach entitles the other party to remedies, and *conditions*, the basic form of qualification on a promise, whose non-occurrence excuses a duty. Conditions fall into two further categories, some that regulate who must go first when performance is sequential and others that operate when parties must render their respective performances simultaneously.

10. *See* Celia R. Taylor, Self-Help in Contract Law: An Exploration and Proposal, *Wake Forest Law Review* 33 (1998): 839.

11. *Ziehen v. Smith*, 42 N.E. 1080 (N.Y. 1896).

12. *Stewart v. Newbury*, 115 N.E. 984 (NY 1917).

13. Contract law has a separate approach to conditions that hinge on the satisfaction of a party. Although people are free to contract for whatever conditions of satisfaction they wish, when a party to a contract must be personally satisfied with some performance, there is a danger of subterfuge. Accordingly, conditions of personal satisfaction concerning utilitarian performances (such as a commercial painting job) are evaluated according to a reasonableness standard – whether reasonable commercial actors would find the performance satisfactory. Conditions of personal satisfaction concerning idiosyncratic performance, however, such as the painting of a portrait, are evaluated according to personal subjective taste, although any objection must be held in good faith. *See Fursmidt v. Hotel Abbey Holding Corp.*, 200 N.Y.S.2d 256 (N.Y. App. Div. 1960); *Morin Building Products v. Baystone Construction*, 717 F.2d 413 (7th Cir. 1983). Some states insist on strict compliance with conditions of satisfaction concerning a product that can be returned, such as freestanding goods, while allowing for a looser standard of acceptability for those that cannot, such as a construction project wrought into a physical structure. *Compare Van Iderstine Co. v. Barnet Leather Co.*, 152 N.E. 250 (N.Y. 1926) with *Nolan v. Whitney*, 88 N.Y. 648 (1882).

14. For more on this topic, see Edwin Patterson, Constructive Conditions in Contracts, *Columbia Law Review* 42 (1942): 903.

15. Restatement (Second) of Contracts § 251(a) (1982); *see* Larry T. Garvin, Adequate Assurance of Due Performance: Of Risk, Duress, and Cognition, *Colorado Law Review* 69 (1998): 71.

16. *See* Mark P. Gergen, A Theory of Self-Help Remedies in Contract, *Boston University Law Review* 89 (2009): 1397.

17. *See* Eric G. Anderson, A New Look at Material Breach in the Law of Contracts, *U.C. Davis Law Review* 21 (1988): 1073.

18. *K&G Construction Co. v. Harris*, 164 A.2d 451 (Md. 1960).

19. Complaint, *Sheen v. Lorre*, Case No.SC111794, 2011 WL 817781 (Cal. Superior Court March 10, 2011), ¶ 3.
20. *West v. Clark*, 86 N.E. 1 (N.Y. 1908).
21. Section A of Chapter 2 explains this point.
22. *Daneshjou Co. Inc. v. Bullock*, 2009 WL 790200 (Tex. App., Austin, March 27, 2009). Sources for some factual background in the Bullock case include Voir Dire, Nightmare House, *National Law Journal* (Aug. 30, 2004); Guillermo X. Garcia, Actress Takes Stand in Mansion Lawsuit, *San Antonio Express-News* (Sept. 1, 2004); Peggy Fikac, Trial Has Happy Ending for Actress, *San Antonio Express-News* (Oct. 15, 2004); Mary Alice Robbins, Builder Promises Sequel in Suit Involving Star Sandra Bullock, *Texas Lawyer* (Oct. 25, 2004).
23. *Stark v. Parker*, 19 Mass. 267 (Mass. 1824).
24. *Id.*
25. *Britton v. Turner*, 6 N.H. 481 (N.H. 1834).
26. This is called the "perfect tender rule" and is of ancient vintage in commercial law. It is codified in Section 2–601 of the Uniform Commercial Code adopted in all the states. However, there are several exceptions and qualifications to this provision so that it often operates more like a flexible standard than a rigid rule. *See Plateq Corp. v. Machlett Laboratories, Inc.*, 456 A.2d 786 (Conn. 1983).
27. *Jacob & Youngs, Inc. v. Kent*, 129 N.E. 889 (N.Y. 1921); *see* Amy B. Cohen, Reviving Jacob & Youngs, Inc. v. Kent: Material Breach Doctrine Reconsidered, *Villanova Law Review* 42 (1997): 65.
28. *Plante v. Jacobs*, 103 N.W.2d 296 (Wisconsin 1960).
29. *Peevyhouse v. Garland Coal*, 382 P.2d 109 (Oklahoma 1962); *see* Judith L. Maute, Peevyhouse v. Garland Coal & Mining Co. Revisited: The Ballad of Willie and Lucille, *Northwestern U. Law Review* 89 (1995): 1341.
30. *Groves v. John Wunder Co.*, 286 N.W.2d 235 (Minn. 1939); *see* Richard S. Wirtz, Cost of Performance or Difference in Value? *Case Western Reserve Law Review* 59 (2008): 61.
31. *Advanced Ink v. Wilks*, 711 AP.2d 524 (Alaska 1985).
32. John Harlow, Bullock to End Dream-Home Nightmare, *Times of London* (Feb. 6, 2006).
33. *See, e.g., Laurin v. DeCarolis Construction Co.*, 363 N.E.2d 675 (Mass. 1977). For more on the curious and subtle role that fault can sometimes play in contract law, see the various articles in Symposium, Fault in American Contract Law, *Michigan Law Review* 107 (2009): 1341.

## 9. Considering Others: Third Parties and Society

1. *Doe v. Wal-Mart Stores, Inc.*, 572 F.3d 677 (9th Cir. 2009). This discussion is based on both the court's opinion in the case and the briefs filed by the parties.

2. *Lawrence v. Fox*, 20 N.Y. 268 (1859); *see* Anthony Jon Waters, The Property in the Promise: A Study of the Third Party Beneficiary Rule, *Harvard Law Review* 98 (1985): 109.

3. *Seaver v. Ransom*, 120 N.E. 639 (N.Y. 1918).

4. *H.R. Moch Co. v. Rensselaer Water Co.*, 159 N.E. 896 (N.Y. 1928) (Cardozo, C.J.).

5. *Chen v. Street Beat Sportswear, Inc.*, 226 F. Supp. 2d 355 (E.D.N.Y. 2002).

6. For more on this topic, see Melvin A. Eisenberg, Third Party Beneficiaries, *Columbia Law Review* 92 (1992): 1358; S. A. Smith, Contracts for the Benefit of Third Parties: In Defense of the Third-Party Rule, *Oxford Journal of Legal Studies* 17 (1997): 643.

7. *Empresas Cablevisión v. JP Morgan Chase Bank*, 680 F. Supp. 625 (S.D.N.Y. 2010), *affirmed* 381 Fed. Appx. 117 (2d Cir. 2010).

8. *Sally Beauty Co. v. Nexxus Products Co.*, 801 F.2d 1001 (7th Cir. 1986).

9. *Berliner Foods Corp. v. Pillsbury Co.*, 633 F. Supp. 577 (D. Md. 1986).

10. *New England Patriots v. StubHub*, 2009 WL 995483 (Mass. Super. Jan. 26, 2009).

11. *Commonwealth v. Sovrensky*, 269 Mass. 460 (1929); *Lanier v. City of Boston*, 95 F.Supp.2d 17 (D. Mass. 2000) (sale outside Fenway Park of a single ticket at face value did not amount to the business of reselling).

12. *City of Santa Barbara v. Superior Court*, 161 P.3d 1095 (Cal. 2007).

13. *Tunkl v. Regents of University of California*, 383 P.2d 441 (Cal. 1963). Justice Tobriner, who authored the opinion in *Tunkl*, also authored the opinion in *Marvin v. Marvin*, discussed in Section C of Chapter 2.

14. *Richards v. Richards*, 513 N.W.2d 118 (Wisconsin 1994).

15. *See Hackbart v. Cincinnati Bengals, Inc.*, 601 F.2d 516 (10th Cir.), *cert. denied*, 444 U.S. 931 (1979).

## Conclusion

1. *See* Gregory S. Crespi, The Influence of Two Decades of Contract Law Scholarship on Judicial Rulings: An Empirical Analysis, *SMU Law Review* 57 (2004): 105.

# TABLE OF CASES

# INDEX